Funded by a State Legislature Grant
Senator Suzi Oppenheimer

RYE FREE READING ROOM
Escape to the Library

Bloom's Modern Critical Views

Bloom's Modern Critical Views

AUGUST WILSON

Edited and with an introduction by
Harold Bloom
Sterling Professor of the Humanities
Yale University

BLOOM'S
LITERARY CRITICISM
An imprint of Infobase Publishing

Bloom's Modern Critical Views: August Wilson

Copyright © 2009 by Infobase Publishing

Introduction © 2009 by Harold Bloom

Bloom's Literary Criticism
An imprint of Infobase Publishing
132 West 31st Street
New York NY 10001

Library of Congress Cataloging-in-Publication Data

August Wilson / edited and with an introduction by Harold Bloom.
    p. cm. — (Bloom's modern critical views)
  Includes bibliographical references and index.
  ISBN 978-1-60413-393-6 (acid-free paper) 1. Wilson, August—Criticism and inter-pretation. 2. Historical drama, American—History and criticism. 3. African Americans in literature. I. Bloom, Harold. II. Title.

  PS3573.I45677Z55 2009
  812'.54—dc22

                                        2008040762

Contributing Editor: Pamela Loos
Cover designed by Takeshi Takahashi
Printed in the United States of America
Bang EJB 10 9 8 7 6 5 4 3 2 1

This book is printed on acid-free paper.

Contents

Contents

Editor's Note

My introduction centers on what seems to me August Wilson's strongest play, *Joe Turner's Come and Gone.*

Wilson's southern roots are interpreted by Patricia Gantt, while Sandra G. Shannon broods on Wilson's sense of audience.

Keith Clark sees Wilson as a prophet of ritual regeneration, after which William W. Cook meditates on the dramatist's diction.

Çiğdem Üsekes unsurprisingly traces whiteness as the villain for Wilson, while Amanda M. Rudolph more usefully studies African religion in *Joe Turner's* and *The Piano Lesson.*

The exemplary figure of Booker T. Washington is invoked by Ladrica Menson-Furr, after which Philip D. Beidler celebrates Wilson's general triumph as a dramatist.

Radio Golf, which eludes me, is praised by Margaret Booker, while Harry J. Elam, Jr. concludes this volume by hailing the equally dubious (to me) *Gem of the Ocean.*

HAROLD BLOOM

Introduction

I recall attending a performance of *Joe Turner's Come and Gone* at Yale in 1986 and came away more moved than I had been by *Ma Rainey's Black Bottom* and *Fences*. *Two Trains Running* I have never seen and have just read for the first time, after rereading three earlier plays in the University of Pittsburgh Press's very useful *Three Plays* (1991), which has a stern preface by the dramatist and a useful afterword by Paul Cater Harrison. Returning to the text of *Joe Turner's Come and Gone* after a decade is a remarkable experience in reading, since few plays by American dramatists hold up well away from the stage. As a literary work, *Joe Turner's Come and Gone* is authentically impressive, particularly in its spiritual insights. August Wilson's political stance as a black nationalist is present in *Joe Turner's* (to give it a short title), but his art as a dramatist surmounts the tendentiousness that elsewhere distracts me. Whether or not his other celebrated plays may prove to be period pieces (like those of Bullins and Baraka), I am uncertain, but there is a likely permanence in *Joe Turner's*, perhaps because of its profound depiction of the African-American roots of what I have learned to call the American Religion, the actual faith of white Protestants in the United States.

Wilson, in his preface to *Three Plays*, offers a powerful reading of his masterwork:

> There is a moment in *Joe Turner's Come and Gone* at the end
> of the first act when the residents of the household, in an act of
> tribal solidarity and recognition of communal history, dance a

Juba. Herald Loomis interrupts it to release a terrifying vision of bones walking on the water. From the outset he has been a man who has suffered a spiritual dislocation and is searching for a world that contains his image. The years of bondage to Joe Turner have disrupted his life and severed his connection with his past. His vision is of bones walking on water that sink and wash up on the shore as fully fleshed humans. It is not the bones walking on the water that is the terrifying part of the vision—it is when they take on flesh and reveal themselves to be like him. "They black. Just like you and me. Ain't no difference." It is the shock of recognition that his birth has origins in the manifest act of the creator, that he is in fact akin to the gods. Somewhere in the Atlantic Ocean lie the bones of millions of Africans who died before reaching the New World. The flesh of their flesh populates the Americas from Mississippi to Montevideo. Loomis is made witness to the resurrection and restoration of these bones. He has only to reconcile this vision with his learned experiences and recognize he is one of the "bones people." At the end of the play he repudiates the idea that salvation comes from outside of himself and claims his moral personality by slashing his chest in a bloodletting rite that severs his bonds and demonstrates his willingness to bleed as an act of redemption.

Spiritually, this is both greatly suggestive and not unconfusing. Why does Loomis slash himself? There is a deep pattern of African gnosticism in the colonial black Baptists, who carried on from their heritage in affirming "the little me within the big me," the spark of the Alien God that was the best and oldest part of them, free of the Creation-Fall. Michal Sobel has shown how this pattern recurs in African-American religion, and I suspect it was transmitted by the African Baptists to the original Southern Baptists. If Loomis slashes himself as a parody of and against Christian blood atonement, I could understand it more readily, but Wilson violates African tradition by the chest-slashing that is a bloodletting, bond-severing act of redemption. Perhaps Wilson felt he needed this self-violence as a dramatic gesture, and yet it may detract from the rebirth of Loomis. If this is a flaw, it is a small one in so strong a play.

The summer of 2001 was hardly a good time to argue nationalist stances among African Americans, now that the full extent of black disenfranchisement in Jeb Bush's Florida is being revealed. It is clear that if there had been an unimpeded African-American vote in Florida, the Supreme Court would not have been able to appoint George W. Bush as president.

I write now in September 2008 in what I would hesitate to call a very different America. Nevertheless, Barack Obama is running at least on even terms for the presidency of the United States as the candidate for the Democratic Party. August Wilson, alas, is now gone. I met him only once, was impressed by his barely controlled fury, but wonder if he would have been softened by the Obama candidacy. Perhaps one should wait to see whether the election of November 2008 finally repairs the Florida Outrage.

PATRICIA GANTT

Ghosts from "Down There": The Southernness of August Wilson

Audre Lorde, speaking of the impetus for her poetry, says, "I cannot recall the words of my first poem / but I remember a promise / I made my pen / never to leave it / lying / in somebody else's blood" (39–40). August Wilson appears to have made a similar aesthetic vow of experiential fidelity: using what he himself calls "the blood's memory as my only guide and companion," Wilson has filled his five major dramatic works with characters whose psyches are rooted in the realities of the African American past, especially its complex Southern component (*Three Plays* xii). These plays constitute an investigation of that southern past and a substantive testimony to its legacies to twentieth-century experience, wherever it is lived.

As produced under the direction of Lloyd Richards and as published, the sequence of Wilson's plays begins with *Ma Rainey's Black Bottom* (1984) and concludes with his most recent success, *Two Trains Running* (1993), with *Fences* (1985), *Joe Turner's Come and Gone* (1986), and *The Piano Lesson* (1990) created in between.[1] Significantly, Wilson focuses on a different decade in each play: *Joe Turner* takes place in 1911; *Ma Rainey*, in the late 1920s; *Piano Lesson*, in the Depression; *Fences*, in 1957; and *Two Trains Running*, in 1969. To examine the African American historiography that the works create together, it is intriguing to approach them not from their actual order of composition, but as viewed from the playwright's chosen

From *August Wilson: A Casebook*, edited by Marilyn Elkins, pp. 69–88. © 2000, 1994 by Marilyn Elkins.

chronology. Doing so enables us to see how the plays express Wilson's artistic vision of the African American search for identity, as transfigured through generations of individuals and their memories.

At first glance it may seem peculiar to speak of the "southernness" of Wilson's drama. The playwright was, after all, born in Pittsburgh, Pennsylvania, and has lived most of his life there or in St. Paul, Minnesota. Nor do his plays take place in the South: Wilson sets all of them in Pittsburgh, except for *Ma Rainey*, which is set in Chicago. Yet each is replete with vestiges of a mysterious, fascinating locale characters have in common but often fear or reverence so much that they refuse to name. It is the South. Again and again they refer to the South as "down there" (a euphemism suggesting the forbidden locus of human sexuality as well as the geographic home of the slave past). This territory is for Wilson's characters variously a scene of slavery and sharecropping, of oppression and cruelty, of rejection, bittersweet yearning, and only restricted happiness. It lingers in memories and suffuses speech. It figures abundantly in each decade's play and is part of the "fabric of remembrance August Wilson summons up" (Wilde 74). Names (whether of characters or recalled places), music, art, vernacular expression, religion, food, folk wisdom, material culture, stories passed down in oral tradition, and often painful memories of incidents experienced there all serve as shadowy reminders of the South.

The first play in the historic cycle *is Joe Turner's Come and Gone*, a drama full of the sounds and memories of the South. Because the majority of the characters were born in the South or are only a generation away from it, it is no surprise that the texture of southern life is evident in much they say and do. Pittsburgh city people now, they still use a language laden with rural vernacular: a man is "hungrier than a mule"; a child who will not eat is "skinny as a bean pole"; a person on the edge of an action is "fixing to" do it; things beneath consideration are those a person "ain't studying" (5, 85, 13, 12). Characters' speech is often rich with folk lyrics, as when a man recalls John Henry's "ten-pound hammer" in bragging about his own sexual prowess (26). Folk belief and folk wisdom, too, are part of the play. One of the chief characters is Bynum, a conjure man skilled in the old ways of roots and potions. Consulted by a woman grieving for her missing man, Bynum gives her a packet to put under her pillow to "bring good luck to you. Draw it to you like a magnet" (24). Southern foodways, too, have made the northern journey, as folks gathered around the table share grits, yams, biscuits, or fried chicken. Out of the physical South themselves, *Joe Turner's* people carry much of the South within.

The principal southern legacy they share, however, is their memory of the slave past, which Wilson brings into the play from its inception. The prologue places the action in the context of the diaspora—especially southern slavery—with a lyrical description of the migration of the "sons and daughters of newly freed African slaves" to the great cities of the north, where they hope to shape "a new identity as free men of definite and sincere worth" (iii). "Foreigners in a strange land . . . Isolated, cut off from memory . . . they arrive dazed and stunned" by all they have endured, mostly in the rural South (iii). The psychological baggage they carry is considerable: refused full access both to their African heritage and to modern financial and political power, they desire ways to "give clear and luminous meaning" to the as-yet unarticulated song they carry within, one composed of both "a wail and a whelp of joy" (iii). They arrive "carrying Bibles and guitars," symbols of old faith and new songs (iii). In this play, as in others, Wilson is not reluctant to explore the slave past, about which he says: "Blacks in America want to forget about slavery—the stigma, the shame. That's the wrong move. If you can't be who you are, who can you be? How can you know what to do?" (Freedman 40). For *Joe Turner's* characters, the quest for identity and the pain of slavery's memories are inextricably bound.

The chief wanderer in *Joe Turner* is Herald Loomis who, after seven years' innocent entrapment on Joe Turner's Tennessee chain gang, wanders the country with Zonia, his young daughter. The seven years of Loomis' forced labor, according to Wilson, "can in fact represent the four hundred years of slavery" (Powers 54). Loomis searches for his wife Martha, whom he has not seen since his capture. He clings to the mistaken belief that if he can find Martha and bring her back into the ruptured family circle, he can be free of painful memories and construct a new identity for himself. Loomis longs for "a starting place in the world" (*Joe Turner* 73). "Got to find my wife," he says; "That be my starting place" (76). After almost four years of searching, he and Zonia arrive at Seth Holly's Pittsburgh boardinghouse, a microcosmic "community" in which various types can come together.

Seth, an independent craftsman besides owning the boardinghouse, is adamant about *not* having the recent Southern backgrounds several others share. When another character muses, "I reckon everybody done picked some cotton," Seth insists, "I ain't never picked no cotton . . . I ain't never even seen no cotton" (70). Son of free parents, he disdains "that old backward country style of living" he ascribes to southern immigrants "from the backwoods" (5, 6). He characterizes these travelers as "foolish-acting niggers" for naively believing they can find the good life in the city or its steel mills (6). "They got a rude awakening," Seth tells his wife Bertha; he has been in the North all his life and knows prejudice is not isolated below the Mason-Dixon Line (6).

A regular visitor at Seth's boardinghouse is Rutherford Selig, a peddler also known as the "People Finder" (6). When Loomis hears of Selig's ability to find people, he enlists his assistance in locating Martha. Selig reveals a sinister twist to his talent when elaborating his credentials to Loomis. A white man, he, too, is directly connected to the slave past: "[W]e been finders in my family for a long time. Bringers and finders. My great-granddaddy used to bring Nigras across the ocean on ships. . . . My daddy, rest his soul, used to find runaway slaves for the plantation bosses" (41). The irony of Loomis' requesting Selig's help is apparent.

Bynum, the rootworker and conjure man, is in many ways the most intriguing individual in the play, and figures significantly in Edith Oliver's characterizing *Joe Turner* as "the most mystical, most remote and dispersed of all Mr. Wilson's plays" (107). Bynum seems always "lost in a world of his own making" where metaphysics, rather than the clear reality which guides Seth, is the order of the day (Wilson, *Joe Turner* 4). Like others in the play, Bynum is searching—but his search is a different kind: he is looking for his "shiny man," a person he has seen in a dreamlike vision experienced on the road one day (6). In Bynum's symbolically-laden vision, the stranger promises to show him the "Secret of Life," but instead leads him to a mystic place where everything is disproportionately sized and infused with a blinding light (9). There Bynum encounters the ghost of his father, who encourages him not to sing someone else's song, but to find one of his own. The ghost tells Bynum to find the "shiny man"; then Bynum will know his song has been "accepted and worked its full power in the world" (10). Bynum's vision is heavy with symbolic meaning for the African American search for identity. Forced for so long to sing others' songs, African Americans must find their own and sing them boldly. Bynum's father had a "Healing Song" which, although it might sound "no different than any other song" to its hearers, had curative power (61). Bynum chooses a "Binding Song," for he observes the lack of unity in his people and sees this forceful melody as a cure for their separation and mutual lack of power (10).

Song—particularly the significance of finding one's own song to sing—becomes a vital element in *Joe Turner* from the time Bynum recounts his vision. The music sought is Houston A. Baker, Jr.'s "long black song," one in which interconnections of past, present, and people spiral together into a unified whole (*Song* xi). Both dialogue and stage direction frequently depict the searchers who people this play in terms of their progress in achieving a personal or collective song, one "useful in making sense of this world" (143). When Jeremy, a young man who lives at the boardinghouse, enters, for example, stage directions depict him as one whose "spirit has yet to be molded into song" (Wilson, *Joe Turner* 12). Later, when Bynum speaks with Mattie Campbell, a woman searching for a man she can feel a sense of belonging with, he tells her that she and her man are "lost from yourselves," but that "where you're supposed to be alive, your heart [is] kicking in your chest with a song worth singing" (22). Most importantly, Herald Loomis is said to be a man "unable to harmonize the forces that swirl around him"

(14). Injustices suffered in Tennessee have robbed him of his song. "Herald" in name only, he cannot sing because he has no sense of self or belonging.

Act One culminates in Bynum's leading the people at the boardinghouse in an impromptu *Juba*, a dance/song of call and response, "reminiscent of the Ring Shouts of the African slaves," and interconnecting participants with the antebellum South and beyond to the African past (52). Loomis screams at them to stop, when suddenly he is overtaken by his own vision—one of bones walking on the water. The dance becomes a call-and-response folk sermon, with Loomis describing his vision and Bynum leading him on. This scene is full of what Clive Barnes calls the "verbal riffs and emotional cadenzas" that fill the play, and allows Loomis to begin articulating his song ("O'Neill"). Frantically he chants his vision about disunity and dispersion, in which dead bones walking across the water are impelled to stand and "get up on the road" toward healing (Wilson, *Joe Turner* 56). Only by expressing their connection with the past can the boardinghouse residents attain what Frank Rich terms "a degree of unity and peace" ("Panoramic" C15).

Act Two finds Bynum repeating a disturbing song of the South—W.C. Handy's blues ballad which gives the play its title. The song tells the story of Joe Turner's notorious cruelty, which Loomis knows firsthand. Bynum hopes with this particular tune, a reminder of the past and its dominance by the white oppressor, to provoke Loomis into remembering his own song. He says, "Now, I can look at you, Mr. Loomis, and see you a man who done forgot his song. Forgot how to sing it. A fellow forget that and he forget who he is" (Wilson, *Joe Turner* 71). If Bynum can help Loomis recall his song, he will salvage both their identities. He assures Loomis that his song—his sense of independent worth—has not vanished, just gone underground. But Loomis is resistant to Bynum's pleas.

Selig reappears, justifying his title of "People Finder" by bringing Martha with him. In revealing why she has not waited for Loomis in Tennessee, Martha recalls the demeaning weariness and the danger inherent to staying "down there" in the South (89). She explains: "They told me Joe Turner had you and my whole world split half in two. . . . So I killed you in my heart . . . then I picked up what was left and went on to make life without you. . . . I couldn't drag you behind me like a sack of cotton" (90). Martha expresses the griefs and troubles provoked in the South through a metaphor of the southern landscape. Even more deeply embittered now, Loomis turns on Bynum, who, along with Martha, is urging him to wrest his own meaning from life. Told he must be cleansed in "the blood of the lamb," Loomis rejects the Lamb of formulated Christianity (93). He perceives himself as the innocent sacrifice, rather than "Mr. Jesus Christ," who has looked on for generations without intervening while "enemies all around me picking the flesh from my bones" (92, 93). But if blood is required to achieve purity, he will oblige. "I don't need nobody to bleed for me," he says, "I can bleed for myself" (93). Loomis then takes out a knife and slashes himself, smearing blood from his lacerated chest onto his face in an inclusive, horrific ritual of death and rebirth as old as West African scarring *rites de passage* and as new as the victorious pronouncement he makes in that Pittsburgh kitchen. At that point Loomis is able to stand alone; he regains his song, one of "self-sufficiency, . . . free from any encumberance other than the workings of his own heart and the bonds of the flesh" (94). Accepting responsibility for putting his world together, he is at last free. His northern migration has proved liberating in both physical and spiritual terms. Loomis, "shining like new money," is newly minted in the wholeness Wilson finds essential to his vision for modern African Americans (94). That wholeness can come only when, like Loomis, one looks squarely at the past, however painful, and moves resolutely forward, taking only those legacies which can help him on his way. Then he, too, will be "free to soar above the environs that weighed and pushed his spirit into terrifying contractions" and can stand alone (94).

Ma Rainey's part in Wilson's "grand dramatic design of providing a panoramic view of the American black experience since the days of Lincoln" also relies on repeated echoes of the South (Barnes "O'Neill"). The play takes place in 1927 Chicago at a rundown recording studio on the Southside, where members of a blues band wait to record a session with Ma Rainey, legendary blues queen. The blues, *Ma Rainey*'s symbol of the African American heritage, could "instruct and allow [free men of definite and sincere worth] to reconnect" if it were truly heard as Ma herself hears it, as a personal song to be improvised and sung with fervor (Wilson, *Ma Rainey* xvi). Ma values the blues as "life's way of talking . . . a way of understanding life . . . [and] keep[ing] things balanced" (82). Yet the blues does not function in this play as what Houston A. Baker, Jr., terms a "vibrant network . . . the multiplex, enabling *script* in which Afro-American cultural discourse is inscribed" (*Blues* 4). For Sturdyvant and Irvin, who have set up the session, the music is only a way to "make a bundle" (Wilson, *Ma Rainey* 19). Ma's song has been stolen from her and claimed by another, thus making the blues a means of pointing out black victimization by societal racism.

Although once again basing the dramatic context in allusions to the South, Wilson's prologue indicates that southernness will not be so essential to *Ma Rainey's Black Bottom* as it is to his other productions, despite its being centered on music born in the South:

Whether this music came from Alabama or Mississippi or other parts of the South doesn't matter anymore. The men and women who make this music have learned it from the narrow crooked

streets of East St. Louis, or the streets of the city's Southside, and
the Alabama or Mississippi roots have been strangled . . . (xvi)

The birthplace of the blues is just one entity in the racist culture that pervades America and dominates this play.

Nevertheless, southern cultural background is just as evident in *Ma Rainey* as it is in *Joe Turner*. The headnote to the play is a portion of a song by southern bluesman, Blind Lemon Jefferson. There are references to slavery, to farming in the rural South, and specifically to sharecropping; the city bluesmen's disgust for menial work in the city—emblematized through mention of an acquaintance who runs an elevator in St. Louis—is expressed as being "better than stepping in muleshit" (93). Wilson has received considerable praise for the "extraordinary acuity" of his ear—"a quality that has a black audience murmuring 'That's right' or 'Tell it' during his plays, as they might at a Jesse Jackson speech or a B. B. King concert"—and the playwright's "virtuosity with the vernacular" is a part of each page of *Ma Rainey*'s dialogue (Freedman 49). This authenticity, clear in the blues musicians' speech, marks such lines as "It sure done got quiet in here" (Ma Rainey), "Why you be asking?" (Toledo), "She out for what she can get" (Cutler), "Ain't nothing wrong with hauling wood. I done hauled plenty wood" (Slow Drag), or "We's in Chicago, we ain't in Memphis!" (Levee) (Wilson, *Ma Rainey* 82, 29, 22, 93, 38). The South, though background for most of the characters, is seen almost exclusively in pejorative terms.

The South's main detractor is Levee, *Ma Rainey*'s protagonist, who ironically takes his name from the embankments along the Mississippi; his name, according to Paul Carter Harrison, suggests an affiliation with the "new music soundings of jazz" and a possible rejection of the blues (308). The most frequent targets of Levee's abuse are Christianity and Toledo's philosophical talk about building a better life. He demeans Toledo's ideas as ineffectual nonsense, calling him "Booker T. Washington" and telling him he's "just a whole lot of mouth" with his "highfalutin ideas" and "that old philosophy bullshit" (Wilson, *Ma Rainey* 41, 42). Levee feels that "if there's a god up there, he done went to sleep. . . . God don't mean nothing to me," and would agree that religion is only a "white man's palliative" (43, 46; Walker 18).[2] He becomes increasingly antagonistic towards Toledo, equating Toledo's frequent expressions of religious faith and his references to "making the lot of the colored man better for him here in America" with the oppressive life in the rural South, a backward place of horrific memories for Levee (Wilson, *Ma Rainey* 41).

Alice Walker's characterization of rural Southern life would suit Levee well: "I can recall that I hated it, generally. The hard work in the fields, the shabby houses, the evil greedy men who worked my father to death and almost broke the courage of that strong woman, my mother" (21). Levee fixates on Toledo's rough shoes, symbol to him of what life might be like without music, and says, "Nigger got them clodhoppers! Old brogans! He ain't nothing but a sharecropper. . . . Got nerve to put on a suit and tie with them farming boots" (Wilson, *Ma Rainey* 40). The racial brutality Levee has witnessed in the South fuels his relentless bitterness. When he was eight years old, he witnessed his mother's gang rape by eight or nine white men; trying to defend her, he was slashed across the chest by one of the rapists, and still carries the scar. Levee's father Memphis, whose hard work and savings earned him "nearly fifty acres of good farming land" in Mississippi, was away buying seed and fertilizer at the time (69). Upon Memphis' return, he "acted like he done accepted the facts" of his wife's rape, "smiled in the face of one of them crackers who had been with my mama . . . and sold him our land" (70). Pretending to leave, Memphis then doubled back and killed four of the rapists before the white establishment caught him, lynched him, and set his body afire. Levee learns from his father to handle whites by masking and waiting for his chance for revenge: "I can smile and say yessir to whoever I please," he tells the other bluesmen, "I got time coming to me" (70). This is a man who "cannot bear the weight of his own rage" (Smith 184). At the climax of the play, Levee's rage finally erupts into violence.

Much of Act Two consists of a series of debates between Toledo and Levee about the fairness of life and the powerlessness of blacks in white society. Finally Cutler, the leader of the blues band, brings the discussion home by pointing out how unimportant the band and their music are to whites: "white folks don't care nothing about Ma Rainey. She's just another nigger who they can use to make some money" (Wilson, *Ma Rainey* 97). Cutler shares a bitter memory, in which the Reverend Gates, a black preacher, gets off a train at a small southern crossroads. In this place "the only colored rest room is an outhouse they got sitting way back two hundred yards or so from the station" (96). The train leaves before the minister can get back. A group of whites with guns torment him, tearing the cross from his neck, ripping his Bible, and making him dance. Hearing this story, Levee is incensed:

> "Why didn't God strike some of them crackers down? . . . 'Cause he a white man's God. That's why. God ain't never listened to no nigger's prayers. God take a nigger's prayers and throw them in the garbage. . . . In fact . . . God hate niggers! Hate them with all the fury in his heart. . . . God can kiss my ass." (98).

Hearing this, Cutler leaps to his feet and punches Levee in the mouth. Levee, overwrought, pulls a knife, but begins screaming—not at Cutler, but at God, demanding to know where God was when his mother was being raped and calling on Jesus to have mercy: "Did you turn your back, motherfucker? Did you turn your back?" (99). His encounter with Cutler unleashes the wrath Levee has suppressed for so long.

Soon after this incident, Levee tries to interest Sturdyvant in his arrangements, hoping through his music to find the control over his life that is missing everywhere else. Sturdyvant rejects Levee's music and condescendingly dismisses him, and Levee then turns on the first person he sees. It happens to be Toledo, who accidentally steps on Levee's shoe with his "raggedy-ass clodhoppers" (110). Displacing all his pent-up frustrations from the racism he and the others have suffered North and South onto Toledo's heavy farmer's shoes, Levee again pulls his knife. Before he knows what he is doing, Toledo is dead. This recording session—not a rehearsal of music so much as of the evils of the American racist society—ends in further victimization. By killing Toledo, Levee "has not only desecrated a natural life, but also cut himself off from ontological continuity, a sort of cosmic suicide" (Harrison 311). He rejects the unity Toledo, through his philosophy, has tried to extend, just as he rejects all contact with Toledo's southern farm boots.

The southern heritage, the "whole solid past" which will not be rejected, but must be faced and dealt with, is strongest in Wilson's drama of the Depression years, *The Piano Lesson* (Welty 206). The "lesson" mentioned in the title is not merely one conducted on the actual keys of an upright piano which fills the Charles family's Pittsburgh parlor. The piano's lesson is also inscribed in the wooden carvings the upright bears, mask-like carvings reminiscent of African sculptures, "rendered with a grace and power of invention that lifts them . . . into the realm of art" (Wilson, *Piano Lesson* xiii). Further, this lesson is dramatically foregrounded through the Charleses' confrontations about whether to sell the piano to finance Boy Willie's dream of land ownership "down there" in the South, or to hold onto it for what it represents to his sister Berniece of both their flesh-and-blood heritage and their proud spiritual legacy of reverence for family and the past (3). According to Frank Rich, "the disposition of the piano becomes synonymous with the use to which the characters put their ancestral legacy . . . somber shrine to a tragic past [or] stake to freedom" (C15). "The past has never passed" for this haunted brother and sister, but exists in ghosts of their southern heritage that are both actual and psychological (Ching 71). In *The Piano Lesson* Wilson invites his audience to consider a number of crucial questions: What is the place of tradition? of community? of family? of the past? What do we owe them and memory? To examine these questions, *Piano Lesson*'s people must look back to their shared southernness, which pervades August Wilson's imagination and theirs.

Boy Willie, part owner of the piano, is eager to go South again. He sees his chance to own a piece of Mississippi farm land as his chance to be somebody. He tells his uncle Doaker, "I ain't got no advantages to offer nobody," but that if he had land, "something under his feet that belonged to him," he could "stand up taller" (91, 92). "1 ain't gonna be no fool about no sentimental value," Boy Willie proclaims (51). He does not understand why Berniece will not play the piano if it means so much to her, or at least pass its story on to her daughter Maretha so she could "know where she at in the world" (91). Berniece, however, would rather keep the piano in the parlor, dusted but never played, as a memento of the sacrifice of their ancestors. She remembers her late mother's playing the piano and saying she could hear the spirits of her ancestors talking to her when she did so.

Berniece is apprehensive, too, about the ghost of Robert Sutter, the slave owner who laid claim to their family long ago, and split them up to buy the piano for his bride. The first Boy Willie, a slave with the gift of woodworking, is forced to carve the images of his wife, the first Berniece, and their son into the piano.[3] The master woodworker does not stop there, but goes on to fashion a pictorial history of the entire family into the wood of the piano. Eventually Boy Charles, father of the present Boy Willie and Berniece, goes into the Sutter home and takes the piano. Disturbed for years because the Sutters own it, Boy Charles feels that whoever possesses the family's pictographs—and therefore the stories of their past—somehow controls their spirits. Vindictive whites burn Boy Charles alive in the boxcar where he is hiding; he has given his life to reclaim the visual symbol of the family's past. His ghost walks, too, mysteriously dealing retribution to Mississippi whites. Berniece believes that if she does not play the piano, she can avoid disturbing the troubled spirits, and, thereby, spare Maretha the burden of the past. At the same time, Berniece is convinced that "Money can't buy what that piano cost. You can't sell your soul for money. It won't go with the buyer. It'll shrivel and shrink" (50). But Sutter's ghost walks their house, and Maretha has already seen it. The burden of the past, as well as its beauty, belongs to all of them.

Wilson skillfully conducts the debate between brother and sister, with each confrontation adding more details to the family story and increasing his audience's tension at the lack of resolution. Wining Boy, Doaker's older brother, brings matters to a climax with his musical tribute to memory. All at once the presence of Sutter's ghost is felt, and various people gathered in the Charleses' home try to exorcise it, including Avery, a minister. All efforts are useless. Boy Willie wrestles with Sutter's ghost, but is thrown. Berniece then realizes that she must save them from Sutter's evil presence by playing the piano. She can neither ignore the past nor let it lie dormant nor sell it nor give it away. She must take it up and "play" it, make it a part of her. She sits at the piano and begins a powerful song, playing and singing her incantation to Mama Berniece, Mama Esther, Papa Boy Charles, and Mama Ola—the old ones who have kept the past from being forgotten—asking them repeatedly to help her preserve her loved ones from their common enemy. Her prayer is granted, and Sutter's ghost vanishes. Berniece, in whose name kinship is embedded, liberates her family by confronting the past she has steadfastly avoided throughout the play. She finds comfort in the confrontation. Berniece learns, as Wilson insists his people must, that she cannot suppress any portion of her selfhood if she and her loved ones are to move on with their lives, balanced and whole. At the conclusion of *The Piano Lesson* Boy Willie leaves for Mississippi, content for Berniece to keep the piano so long as someone will make use of it to bring music and meaning to the present. Through music, the piano's song reaffirms the stories of the past, transforming the ugly and awful, along with the beautiful and tender, into a joyous melody of hope.

By the decade explored in his 1950s play, *Fences*, Wilson's characters are more concerned with coping with the present than with looking to their southern past. Wilson makes this focus clear in his prologue: Unlike European immigrants and their descendants, he writes:

> descendants of African slaves were offered no such welcome or participation [in the city]. They came from places called the Carolinas and the Virginias, Georgia, Alabama, Mississippi, and Tennessee. They came strong, eager, searching. The city rejected them and they ... [lived] in quiet desperation and vengeful pride ... in pursuit of their own dream. That they could breathe free, finally, and stand to meet life with the force of dignity and whatever eloquence the heart could call upon. (xvii)

Reminders of the South are plentiful enough—in Troy Maxson's recollections of coming to manhood on his father's Alabama farm, in the collard greens and cornbread Rose Maxson serves up in her kitchen, in Troy's yearning for the exoticism of "one of them Florida gals . . . [with] some Indian blood in them" and Bono's longing for a woman "got them great big old legs and hips wide as the Mississippi River," or in a reference to Troy's storytelling ability as having "some Uncle Remus in your blood" (4, 5, 13). *Fences* again displays the "authentic root" of Wilson's dialogue in southern dialect, noted in the discussion of earlier plays and evident throughout, as when Rose admonishes Cory, "Your daddy like to had a fit with you running out of here this morning without doing your chores" (Henderson 67, Wilson, *Fences* 29). These southern echoes are secondary, however, to the main consideration of the play, the fences society builds up around us and those we construct, willingly or unwillingly, around ourselves.

The theme of this play, articulated so strongly before in Wilson's drama (particularly in *Joe Turner's Come and Gone* and *Ma Rainey's Black Bottom*) is the need to sing one's own song. The recurrent melody in *Fences* is a traditional folksong from Troy's childhood, about a dog named Blue that "treed a possum out on a limb" (99). On the day of Troy's funeral, when Cory Maxson comes home and confronts his connections with the past, including his embattled relationship with his dead father and his tie to his half-sister Raynell, he affirms his part "in a continuum that runs from Pittsburgh to the antebellum South and finally to Mother Africa" (Freedman 36). Cory and Raynell are able to sing the song together. It is at once theirs and Troy's and older than all of them, a melody of their interconnectedness. Inappropriate as the song of dog and possum may seem on such a solemn occasion, it signifies, as Ralph Ellison says of the blues,

> an impulse to keep the painful details and episodes of a brutal experience alive in one's aching consciousness, to finger its jagged grain, and to transcend it, not by the consolation of philosophy but by squeezing from it a near-tragic, near-comic lyricism. (90)

Threading backward through time, the song binds brother and sister to each other and to the mixture of pain and inarticulated love which is their common legacy. At the song's conclusion, they are for the first time truly a family.

In *Two Trains Running*, Wilson goes to the late sixties, "a turbulent, racing, dangerous, and provocative decade," and sets his drama in a Pittsburgh restaurant symbolically placed between life (Lutz's Meat Market) and death (West's Funeral Home) (Wilson, *Two Trains Running* xviii). Vernacular language, southern place names, foodways, songs, and cultural customs are all as evident in *Two Trains Running* as in Wilson's earlier works and are as seamlessly incorporated as before. For this play, as in *The Piano Lesson*, the oral history of the southern past is focal. Restaurant owner Memphis, who has witnessed tremendous change since leaving the Jackson, Mississippi, farm where he grew up to settle in Pittsburgh, sees every occurrence as an occasion for a story. He keeps southern oral tradition alive. Memphis and his friend Holloway, a regular at the restaurant and something of a historian, constantly swap memories. Now Memphis faces the possibility that his restaurant will be torn down, a risk which provokes his recollecting the past with even greater intensity than he has done before.

Memphis has been out of the South for almost forty years, but intends one day to catch one of the two daily trains running there and go back, to flaunt his material successes in Jackson, where he was robbed of his land

and run out of town. He believes in working hard and saving money, and has no use for Wolf, who plays the numbers, or Sterling, a young man who will not or cannot keep a series of menial jobs, his only option since release from prison. When Memphis voices his opinion that Sterling is "lazy," he provokes a history lesson from Holloway:

> People kill me talking about niggers is lazy. Niggers is the most hard-working people in the world. Worked three hundred years for free. And didn't take no lunch hour. . . . If it wasn't for you the white man would be poor. Every little bit he got he got standing on top of you. That's why he could reach so high. (34).

Holloway goes beyond the slave past to the Middle Passage, then returns to present inequities. To him, Memphis needs the sense of perspective that history can provide. But Memphis does not seem to care about the long view: he has watched civil rights leaders come and go, and nothing seems to have improved much, as far as he can tell. "Malcolm X is dead," Memphis says (40). "They killed Martin. If they did that to him you can imagine what they do to me or you. If they kill the sheep you know what they do to the wolf. . . . Ain't no justice. That's why they got that statue of her and got her blindfolded" (41, 42). Memphis wants nothing to do with history or with politics. His credo is that God blesses the child that's got his own, and he intends to mind his own business and protect his property as best he can.

Memphis goes to the courthouse on the day city officials are planning to make a decision about taking his property, sure they will try to cheat him. According to his observations, "the only way to recover what has been lost or stolen is by following the dominant culture's tactics: robbery, burning buildings for insurance, carrying guns to assert power," or cheating someone out of control (Wilde 74). To his surprise, the city offers him thirty-five thousand dollars for his property, ten thousand more than he has declared himself ready to fight for. Confused at this sudden turn, Memphis looks for guidance. He goes to Aunt Ester, the local prophetess; she tells him he must "go back and pick up the ball" (109). Memphis interprets her advice as a mandate to return to the South, face things there, and reclaim his farm. By dealing with the past, he can be free to go forward. Thus *Two Trains Running* carries a question which resonates through all Wilson's plays: how can we know who we are and where we are going, if we do not face our past, struggle towards understanding it, and reconcile ourselves to its present legacy to us?

August Wilson's dramatic works, ranging freely across the decades of American history, perform what Addell Austin terms a "vital function of the black theatre" (89). Lyrical works of art, these plays operate on another level as well. They hold up a "live mirror for helping black people to see, to cope with, and to redefine their perceptions of their own humanity" (Bass 64). A very essential part of that humanity, Wilson suggests, comes directly from the influences and inheritances of the southern past.

The five major plays written so far—full of fresh, inclusive portraits of America—provide multiple opportunities for the redefinition and self-identification their creator has often expressed as being crucial for African Americans. Wilson elaborates his reasons for redrawing the American past, and in doing so explains his vision for his work: "The message of America is 'Leave your Africanness outside the door.' My message is 'Claim what is yours' " (Freedman 36). Recasting the past allows one to turn with clarified vision toward the future. By looking to the southern past and incorporating its knotty, conflicted legacy of language, custom, history, belief, and deep pain, Wilson seeks a reaffirmation which can inform, strengthen, and empower. His plays tell us that strength does not lie in avoidance of the past, even one as fraught with complexity as the southern past is. If we seek today to find "the real person, the whole person" within, we must look to *all* our yesterdays (Powers 52). Then we can find our own songs, vigorous and enabling. Acknowledging the vestiges of the past within ourselves, we can truly lay claim to what is ours.

NOTES

1. References to the dates of Wilson's plays are to their publication in paperback, rather than to their earlier openings at the Yale Repertory Theater or to any appearance elsewhere.

2. Wilson has commented several times on the failure of Christianity to serve African Americans. Ishmael Reed quotes him as saying, "God does not hear the prayers of blacks" (93). Wilson also told Kim Powers, "Your god should resemble you. When you look in the mirror you should see your god. If you don't, then you have the wrong god" (54).

3. Names repeated in *The Piano Lesson* exhibit Wilson's talent for incorporating something Kimberly W. Benston notes as an important feature of Richard Wright's work, as well, the "shamanistic voice [that] keeps the ancestral names alive and resonant" (10).

WORKS CITED

Austin, Addell. "The Present State of Black Theatre." *Drama Review* 32.3 (Fall 1988): 85–100.

Baker, Houston A., Jr. *Blues, Ideology, and Afro-American Literature.* Chicago: University of Chicago Press, 1984, 1987.

———. *Long Black Song: Essays in Black American Literature and Culture.* Charlottesville: University Press of Virginia, 1972, 1990.

Barnes, Clive. "O'Neill in Blackface." *New York Post* 28 March 1988.

Bass, George Houston. "Theatre and the Afro-American Rite of Being." *Black American Literature Forum* 17.2 (Summer 1983): 60–64.

Benston, Kimberly W. " 'I Yam What I Am': Naming and Unnaming in Afro-American Literature." *Black American Literature Forum* 16.1 (Spring 1982): 3–11.

Ching, Mei-Ling. "Wrestling Against History." *Theater* 19.3 (Summer/Fall 1988): 70–71.

Ellison, Ralph. *Shadow and Act*. New York: Random House, 1964.

Freedman, Samuel G. "A Voice from the Streets." *New York Times Magazine* 10 June 1987: 36, 40, 49, 70.

Harrison, Paul Carter. "August Wilson's Blues Poetics." In *Three Plays* by August Wilson. Pittsburgh: University of Pittsburgh Press, 1991.

Henderson, Heather. "Building *Fences*: An Interview with Mary Alice and James Earl Jones." *Theater* 16.3 (Spring/Fall 1985): 67–70.

Lorde, Audre. "To the Poet Who Happens to Be Black and the Black Poet Who Happens to Be a Woman." *Callaloo* 14.1 (Winter 1991): 39–40.

Oliver, Edith. "Boarding House Blues." *New Yorker* 64.8 (April 11, 1988): 107.

Powers, Kim. "An Interview with August Wilson." *Theater* 16.1 (Fall/Winter 1984): 50–55.

Reed, Ishmael. "In Search of August Wilson." *Connoisseur* 217 (1987): 92–97.

Rich, Frank. "A Family Confronts Its History in August Wilson's *Piano Lesson*." *New York Times* 17 April 1990: C13.

———. "Panoramic History of Blacks in America in Wilson's *Joe Turner*." *New York Times* 28 March 1988: C15.

Shannon, Sandra G. "From Lorraine Hansberry to August Wilson: An Interview with Lloyd Richards." *Callaloo* 14.1 (Winter 1991): 124–135.

———. "The Good Christian's Come and Gone: The Shifting Role of Christianity in August Wilson's Plays." *MELUS* 16.3 (Fall 1989–1990): 127–142.

Smith, Philip E. "*Ma Rainey's Black Bottom*: Playing the Blues as Equipment for Living." In *Within the Dramatic Spectrum* VI. Ed. Karelisa V. Hartigan. New York: University Press of America, 1986.

Walker, Alice. "The Black Writer and the Southern Experience." *In Search of Our Mothers' Gardens*. New York: Harcourt Brace Jovanovich, 1983. 15–21.

Welty, Eudora. *The Optimist's Daughter*. New York: Vintage Books, 1972.

Wilde, Lisa. "Reclaiming the Past: Narrative and Memory in August Wilson's *Two Trains Running*." *Theater* 22.1 (Winter 1990–1991): 73–74.

Wilson, August. *Fences*. New York: Penguin, 1986.

———. *Joe Turner's Come and Gone*. New York: Penguin, 1988.

———. *Ma Rainey's Black Bottom*. New York: Penguin, 1985.

———. *The Piano Lesson*. New York: Penguin, 1990.

———. *Three Plays*. Pittsburgh: University of Pittsburgh Press, 1991.

———. *Two Trains Running*. New York: Penguin, 1993.

SANDRA G. SHANNON

Audience and Africanisms in August Wilson's Dramaturgy: A Case Study

In what is perhaps one of August Wilson's earliest published interviews following the sudden notoriety thrust upon him by the Broadway success of *Ma Rainey's Black Bottom*, he told Kim Powers about his aspirations for his next work, *Joe Turner's Come and Gone*: "My idea is that somewhere, sometime in the course of the play, the audience will discover these are African people. They're black Americans, they speak English, but their worldview is African."[1] Although Wilson's designs for what was shaping up to be the third play in his proposed ten-play series seemed clear enough, this early articulation of his dramatic agenda, posited in 1984, continues to be the source of problematic issues for a specific segment of the American theatergoing public. That is, many of them subscribe to the fantasy-driven and ridiculously fallacious American melting pot theory still embraced by diehard conservatives such as Robert Brustein.[2] Often woefully naive and culturally uninformed, this group regards any effort on Wilson's part to demonstrate that "these are African people" as an attempt to promote separatism and to wage a somewhat arcane and contradictory cultural war against a country into which they have assimilated and prospered.

At issue then—as it has been for centuries—is an imperialist world view that automatically relegates Africa to the margins in matters regarding aesthetics while foregrounding Eurocentric ideals. An extension of this

From *African American Performance and Theater History: A Critical Reader*, edited by Harry J. Elam, Jr. and David Krasner, pp. 149–167. © 2001 by Oxford University Press.

21

tendency to privilege one culture over another is also prevalent among
black theater audiences, in general, and among August Wilson's audiences,
in particular, most noticeably manifesting in the refusal or inability on the
part of spectators and critics alike, white or black, to recognize the African
in African American. Though often advanced in the guise of sophisticated
theater reviews or passed off as informed intellectual discourse, the tendency
to devalue another culture's aesthetic principles while waving the American
flag and advocating Euro-American standards is a dangerous one, which
needs to be exposed for what it is. Nigerian playwright, professor, and critic
Wole Soyinka argues in his important work *Myth, Literature, and the African
World*, "When ideological relations begin to deny, both theoretically and in
action, the reality of a cultural entity which we define as the African world
[and] to sublimate its existence in theirs, we must begin to look seriously
into their political motivation."[3] In what is perhaps the most cogent recent
articulation of this Western tendency to negate and denigrate African cultural
ideologies, Benny Sato Ambush goes to the heart of the matter in his essay
"Culture Wars," which was published in *African American Review*'s Winter
1998 special issue on black theater. He observes:

> This living in at least two worlds while claiming an African-
> derived identity which refuses to abandon itself by assimilation
> into mainstream Euro-centric culture is befuddling for many
> whites who, because of the privilege their white skin carries, have
> not had to negotiate such dualities.[4]

Adding to this, Brenda Gottschild argues, "We desperately need to cut
through the convoluted web of racism that denies acknowledgement of the
African part of the whole."[5] Building on Gottschild's observation, this essay
will demonstrate the African presence in August Wilson's plays.

A close examination of Wilson's confident prediction that his audiences
"will discover these are African people"[6] reveals his pervasive tendency to
privilege memory over history in his work and, by so doing, establish a closed
communication system within a group unified by "blood's memory." As
Pierre Nora notes in "Between Memory and History":

> It [memory] remains in permanent evolution, open to the dialectic
> of remembering and forgetting, unconscious of its successive
> deformations, vulnerable to manipulation and appropriation,
> susceptible to being long dormant and periodically revived....
> Memory, insofar as it is affective and magical, only accommodates
> those facts that suit it.... Memory is blind to all but the group
> it binds.[7]

Regarded as such, certain moments in African American history are filtered through Wilson's memory and recovered on stage through performance. The spectator's ability to acknowledge and identify with Wilson's Africa through performances that respond to memory rather than history depends heavily upon how effective are the actors' portrayals of "gestures and habits, in skills passed down by unspoken traditions, in the body's inherent self-knowledge, in unstudied reflexes and ingrained memories."[8]

In addition to those who view the African American as an exclusively American product whose affinities with Africa are, for all intents and purposes, irrelevant, there is another issue: certain critics "just don't get it." That is, the inability (or unwillingness) to recognize the African memory in its rhythms, rituals, and other signifiers, which are conveyed in the dramatic texts as well as in the performances of Wilson's work, seriously impedes the critic's ability to understand their full import. On one level, Wilson's plays, such as *Joe Turner's Come and Gone*, *The Piano Lesson*, and, to some extent, *Ma Rainey's Black Bottom*, *Fences*, and *Seven Guitars*, provide enough narrative structure and cross-cultural appeal to engage most audiences. However, on another, the African subtexts and the use of memory in his plays more often than not go unnoticed and are, perhaps, dismissed as directorial flourishes rather than acknowledged as components integral to the play's inherent message. Journalist Bill Moyers, for example, challenged Wilson to bring more into focus this blurry zone between his notion of an Africanist agenda and what his audiences should infer from its implementation in select plays. His pointed questions—"What happens when you get in touch with that African sensibility?" and "What does it mean to go back to Africa?"[9]—situate the concerns and misconceptions around how this aesthetic manifests and operates in Wilson's plays.

Getting in touch with an African sensibility is, Wilson believes, a crucial first step that African American artists must take in order to reorder, deconstruct, and make sense out of a world not of the African American's making. It entails the simultaneous acts of rejection and subversion of Western aesthetics by rhetorical and performative means in order to create space in this new world—also known as *America*—to realize the African nexus of his identity. Wilson likens this process to "[searching] for ways to reconnect, to reassemble" (*JT* xi).[10] Moreover, the concept of "getting in touch with an African sensibility" suggests that this mental responsiveness to Africa already exists within today's African American audiences, yet, for many, this sensibility lies dormant, existing only on a subconscious level, or is even suppressed by denial or ignorance of its current relevance. The job of Wilson as playwright, then, is to tease out this suppressed African consciousness. In his dramatic texts, this process entails the manipulation of language to evoke familiar symbols, scenarios, and potentially recognizable

Africanisms for contemporary readers. In performance, this process entails, for the spectator, aural and visual stimuli for reconstructing Africa, such as utterance, ritual, suggestive movement and gesture, and stage machinery.

Closely associated in meaning to Moyers's question "What happens when you get in touch with that African sensibility?" is the other question, which, apparently, is the source of confusion for him and for others who "just don't get it": "What does it mean to go back to Africa?" Although the two questions seem to express essentially identical concerns, the second invites a careful scrutiny of the Africa that Wilson constructs on stage for the modern African American audience, an Africa that is quite different from the Africa that exists for them as a geographically and historically distant continent. The former is a material presence; the latter is a spiritually embodied idea. Hence, in order to follow Wilson's agenda, it is necessary to situate his concept of Africa within the rhetorical and spiritual contexts of his dramatic universe. Wilson is the first to concede to the impracticalities associated with a too literal interpretation of his back-to-Africa agenda. He explains:

> If you take these people [African Americans] back over to Africa, they'll walk around trying to figure out what the hell's going on. There's no way that they can relate to that. But the sensibilities are African. They are Africans who have been removed from Africa, and they are in America four hundred years later. They're still Africans.[11]

Contrary to those who would argue that African Americans do not have a separate and distinct culture, Wilson argues in his plays that "Africanisms did survive the Middle Passage."[12]

In addition to introducing new African space to allow for an African sensibility, Wilson also constructs a new African, who announces his or her presence on stage in ways not possible in the traditional, mainstream sense of the dramatic text. Frequently, this "African" is not immediately recognizable to modern audiences, accustomed as they are to simplistic sound bites and prepackaged images. The ability to recognize any of Wilson's characters as African is bound intimately with the acquisition of an African sensibility; the spectator must, for example, suspend preconceived notions associated with Western logic and accept an African world view. John Conteh-Morgan's concept of "objective materialism" offers help in understanding such potentially overwhelming experiences in the play:

> Traditional African drama does not really depend on the outcome of a plot action, neither is it dependent on character portrayal. Characters are identifiable visually. In this respect

the important factor is ... the sheer power and expressiveness of the [performers'] stage presence and acts.... Meaning is not prosaically represented in words alone but ... finds "objective materialization" in movement, gesture, and sound.[13]

What, then, is the profile of Wilson's reconstructed New World African? What does it mean to be African? And what is this reconfigured dramatic space, which he calls Africa, like in performance? The answers to these key questions form the basis for this study. Thus, attention must be paid to the impact of these new constructs upon the modern audience, African American or otherwise.

For August Wilson, discovering, claiming, and foregrounding his own African identity fuels both a personal and professional odyssey. Due to childhood circumstances in his native Pittsburgh—which involved a wayward German father, a strong-willed and industrious mother, a house full of siblings, and limited financial resources—Wilson had no choice but to fashion his identity from the culture surrounding him and to define his manhood according to terms dictated by his fate. Pittsburgh's Hill District informed the playwright's African American mother, Daisy Wilson, as did her recollections of her southern past, reinforced by the sights, the sounds, the smells, the language of her life. By extension, the sensibilities of this predominantly black urban environment influenced Wilson. Wilson and many of the people he knew and grew up with had grandparents or great-grandparents from the South, and, in some instances, they were aware of actual slave ancestors. Thus, for the young Wilson, who came of age in an era preoccupied by the concepts of cultural nationalism espoused by Malcolm X and Elijah Muhammad as well as by the Black Arts and Black Power movements, Africa became his center of gravity and a symbol for his mother's dominant heritage, a heritage that he wholeheartedly embraced.

At any given performance of an August Wilson play, it has become commonplace to see a largely white, middle- to upper-class audience pack the houses. For me, the question arises: Must white audiences—or Asian audiences, or Latino audiences, or African audiences, for that matter—see, understand, and appreciate the same African contexts that Wilson creates? Is their experience of a play such as *Joe Turner's Come and Gone*, for example, somehow lessened if, for whatever reason, they do not see what is so African about Herald Loomis? Or, if they cannot relate to the African rhythms resurrected in the Juba, do they miss the true meaning of the play? Also, do they miss out on the full meaning of *Seven Guitars* because they see Hedley in a strictly literal sense? I realize that implicit in my line of questioning here is the simplistic notion that only African Americans can understand August Wilson. However, the issue I raise is not one of audience exclusivity; instead, it is one of the performance's communicative ability. A more appropriate question may be: How do Wilson's plays and performances actualize the African presence he seeks?

Joe Turner's Come and Gone (set in 1911) and *The Piano Lesson* (set in 1936) feature Wilson's efforts "to achieve the preservation of black African identity through theater performance in terms that are quite reminiscent of ritual theater."[14] Wilson's Africa also emerges in less conspicuous ways and to a lesser degree in other plays, such as *Ma Rainey's Black Bottom* (set in 1927), *Seven Guitars* (set in 1948), *Fences* (set in 1957), and *Two Trains Running* (set in 1969). The remaining play in Wilson's current repertoire— *Jitney!* (set in 1971)—noticeably lacks African signifiers both in its text and in its performance. In fact, Wilson admits in a recent interview that when *Jitney!* was conceived and written in 1979, he had not yet adopted an artistic agenda that advanced an African presence:

> I don't think it's [African sensibility] there. Here again, it's eighteen years ago. I've become more different. I became more conscious of what I was doing and wanting to do—to the extent that I determine the way the characters act and the way that they talk.[15]

It stands to reason, then, that Africa looms largest in Wilson's plays that are set in close temporal proximity to the slave and preslave historical eras; the African presence assumes a more subtle tone in plays that are set closer to the present. Hence, one may discern a correlation between the level of difficulty Wilson's audiences experience seeing, understanding, and appreciating his renditions of Africa with his plays' evolution from the Reconstruction era to the Harlem Renaissance and Great Depression to the Civil Rights and Black Power years to the decade of racial integration and the Vietnam War. Distanced by time, censored by racism, buttressed by an oral tradition, and muted by amnesia—selective or otherwise—the historical past of African Americans now largely resides in memory. That collective memory or "blood's memory," has become for him a dramatic landscape, a site of reconstruction, a space that allows him to redefine African Americans' identities through the reimagination of their history. In his ground-breaking theoretical study, *Scars of Conquest/Masks of Resistance: The Invention of Cultural Identities in African, African-American, and Caribbean Drama*, Tejumola Olaniyan defines this same space between memory and history by calling it "an empowering post-Afrocentric space, a space that calls to and radically revises the colonialist, triumphalist narrative of European modernity."[16]

The failure to comprehend Wilson's Africanist agenda has manifested in several forms, and one early indication may be traced to the lackluster reception that *Joe Turner's Come and Gone* received during its Broadway run in 1988. Despite his confidence about the play's potential to mirror the Africanness in his characters, *Joe Turner* fared much worse on Broadway than have other Wilson works. I have noted elsewhere that Broadway audiences were not impressed. In fact, the play had a comparatively short season (27 Mar.–26 June 1988) at the Ethel Barrymore Theatre. This lack of enthusiasm, I contend, was due not so much to the absence of a celebrity among its cast (as in *Fences*) or to the play's heavy tragic weight but to the play's difficult premise. Many audiences found Wilson's psychic protagonist and mystical flourishes over their heads and left the theater more confused than enlightened.[17]

What was it that spelled doom for Wilson's second play to reach Broadway in four years? In 1984, *Ma Rainey's Black Bottom* had been an unequivocal hit. However, this time, Wilson's work was greeted by a tougher audience—one apparently not impressed by spending an evening at the theater perplexed about the playwright's lessons on being Africans in America. Lloyd Richards, who directed *Joe Turner*, the epic drama of post-Reconstruction African Americans searching for their personal and collective identities while held up at a boardinghouse in Pittsburgh, warded off speculations that the play floundered because its cast did not include a star. He explained in a *New York Times* interview that confusion about *Joe Turner* was due to "the depth and difficulty of the play" and admitted that it "was a much more mystical play than *Fences*, a much more challenging play. . . . It took you deeply into a place where you had never been before. It made you work, and there are people who go to the theater who don't like to work."[18]

One might argue that the short life of *Joe Turner* on Broadway was a commentary on August Wilson's creation of a "closed" performance. That is, *Joe Turner* "anticipate[d] a very precise receiver and demand[ed] well-defined types of 'competence' (encyclopedic, ideological, etc.) for their 'correct' reception."[19] In this sense, the relatively short run of the play was inevitable, given the history of Broadway audiences' lukewarm reception of African-based dramas about black life. But also, I contend, the play did not fare well because the mainstream audience was reluctant to leave its established comfort zone of cultural awareness to examine life—even temporarily—from another's perspective. In order "to do justice to the African presence," Brenda Gottschild favors such a reversal in the dominant point of view. She conjectures, "What if we were to stand on our heads and assume that our American culture is African-rooted, so that the European elements could be regarded from an Africanist perspective?" She sees this revisionist approach of viewing "European elements . . . from an Africanist perspective" particularly useful in communicating the sometimes unconscious exercises in cultural imperialism.[20]

Joe Turner's Come and Gone serves as a paradigm, illuminating the problem between author and critics. Despite Wilson's admission that *Joe Turner* is his favorite play, it was reviewed harshly by critics who just did not get it—the playwright's infusion of Africanisms, that is. Herald Loomis, the darkly clad, brooding tenant at Seth and Bertha Holly's Pittsburgh boardinghouse, bears the brunt of this negative criticism. Those theater critics who detest his character argue that Loomis's "violent rebirth [does not make] dramatic sense," that his religious vision is "so obliquely written, it seems more like an LSD flashback," that his character is "closed mouthed and near crazy," that "the playwright—or Jesus—had struck him with a bolt of lightning," and that "we're left grappling for symbolic explanations and metaphysical justification for his behavior, the knife he wields, and the blood he sheds."[21] This catalog of complaints about Charles Dutton's (Yale Repertory Theatre) and Delroy Lindo's (Broadway) portrayals of Loomis reveals how utterly confounded and ill-equipped these critics were to make sense of the play. Director Lloyd Richards's attempts to convey Wilson's stage note that Loomis is "a man driven not by hellhounds that seemingly bay at his heels, but by his search for a world that speaks to something about himself" were lost on these critics.[22] In fact, Richards saw early on that Loomis would pose problems for audiences and was relatively successful during the play's journey from Yale to Broadway in convincing Wilson to alter the play in order to clarify the character's uncertain motivation and open-ended fate.[23]

The denunciations of Loomis's character are commonplace among those whose sensibilities remain blind to Wilson's Africanist agenda. Nevertheless, as one professor of African literature notes, "Afro-American mythology is not 'strange,' but a common, natural part of life."[24] Viewed according to certain principles of African ritual performance, Dutton and Lindo situate their characters outside the logic of Western thought and within the realm of African sensibility, where "symbolic movements and actions, stylized gestures, patterned dances, and even speech which is molded into a variety of fixed forms, formulaic expressions, and tropes" are expected to be understood as means of communication.[25] Loomis's morbid attire, sullen countenance, ominous narratives of archetypal dimension, and shocking scenes of self-scarification allow each particularity to enter his realm. Thus, without knowledge of African rituals, superstition, religion, or music, which continue to inform Africans in America, audiences are forced to assess Wilson's work using awkward yardsticks that contain little, if any, relevance to Wilson's intentions.

Understanding the actions, gestures, and motivations of Herald Loomis is the toughest challenge of any *Joe Turner* audience. To regard the ominous intruder as an embodiment of Africa requires careful attention to his role in the play. Loomis's prevailing sense of disorientation underscores the degree of devastation he has suffered in the wake of an imposed seven-year work detail, which separated him from his family and, by extension, from his cultural base. When viewed through the lens of an African sensibility, Loomis personifies the aching consciousness of millions of slaves, who were uprooted from their homelands, forced into subjugation, eventually emancipated, and ultimately set out on the road to fend for themselves. He also mirrors the suppressed anxieties of contemporary African Americans, who are haunted by this indelible past. However, despite these African-based perspectives, what has prevented modern audiences and critics alike from regarding Loomis as the conscience of Africa are numerous signals that, in their eyes— and according to Western logic—may be construed as evidence of possible derangement rather than as clues to his symbolic importance. To audiences who experience the play but lack African sensibility or cultural sensitivity to Wilson's agenda, Loomis's nightmares, convulsions, fits of anger, shocking displays of blasphemy, haunting attire, and foreboding appearance impede their understanding of Wilson's loftier regard for his dignity as an African. Still, the majority of the negative assessments that have been compiled by theater critics reveals their ignorance of Africanisms and cultural prejudice and confirms a degree of laziness and shortsightedness regarding cultural differences.

Not only have Herald Loomis's Africanist meanings easily gone unnoted or misconstrued in *Joe Turner*, but other manifestations of this aesthetic have the potential to remain obscure to those insensitive to the culture revealed in the performance text. These include, for example, the tenants dancing the African-based Juba; the conjure man, Bynum, killing pigeons in Seth's garden and relating the tale of Shiny Man; Miss Mabel's ghost actually appearing before the child Reuben; and Loomis claiming to experience atavistic visions of the Middle Passage and, ultimately, inflicting a wound upon his body. Each of these episodes is steeped in African ritual and lore as well as in symbolic aspects of African Americans' slave past, and, taken together, they underscore how the play can operate as a closed performance.

I was witness to intense reactions to one of August Wilson's closed performances when he visited Howard University in September 1995 to participate in an open forum at the Ira Aldridge Theater. During the question-and-answer session, a white woman rose from the predominantly African American audience and admitted that she was unable to observe anything African about the characters in a production of *Joe Turner's Come and Gone*, which she had recently seen, and asked that the playwright expand upon this aspect of the play's premise. Immediately, her question transformed the dynamics of the Howard University audience from collegial and respectful to belligerent and defensive. Before Wilson could address her question, several vocal responses to her statements erupted from the crowd, as if, by admitting her difficulties, she had somehow insulted this particular audience, who evidently had no problems recognizing and accepting the likes of Herald Loomis, Bynum Walker, and Martha Pentacost as Africans. Once the audience had recovered from the initial impact of this woman's query, Wilson responded—not to why she had difficulties seeing Africa but to what, according to his agenda, the play should have revealed to her. In terms quite similar to those he expressed in the interview with Moyers, Wilson explained:

> We are Africans who have been in America since the seventeenth century. We are Americans. But first of all, we are Africans. . . . We have different philosophical ideas and attitudes, different values, different ideas about style and linguistics, different aesthetics.[26]

I cannot recall ever having witnessed a writer, a playwright, a musician, or a dancer being placed in the awkward position of having to explain why a particular member of an audience did not get their meaning. Neither can I recall any artist directly responding to such an honest though artistically intrusive query. Frankly, had Wilson answered this woman's question as forthrightly as she had posed it, he would have likely offended her. In effect, what she wanted to know was how could a white woman sit through a theatrical performance of *Joe Turner*, sharing the same space as African American spectators, and totally miss that the people on stage were Africans? What she revealed instead was that she—like other spectators of various races and cultural backgrounds who share her struggle—had not grasped the manifestations of the Africa that Wilson's plays embrace in performance. These Africanisms do not announce their presence with drum beats, colorful costumes, or expressive dances. Neither are they conveyed in native African tongues. Hence, recognition is not instantaneous or automatic to all members of the audience.

Had Wilson chosen to respond to the woman more directly, his answer might have been, "You don't get it because the play was not intended for you" or "You don't get it because you lack the necessary African sensibility." As if to avert such a scenario, Wilson simply repeated his assertion that these characters were undeniably African and left her to conjecture her own meaning from this.

The imaginary African masks that the Charles family dons in Wilson's *The Piano Lesson* (1988) are less implicit and thus less atavistic than those attempted in *Joe Turner's Come and Gone*. With the notable exception of *New Republic* critic Robert Brustein—whose well-known and widely proclaimed rejection of Africanist ideologies prompted him to denounce the play as "the most poorly composed of Wilson's four produced works"[27]—critics and audiences sensitive to the implications of the play, for the most part, do get it. That they comprehend the ties that bind African Americans living in 1936 Pittsburgh with their slave ancestors is due largely to the clearly didactic message of the play's principal symbolic image: a piano, more than a century old, carved with "African" symbols. Wilson is also more effective in convincing his audiences that the Depression-era Charles family, which has put its roots in Pittsburgh, is actually composed of Africans living in America. Wilson clarifies the ambiguities that he leaves open in *Joe Turner*. In *The Piano Lesson*, he relies upon the speeches of a single character, Doaker Charles, to reveal the crucial narrative of the family's history, which has remained locked in the piano. Conversations dominated by the sage uncle of the family create clear connections between Africa then and Pittsburgh now as he carefully delineates the experiences of his parents and grandparents: "See, now . . . to understand why we say that . . . to understand about that piano . . . you got to go back to slavery time. See, our family was owned by a fellow named Robert Sutter" (*PL* 42). As self-appointed griot, he keeps Africa ever in his family's psyche as well as in the consciousness of the play's audience.

A significant number of critics charge that *The Piano Lesson* is overwritten, devoid of action, repetitious, chatty, excessive in characterization, and (before Lloyd Richards was able to convince Wilson to add an extra scene to answer the unresolved question of the piano's final owner) lacked a resolution.[28] In addition, more than a few regard the supernatural intrusion of the ghost of Robert Sutter as an artificial and forced device.[29] On stage, this spirit announces its presence through the tinkling of the piano's ivory keys, the rustling of Berniece's curtains, and the frightful stares and screams of those who come upon it. Its presence is also confirmed in a physically exaggerated wrestling match, during which it proves a fitting rival for the frantically swinging, punching, tumbling Boy Willie. Thus, for many, Wilson's Africa hinges more upon the piano's profound nonverbal visual message while the supernatural addition of a ghost is relegated to the category of special effects.

Yet, just as the Charles family cannot so easily extract Sutter from the piano, Sutter's place in the Africa that Wilson reconstructs in *The Piano Lesson* must be contended with as well. Although paradoxical in nature, Sutter, the white relative of slave owners who bartered away Berniece's and Boy Willie's ancestors for a piano, is an inextricable part of the Charles family's Africanist past. As such, he is also part of the slave-owning colonialism in Africanist memory. Despite the baggage his ghost brings to the 1936 setting, he remains, until exorcised, a part of the African portrait that Wilson summons to the stage and recreates. Like the painful memories that plague Herald Loomis, Sutter's presence must be acknowledged before it can be understood and overcome.

For audiences of *Seven Guitars*, another one of Wilson's closed performances, the ability to recognize Africa and Africans is far from unanimous. The play has been written off as a disappointing hybrid offspring of Wilson's previous plays. From *Ma Rainey*, it inherits the ambitious though tragic blues musician; from *Joe Turner*, *Two Trains Running*, and *Fences*, it inherits the offbeat mystic; and from *The Piano Lesson*, it inherits a credible manifestation of the spiritual world. For example, in *Seven Guitars*, Hedley, the tubercular Jamaican sandwich vendor, perplexes *New York Times* reviewer Vincent Canby to the extent that he calls him the "most troublesome" aspect of the play's Broadway performance.[30] Hedley does not fit into a conventional scheme of Western drama. The character is, therefore, "unimportant" and deserves some neatly summarized and witty dismissal by critics—in this case the appellation "idiot savant."[31]

But, despite the dismay of those who question Hedley's relevance to *Seven Guitars*, Wilson has remained faithful to his initial conception of this character as a modern-day reflection of Africa. Prior to the start of rehearsals at the Goodman Theatre late in 1994, he told interviewer Tom Creamer:

> Specifically, the character Hedley may carry inside him the largest African response to the world with his concept of the messiah, with the understanding that there's a necessity for the messiah. In that sense he may be the one who carries the political awareness that blacks are not free and are oppressed.... Hedley may be the most African of the characters.[32]

Wilson's views of Hedley as "most African" are antithetical to those who deem him dramatically unworthy and point to the void between what the playwright intends and what certain audiences simply fail to understand. On stage, Hedley's severely stooped posture, his labored walking, and graying hair visibly suggest a man in the twilight of his life, a man whose years have revealed for him many of life's secrets, which he now feels compelled to impart. His desires to father a male child with the sensuous southerner and to get money from the self-taught trumpeter, Buddy Bolden, to build a plantation further underscore Africanist inclinations. However, despite this deceptively uncomplicated view of Hedley, his character, like those of Gabriel (*Fences*) and Hambone (*Two Trains Running*), requires more sophisticated understanding from the "culturally handicapped" audience in order for the African stories to have any serious impact. While the effects of alcohol, dementia, and various other mental impairments understandably lessen the credibility of such characters, Wilson insists that any honest reflection of African American culture must include the stories of these marginalized individuals who, he argues, impart the most useful knowledge of African cosmology, memory, and continuity. As such, Hedley is an example of an Africanism in its most basic, most Wilsonian form.

Although the black and white high school students who shared the audience with me at the spring 1997 Center Stage production of *Seven Guitars* found much to keep their attention for the three-hour performance, many looked dazed as they entered the lobby following the final curtain. A few broke the silence by recalling instances of humor as if to suppress thoughts of the gruesome, bloody images of Hedley slashing the throat of a neighbor's rooster followed soon by a similar bloodletting gesture inflicted upon Floyd Barton. They also chose to keep to themselves their immediate thoughts about a man obsessed with receiving money from a long-dead musician to buy a mythical plantation so that "the white man not going to tell me what to do no more" (*SG* 24). The entire experience prompted me to ask, "What is a teenager in 1997 (or any audience member, for that matter) to make of these images?" What level of knowledge do we need in order to comprehend such a profound performance? As I watched this group exit the theater, I was convinced that *Seven Guitars* had seriously shaken them. However, none spoke of Hedley or of Africa in their bewilderment.

The confused teenagers seemed to lack both the language and the cultural sensitivity needed to articulate clearly an understanding of what they had just experienced. This, of course, is saddening and problematic, for it strongly suggests that primary and secondary educational institutions are grooming another generation of callous, apathetic, and culturally ignorant critics and adult theatergoers to take the place of those now thriving in our adult populations. How are plays of the black experience (or any other experience other than white American) taught in these classrooms? Clearly, without knowledge of African-based rituals and without awareness of the nuances of African American history and culture, these youths—soon to become adults—will remain stunned, speechless, and unable to make sense out of much of what they see.

Perhaps because the symbolic backdrop of Africa lies so much in the distance in *Ma Rainey's Black Bottom*, L. Kenneth Richardson (who directed the Center Stage production of *Ma Rainey* during the fall 1990 season) chose to compensate for this absence in Wilson's 1930s play by adding an African mime dancer. Sensing that Wilson's play had somehow reneged on his agenda by not endowing a more imposing African presence, the director apparently took it upon himself to add the Africanist dimension. At select moments during the course of the more than three-hour performance, an embodiment of African consciousness appears on stage, gesticulating half in the shadows to ensure that the image of Africa remains present. Yet, much to the chagrin of the capacity audience on the night I attended, this "tinkering," as it has been called,[33] was overkill. *Washington Times* critic Hap Erstein concurred: "It [the performance] certainly doesn't need an added symbolic character that Mr. Richardson calls Spirit Dancer, a high-stepping, tribal-minstrel apparition to pop out on occasion and accentuate the obvious with his mute echoes of the action."[34] Interestingly, while Erstein's review of the play may have mirrored some of the audience's sentiments, his argument is significantly weakened by his failure to stipulate his meaning of "obvious" within the context of this performance. Moreover, his reasoning does not extend to the next logical step: a clear explanation of what the African dancer does convey. As is often the tendency of culturally uninformed critics, words can become smoke and mirrors, behind which there is frequently little substance.

Despite popular rejection of this appended device, I believe that the African embellishments made by director Richardson were in accord with August Wilson's Africanist agenda. Richardson's idea was to bridge the gaps he anticipated in the largely white audiences' ability to understand Wilson's African undertones. What the African mime dancer offered the Center Stage audience was an invitation to view the performance they had just seen within an African context informed by an African sensibility. From this site, the motivations, actions, and eventual fates of the characters took on more culturally specific meanings. Although silent, the dancer, who was garbed in African headdress, mask, and beads, communicated with his body that Ma, her band, and her two associates occupy the same space as their ancestors; moreover, the dancer drew attention to the fact that the characters should call upon their ancestors as they try to find their way in the racist America of the late 1920s. As a result of their refusal to set aside Western logic, the audience and critics, once again, opted to reject and dismiss as flawed this Africanist symbol.

For the most part, observing the characters of *Ma Rainey's Black Bottom* as Africans seems to be less important for Wilson in this play, which hinges upon a black man's more immediate concerns for survival in the racist recording industry of the late 1920s. Wilson must have realized that a too-aggressive demonstration of an African presence could overshadow other, equally pressing issues, including survival in a more modern environment. Furthermore, it stands to reason that, as his repertoire of plays moves chronologically toward the 1990s, Africa's presence must correspondingly assume more subtle forms. More important than establishing an African context in *Ma Rainey* is an emphasis upon the band's current sorry predicament, upon Ma's refusal to become a victim, and upon Levee's deferred dream. One might argue that getting to the root of each of these concerns involves going back to their African connections, but this is not an immediate concern for spectators, whose attention is focused upon the surface conflicts of the play. While Africa resonates in the persons of Herald Loomis and Bynum Walker in *Joe Turner* and in the etched-upon piano in *The Piano Lesson*, in *Ma Rainey's Black Bottom*, African sensibility becomes the subject of a built-in counternarrative, at the center of which Wilson places Toledo, the philosopher-pianist and eventual victim of homicide.

In Toledo, August Wilson creates a character who possesses exceptional potential to effect positive change among his people, yet he is never really able to rise to the occasion. This reflects the tradition of the revolutionary antihero popularized in Amiri Baraka's characters Walker Vessels (*The Slave*, 1964) and Clay (*The Dutchman*, 1964). Toledo is apparently the only literate and educated band member, yet he focuses his attention upon belittling Levee's intellect and pontificating pseudointellectual rhetoric about African sensibility. When asked for marijuana, for example, he uses the occasion to ostentatiously display his grasp of African concepts: "That's what you call an African conceptualization. That's when you name the gods and call on the ancestors to achieve whatever your desires are" (*MR* 32). At this moment in the play, Toledo's wisdom is not received well by the group, which deems it to be irrelevant to their present circumstances.

As antihero, Toledo forms a counternarrative, which underscores a misguided African sensibility. His non-warriorlike demeanor and his seemingly pretentious African idealism place him in opposition to Wilson's pronouncement that these characters are African. Toledo fails to use his knowledge of Africa to assist his comrades in transcending their dead-end conditions; instead, he flaunts it before them as evidence of his superior intelligence. Understood in these terms, his death becomes the supreme payment he must render to appease the gods, for he has failed them. Outside of this African-based logic, Toledo's death may be perceived as the last link in a causal chain of major disappointing events, which frequently culminates in black-on-black violence. His death comes at the hands of Levee, an individual who has witnessed his mother's rape and his father's murder and who has been duped out of his song lyrics—all acts perpetrated by white men. But, rather than focus his rage on the real oppressor, Levee makes Toledo his target.

Africa also finds indirect or built-in expression in the music of *Ma Rainey's Black Bottom*. The actors of the Center Stage production—coached by composer Olu Dara to "become" musicians for this performance—negotiate their own musical tunes during the mock rehearsal sessions they hold while waiting for Ma. In addition to their blues tunes, distinctly African sounds permeate the production to convey the potentially explosive emotional undercurrents of the male band members' separate and collective fates. In a combined mixture of rhythmical blues guitars, trumpets, and flutes, Dara attempted to infuse the play with Africa's presence by "[underscoring] various narrative passages, including a deft blues tune that accompanies August Wilson's text, a ballad Rainey sings to her tired, hurting feet."[35] Taking his cues from his "cultural ancestors in Africa and Mississippi,"[36] Dara conjured up a musical recipe for *Ma Rainey* made up of ingredients from his own cultural past. In addition, Dwight Andrews, Wilson's principal musician, whose long-time role has been to select and fine-tune the musical accompaniments for the plays, also locates Africa in the music by looking inward for the necessary inspiration. He stresses "how people hear" in determining the most appropriate music for the contemporary audience. That is, he sees as his mission not merely trying to create what Ma may have sounded like in the 1920s but determining how to modify her music to permit the modern audience an opportunity to go from patting their feet to comprehending the profound narratives of these characters' lives.[37]

A restaurant in Pittsburgh in 1969 is perhaps one of the least likely settings to introduce African-inspired characters. On the surface, Wilson's *Two Trains Running* appears to be the farthest removed from Africa, yet, just as in *Joe Turner's Come and Gone*, *The Piano Lesson*, *Ma Rainey's Black Bottom*, and *Seven Guitars*, Wilson tries to convince audiences that, in this play, too, "Africanisms did survive the Middle Passage."[38] The play presents a close look into the lives of black people who come regularly to commune about their despair in a Pittsburgh restaurant slated for demolition. The characters are a diverse group, and several story lines compete for emphasis, ranging from the battle of the restaurant owner to get a fair price from the city for his business to a fragile yet poignant romance between an ex-convict, Sterling, and the restaurant waitress, Risa.

Because *Two Trains Running* is the most historically distant from Africa to date, Wilson's toughest challenge is evoking a sense of an African presence in modern audiences. Previous experience seems to have taught him that the African connection must be subtly conveyed. No doubt in order to elicit the attention of the 1990s audience, which, I contend, has become somewhat numbed by the impact of special effects offered by electronic media, Wilson, in response, sought to modify his presentation of African sensibilities. As a result, the most prominent image of Africa in *Two Trains Running* is a 322-year-old woman, who never appears on stage. The Africanist embodiment is unmistakably signified in Methuselah-like Aunt Ester, the neighborhood faith healer and confidante. While her age is the historical equivalent of the number of years Africans have been in America, her character, like memory, defies exactness and, in fact, encourages belief in otherworldliness. Moreover, since she is never present on stage, Aunt Ester embodies the collisions of history and memory. Her looming presence in the minds of the characters strongly suggests that she is a force with which Memphis Lee's clients must reckon. Her absence from the stage facilitates her role as the distant voice of Africa, but her spiritual presence influences the behaviors on stage. She must be sought after to give counsel and solace and her patrons must act on the faith she supplies rather than on the logic of Western rationalism. We realize that she has absorbed centuries of cultural knowledge and strength, which she imparts on a pay-as-you-go basis. Although Ester never appears on stage, the *idea* of her presence is highly significant to Wilson's neo-Africanist agenda. According to Wilson, "we have [in Aunt Ester] a tradition to remember and fall back on."[39] Her ubiquitous presence in the minds and conversations of the characters is very much analogous to the modern and practical role that Wilson wills between Africa and his contemporary African American audience. Like the image of Africa, she need not surface as a literal or visible presence in the play in order to affect the well-being of her followers in Memphis Lee's Home-Style Restaurant. Instead, though absent, she raises the consciousness of the characters and the audience in subtle but profound ways. She is the link, through thought and memory, to ancestral roots. She is kept alive in the minds and imaginations of the characters and the audience, and as long as they believe she can be of service to them, the African presence hovers over us all.

Such is the ideal African world view that Wilson sketches in *Two Trains Running*, yet as in each of the previous plays discussed, the ideal does not always coincide with the real. When viewed through the lens of an Africanist aesthetic, what is so often classified by certain critics as "muddled" and "out of control," becomes significant in *Two Trains Running*. If, for example, one considers Brenda Gottschild's assertion that "African-based cultural forms and practices in the Americas . . . have signposts that differentiate them from European-based forms and practices,"[40] we will have a more solid basis for critiquing African-based works, such as those of August Wilson. When, for example, we observe Aunt Ester from a spiritual rather than material perspective, we enter the African cosmology that Wilson intends. What appears as "muddle" is redefined as ritual; what is taken for "out of control" is reinterpreted as Africanist expressivity; what is absent from the stage becomes present in the body; and what is seen as devoid of plot will be reconsidered as the flexibility of the griot, the African storyteller roots. Similar enlightenment on differences too automatically perceived as weaknesses in *Two Trains* may result upon acknowledging Gottschild's well-informed description of what shapes African performance. She notes:

> Another example [of opposing African and European elements in American culture] lies in African "dilemma" tales that illustrate a principle of contrariety, open-endedness, or living

with opposition, without the necessity of resolution or closure. These are stories that end with a question or call for a discussion, rather than a solution.[41]

Mainstream critics who adhere to single standards of excellence need to acknowledge the cultural signatures of other peoples and values. On those who continue to question how much of this is African and how much is loss of control, Paul Carter Harrison pins the label "sociological explication[s],"[42] and he attributes such misunderstanding to widespread indoctrination by contemporary modes of thought:

> Lost, for example, is the aesthetic appreciation of discontinuity— rather than linear continuity—as a rhythmic device in the expressive modes of African socialization, including the polymorphic orchestration of offbeats, counter beats, and breaks in music and storytelling, and the visual tension of asymmetrical patterns woven in West African Kente cloth and the African-American quilts of the rural south.[43]

What several of the play's critics claim to be plotless, motiveless, snail-paced performances, Harrison redefines as "a polymorphic orchestration." That is, the unpredictable rhythms and patterns throughout *Two Trains* correspond to the discordant nature that is so prevalent in an African aesthetic.

Fences (set in 1957) features muted African presence different from any others discussed here. As may be deduced by the play's Pulitzer Prize-winning status and the widespread popularity of the domestic drama in both theaters and anthologies, audiences as well as readers connect with the characters and see themselves in the process. Moreover, the numerous universal emotions evoked in *Fences* make it a play that crosses boundaries of time, age, race, gender, and culture. The major story line does not limit itself to a symbolic African landscape. Instead, it involves a garbage collector's war waged against himself, his coworkers, and his family for missing his dream of playing major league baseball.

The play, however, reveals an African presence in basic albeit subtle fashion. Troy Maxson's war-injured brother, Gabriel, whose mental condition leads Gabriel to believe that he is Archangel Gabriel and that he sees Saint Peter on a regular basis, is the conduit through which Wilson transmits an African sensibility in *Fences*. It is not coincidental that Gabriel is both mentally challenged and spiritually gifted, as he joins a number of similar Wilsonian characters whose sensitivity exceeds those around them, even if their mental capabilities do not. As Gabriel attempts to blow his trumpet at the end of the play to signal to Saint Peter to open the Pearly Gates for his brother, he introduces another dimension of *Fences* heretofore unseen; he enters a spiritual realm believed to be inhabited by his African ancestors, where the sound of his horn is, in fact, quite audible. Here again, Wilson subverts Western logic and interrupts the play's naturalistic premise by stepping outside of the borders defined by Eurocentric conventions.

Despite the best Africanist defense, however, this ending seemed to be an awkward attachment for Broadway producer Carol Shorenstein, who threatened to fire Lloyd Richards if he did not clip Gabriel's final gestures. She failed to see the significance of Gabriel's ending and feared it would cause doom for *Fences* in New York. Her decision went beyond personal taste; her reservations also mirrored those of regional theater audiences, which could not decipher Gabriel's "slow strange dance" (*F* 101), his awkward attempt to sing, and his failed efforts to blow his horn for Saint Peter. After months of haggling among Wilson, Richards, and Shorenstein, the three finally made no changes to the script. As a result, Wilson's agenda remained intact, despite efforts by those unfamiliar with his objectives.

The gaps that exist between Wilson's presentation of Africa on stage—in performance and in dialogue—and his audiences' ability to comprehend its depths are not without reason. Filling in these gaps, however, requires honest, conscientious, and willful work on the part of critics and audiences (and producers). Given the playwright's personal quest to negotiate his own African-German heritage, the problematic presence of Africa in his work parallels his maturing awareness of the importance of Africa in claiming his cultural background. Many of Wilson's white critics have been less than kind in their dissecting analyses of such devices, however, revealing evidence of a disturbing lack of cultural sensitivity exacerbated by a refusal to consider any other standards of excellence than their own. We must move beyond one-dimensional critiques, which fail to acknowledge cultural diversity and the plethora of cultural contributions.

August Wilson realizes a crucial and revolutionary role for Africa in his works. No longer can the portrayal of negative stereotypes, such as those that plague *Ma Rainey*'s Levee ("You don't see me running around in no jungle with no bone between my nose" [32]) or *Joe Turner*'s Seth ("that heebie-jeebie stuff" [2]), define Africa for contemporary audiences. In order to advance beyond this, we must recognize what Wole Soyinka refers to as "a prescriptive validation of African self-apprehension," what Paul Carter Harrison refers to as the "African continuum," what Tejumola Olaniyan refers to as "empowering post-Afrocentric space," what Brenda Gottschild refers to as "revisionist thinking,"[44] and what August Wilson consistently refers to as "blood's memory." The stage, as it has done historically, presents enormous opportunity to effect change, and Wilson is in the forefront of playwrights who are experimenting with performance techniques to usher in a new activist-artistic era. In the initially unexplained convulsions of Herald Loomis, in the lively Juba dance of his fellow tenants, in the bloodletting and chanting rituals of Bynum and Hedley, and in the sage advice of the 322-year-old Aunt Ester, Africa is summoned on stage.

NOTES

1. Kim Powers, "An Interview with August Wilson," *Theater* 16 (1984): 53.

2. Robert Brustein has been August Wilson's long-time adversary, harshly criticizing the playwright as well as the former dean of the Yale School of Drama and Wilson's former director, Lloyd Richards, for using the Yale Repertory Theatre as a steppingstone for Wilson's plays before they proceeded to Broadway. Brustein is director of the American Repertory Theater at the Loeb Drama Center, professor of English at Harvard, and drama critic for the *New Republic*.

3. Wole Soyinka, *Myth, Literature, and the African* World (Cambridge: Cambridge University Press, 1976), xi.

4. Benny Sato Ambush, "Culture Wars," *African American Review* 31 (1998): 582.

5. Brenda Gottschild, *Digging the Africanist Presence in American Performance* (Westport, Conn.: Greenwood, 1996), 3.

6. Powers 53.

7. Pierre Nora, "Between Memory and History," in *History and Memory in African American Culture* ed. Geneviève Fabre and Robert O'Meally (New York: Oxford University Press, 1994), 285–286.

8. Nora 289.

9. Bill Moyers, *A World of Ideas* (New York: Doubleday, 1989), 172–174.

10. Following is the key to the list of play abbreviations used in this chapter:

F	*Fences*
JT	*Joe Turner's Come and Gone*
JY	*Jitney!*
MR	*Ma Rainey's Black Bottom*
PL	*The Piano Lesson*
SG	*Seven Guitars*
TT	*Two Trains Running*

11. Quoted in Moyers 172.

12. James V. Hatch, review of *Digging the Africanist Presence in American Performance*, by Brenda Gottschild, in *African American Review* 3 (Fall 1997): 540.

13. John Conteh-Morgan, "African Traditional Drama and Issues in Theater Performance Criticism," *Comparative Drama* 28 (1994): 12.

14. Amadou Bissiri, "Aspects of Africanness in August Wilson's Drama: Reading *The Piano Lesson* through Wole Soyinka's Drama," *African American Review* 30 (1996): 111.

15. August Wilson, interview by author, tape recording, Baltimore, 25 Apr. 1996.

16. Tejumola Olaniyan, *Scars of Conquest/Masks of Resistance: The Invention of Cultural Identities in African, African American, and Caribbean Drama* (New York: Oxford University Press, 1995), 139.

17. Sandra G. Shannon, *The Dramatic Vision of August Wilson* (Washington, D.C.: Howard University Press, 1995), 133.

18. Mervyn Rothstein, "Round Five for the Theatrical Heavyweight," *New York Times* (15 Apr. 1990): H8.

19. Marco De Marinis, "Dramaturgy of the Spectator," *Drama Review* 31 (1987): 103.

20. Gottschild 6.

21. This series of exaggerated and off-base assessments of Herald Loomis's physical bout with the demons of his past come from the following reviews: David Richards, "The Tortured Spirit of 'Joe Turner,'" *Washington Post* (9 Oct. 1987): B1, B12; David Stearn, "'Turner' Comes to a Near-Halt," *USA Today* (29 Mar. 1988): 4D; and M. A. Scherer, "'Turner' Never Comes at All," *Evening Capital* (13 Oct. 1987): B10.

22. *JT* 14.

23. During *Joe Turner's* rehearsal for the 1986 production at Yale, Wilson, Richards, and several observers noted that the script ended with a lingering question as to whether Herald Loomis "finds his song." What audiences needed, according to Richards, was a more emotionally rewarding catharsis after Loomis's frustrated search for his wife for much of the play. Yet it was not until Wilson sat through several intensive rehearsals of the play that he discovered a solution for Loomis's unsatisfying depiction: "I came up with the idea of ending the first act with him on the floor unable to stand up. When he stands at the end, you can read that as him finding his song." For more on the process of revising *Joe Turner*, see Tom Killens, "Black Theater Triumphant: A Dynamic Duo from the Yale Repertory," *The World and I* (Dec. 1987), 236–239.

24. Bissiri 99.

25. Ibid.

26. Moyers 172.

27. Robert Brustein, "The Lessons of 'The Piano,'" *New Republic* (21 May 1990): 29.

28. To learn more about the process of revising *The Piano Lesson*, see Irene Backalenick, "Fine-Tuning *The Piano Lesson*: An Interview with Lloyd Richards," *Theater Week* (16–22 Apr. 1990): 1–19.

29. Dwight Andrews, telephone interview by author, Emory University, Atlanta, 28 Aug. 1997.

30. Vincent Canby, "Unrepentant, Defiant Blues for Seven Strong Voices," *New York Times* (28 Mar. 1996): C32.

31. Ibid.

32. Tom Creamer, "Men with Knives and Steel and Guitar Strings': An Interview with August Wilson," *On Stage* 9 (Goodman Theater Series, 1994–1995): E3.

33. Hap Erstein, "'Ma Rainey' Triumphs over Racism, Director," *Washington Times* (8 Oct. 1990): E3.

34. Ibid.

35. Stephanie Shapiro, "Olu Dara and All the World's Music," *Evening Sun* (16 Oct. 1990): D1.

36. Ibid.

37. See select reviews in Sandra G. Shannon, "Annotated Bibliography on Works by and about August Wilson since 1992," in *May All Your Fences Have Gates: Essays on the Drama of August Wilson*, ed. Alan Nadel (Iowa City: Iowa University Press, 1994), 230–266.

38. Hatch 540.

39. William K. Gale, "August Wilson's Vision of Light at End of the Tunnel," *Providence Journal-Bulletin* (6 Apr. 1990): D5.

40. Gottschild 7.

41. Ibid., 8.

42. Paul Carter Harrison, "August Wilson's Blues Poetics," in *August Wilson: Three Plays* (Pittsburgh: Pittsburgh University Press, 1991), 295.

43. Ibid.

44. Soyinka xii; Harrison 292; Olaniyan 139; and Gottschild 6.

KEITH CLARK

Race, Ritual, Reconnection, Reclamation:
August Wilson and the Refiguration
of the Male Dramatic Subject

V ery rarely does an author articulate his artistic strategy as concisely as does August Wilson in this 1991 interview in the *New York Times*:

> Part of my process is that I assemble all these things and later
> try to make sense out of them and sort of plug them in to what
> is my larger artistic agenda. That agenda is answering James
> Baldwin when he called for "a profound articulation of the black
> tradition," which he defined as "that field of manners and ritual
> of intercourse that will sustain a man once he's left his father's
> house." . . . In terms of influence on my work, I have what I call
> my four B's: Romare Bearden; Imamu Amiri Baraka, the writer;
> Jorge Luis Borges, the Argentine short-story writer; and the
> biggest B of all: the blues. (Wilson, "How" 5)

These comments encapsulate the playwright's "artistic agenda" and his place within the larger context of black male writers. With the production of several plays, including two Pulitzer Prize winners, the degree to which other art forms—the blues being paramount—influence Wilson's writing is well documented. His comments also illustrate the extent to which he situates himself within a twentieth-century black male artistic community.

From *Black Manhood in James Baldwin, Ernest J. Gaines, and August Wilson*, pp. 94–125. © 2002 by the Board of Trustees of the University of Illinois.

Wilson summons Baldwin's and Baraka's ancestral voices, affirming how they cultivated the cultural and artistic ground on which his feet are solidly planted. Wilson resituates the writer as subject: he claims and mines a fertile artistic heritage without "dissing" those who wrote before—no anxiety about his influences. That he places himself within a collectivity of African-American male writers underscores how his plays chronicle black men's exacting struggle to locate an inspiriting and uplifting environment in which they can realize a radical, authentic subjectivity.

For this chapter's title, I invoke Baraka's 1971 essay collection *Raise, Race, Rays, Raze* to suggest points of convergence and divergence vis-à-vis Wilson and other Black Arts dramatists. Wilson is indelibly marked with the cultural stamp of the 1960s Black Arts Movement.[1] His dramas, anchored in African-centered rituals and cosmology, evoke Ed Bullins's Afrocentric dramatic principles: "The future of Black theater will be in its evolution into a profound instrument of altering the slave mentality of Black Americans. In an evil, white world of ever shifting values and reality, for the Black man there must be a sanctuary for re-creation of the Black spirit and African identity" (Bullins 14). Wilson subscribes to the Black Arts Movement's aesthetic dictate that art be rooted in the cultural exigencies of black people; he proudly claims this as his artistic template. But underlying his dramatic vision is not a doctrinaire conception of race that calls for black drama to "raise" and "raze"—that it simultaneously uplift and bludgeon, as Baraka and Bullins mandated. Instead, he centers the boundless possibilities for his black male subjects, their pressing desire to reconnect and reclaim a sense of self, community, and history. By no means am I suggesting that he depicts culturally indifferent or amputated black men who lack racial animus. But even more so than Baraka's stentorian dramatic call to arms, Baldwin's own call issued in *Notes of a Native Son* for the inscription of a "field of manners and ritual of intercourse" (35–36) is the creative appeal to which Wilson responds. Challenging atavistic figurations of the black male dramatic protagonist, the playwright offers innovative forms through which he presents his reconceptualized subjects. He downplays ideological blandishments and centers the rituals that might reconnect not merely fragmented selves but experientially and historically related black men. Though he does not present unfettered and "whole" black men in plays such as *Ma Rainey's Black Bottom* (1984) and *Seven Guitars* (1996), he assiduously chronicles black men's resolute desire for intimacy and community—an impulse that is sometimes thwarted, sometimes realized, but never abandoned.

While some critics—Wilson's nemesis Robert Brustein being the most zealous—have assailed Wilson for covering familiar dramatic terrain, he is grounded in both American and African-American dramatic traditions.[2] Having garnered Pulitzer Prizes for *Fences* (1985) and *The Piano Lesson* (1991), his works evoke comparisons to the pantheon of "great" white dramatists (O'Neill, Miller, and Williams). Craig Hansen Werner has commented on this coterminous relationship:

> Wilson employs numerous themes and motifs familiar to theater audiences grounded in the O'Neill tradition, which includes Tennessee Williams, Sam Shepherd, Lillian Hellman, Lanford Wilson, Beth Henley, and numerous others. Among these are the disruption of the surface of family life by repressed or buried secrets, the blurring of the line separating "psychological" and "physical" realities, and the transformation of everyday diction and syntax into a heightened vernacular poetry. (*Playing* 278)

However, if one can argue that there exists an archetypal twentieth-century American dramatic story, it might be the staging of men's internecine conflicts. Vestiges of the psychological torpor of O'Neill's tortured male Tyrone triumvirate in *Long Day's Journey into Night* (1957) or the verbal bloodletting that occurs between the male real estate agents in David Mamet's *Glengarry Glen Ross* (1984) surface in the same-gender conflicts that pervade Wilson's plays. This is not to say that Wilson's dramatic design is strictly mimetic. However, denying these intersections would be tantamount to overlooking Ellison's discursive conversations with Dostoevsky, Twain, Poe, Whitman, and other European and Anglo-American male writers.

Notwithstanding Wilson's place in this American dramatic tradition, his plays ultimately transcend such parochial comparisons. The centering of black music stands as his most striking modal departure from his white dramatic predecessors, as Wilson venerates it in ways that echo Baraka's observations in his seminal study of African-American music, *Blues People*. As Wilson makes clear in his interview with Sandra G. Shannon, "I have always consciously been chasing the musicians. You see their expression has been so highly developed, and it has been one expression of African American life. It's like culture is in the music. And the writers are way behind the musicians I see" (Shannon, *Dramatic* 234). Though Wilson repeatedly claims the blues as his artistic reservoir, his plays have their thematic origins in the blues while simulating the structure of jazz—"blues tales" related in a "jazz mode."[3] While the distinction between blues and jazz modalities can be alternatively contrived and amorphous, Werner observes that, "Seen in relation to the blues impulse, the jazz impulse provides a way of exploring implications, of realizing the relational possibilities of the self, and of expanding consciousness (of self and community) through a process of continual improvisation" (*Playing* 268–69). One might therefore interpret Wilson's blues plays as being comparable to jazz compositions: his protagonists' sagas of personal, artistic, and familial turmoil are thematically hewn from the blues, while the plays' improvisational strategies of revelation through performance approximate jazz structurally. Not coincidentally, Wilson consistently configures his plays around quartets of black men: Levee, Slow Drag, Cutler, and Toledo in *Ma Rainey* and Floyd, Canewell, Red Carter, and Hedley in *Seven Guitars*. Hence, he invokes the organic and polyvoiced qualities of the jazz combo, replete with unfurling statements and counterstatements, restatements and revisions. This distinctly African-American discursive practice distinguishes his plays from the well-trodden paths of realism and naturalism, which often mute the black playwright's "blues voice."[4] Analogous to Baldwin's claim that the English language is anathema to the "spirits and patterns" of his fellow Harlemites and that he had to "find a way to bend it the way a blues singer bends a note" (Gresham 162), Wilson's elastic dramatic language and dramaturgy permit him to record the multiexpressiveness of African-American life and culture.

Simultaneously drawing on and departing from American dramatic conventions, Wilson constructs his plays in ways that are comparable to Gaines's fictive apparatus, which focuses less on emplotment and more on the stories of black people, especially black men. To this end, he abandons the hallmarks of the well-made play. Contrary to the specious claim that "our most highly acclaimed dramatists are still shaping their works to sequential diagrams" (Brustein, *Reimagining* 25), Wilson is less concerned with causality, linearity, or verisimilitude, which explains why his "history cycle" has not been composed chronologically. Comparing his formal design to the collages of the African-American painter Romare Bearden, he posits that "I've got all these images, and the point is how I put them together. The pieces are always there; it's how I put them together, the relationships between them that counts" (Rocha, "Conversation" 32). Because he constructs action associatively rather than chronologically, the dramatist doesn't so much abjure "sequential diagrams" as he de-emphasizes emplotment. He opens dramatic space for his characters' attempts to "sing their songs," a recurrent trope Wilson uses to signify his black male protagonists' wrenching but exigent spiritual journeys—a prerequisite for wholeness.

Wilson does not jettison plot in the vein of the absurdist dramatists of the 1950s (i.e., Eugene Ionesco or Jean-Paul Sartre). Nor does he metadramatically bring attention to the medium itself as a comment on the efficacy of form. Nor is Wilson a proponent of a neo-"theatre of cruelty," which reflects the French playwright and theorist Antonin Artaud's core belief that theater should incite and catapult spectators into revolutionary action.[5] Rather, Wilson's multiple dramatic discourses—simultaneously realist and naturalist, fabulist and mystic, ritual and spiritual—are rooted in black men's retrieval and voicing of personal histories, which inform the plays' thematic and formal configurations. Hence, personal story takes precedence over the erection of a seamlessly crafted dramatic story.

The lexicon critics use to describe Wilson's plays—words such as "ritualistic," "vernacular," and "musical" recur—invites comparisons between his plays and the revolutionary drama of the 1960s. From a dramaturgical standpoint, his works employ many of that genre's conventions, which Bullins particularizes:

> Some of the obvious elements that make up the alphabet of the secret language used in Black theater are, naturally, rhythm—black, blues, African; the racial consciousness and subconsciousness of Third World peoples; Black Cultural Nationalism, Black Revolutionary Nationalism and traditional Black people's familial nationalism; dance, as in Black life style and patterns; Black religion in its numerous forms—gospel, negro spiritualism to African spirit, sun, moon, stars and ancestor worship; Black astrology, numerology and symbolism; Black mysticism, magic and myth-science; also, history, fable and legend, vodun ritual-ceremony, Afro-American nigger street styles, and, of course, Black music. (9)

A cursory glance at the Wilson oeuvre reveals his indebtedness and adherence to 1960s dramatic aesthetics: the quasi nationalism of characters such as Toledo (*Ma Rainey*) and Sterling (*Two Trains Running*); the African-imbued cultural rituals and myths of *Joe Turner's Come and Gone*; and the seven disjointed, blues-inspired characters in *Seven Guitars* whose lives converge with tragic and transformative consequences. His "polyrhythmic"[6] dramas are undeniably the by-products of this watershed artistic moment.

Though Wilson's plays abound with connections to Black Arts drama, there are substantive differences. The poet and critic Larry Neal's 1968 essay "The Black Arts Movement," considered the cultural manifesto for Black Arts drama, lays bare the distinctions between Wilson and his acknowledged dramatic standard-bearers. Neal earnestly proclaims that the Black Arts Movement eschews "protest literature" but paradoxically insists that "The motive behind the Black aesthetic is the destruction of the white thing, the destruction of white ideas, and white ways of looking at the world" (258–59). It would be erroneous and critically irresponsible to extract these comments from their social and cultural contexts, but it would also be myopic to overlook the race-speak that sometimes diluted the movement's aesthetic aims. A percipient observation by the drama scholar Tejumola Olaniyan addresses the problems of such binary thinking. According to him, there is an inherent "problematic feature of counterdiscourses: their deep and intricate relations with the dominant. They share the same ground with the dominant and thus run the risk of a fixation with the restrictive binary logics of the latter and of recycling its epistemological premises" (20). At the heart of Neal's treatise lies a symbiotic relationship with the dominant, an unshakeable need to invert the cultural and artistic hegemony, to replace one orthodoxy with another.

I interpret Wilsonian aesthetics as less counterdiscursive than recursive and reclamative. Refusing to privilege or valorize Anglo-American culture as dominant, Wilson strives to reposition and recapture blackness not as the mirror opposite of whiteness but for its own historical resonance and complexity. By vowing to compose what he calls a "dramatic history of black Americans" (Shannon, *Dramatic* 232), he has committed to interrogating and displaying the rituals and intricate relationships that unify and/or estrange blacks from each other—again, what Baldwin labeled a "field of manners." Much less a dramatist of didacticism than a dramatist of ideas, Wilson distills the blackness of blackness, that unique and contradictory web of individual and collective narratives of blues people, irrespective of the cultural forces committed to their evisceration. Throughout his work, he dissects the codes of conduct that govern blacks' relationships to each other, foregrounding especially black men's excruciating attempts to gather together in the name of individual and collective affirmation.

Talking B(l)ack, Talking Blues: Repositioning the Black Male Dramatic Subject

By placing black vernacular, oral, and performance traditions at the heart of his art, August Wilson foregrounds the intersection of African-American cultural practices and identity formation. Expounding on the dramatist's literary apprenticeship, the novelist Ishmael Reed conveys how Wilson's native Pittsburgh shaped his artistic ethos as definitively as Louisiana informed Gaines's:

> Wilson's official education ended in the ninth grade, but another education took place in the highest academies of the African literary oral tradition: the gambling dens, or the street corners like the one at Fullerton and Wylie in Pittsburgh, which the Harlem Renaissance author Claude McKay called "the crossroads of the world." Then there were the restaurants, also in Pittsburgh: Eddie's restaurant, on Centre Avenue, Sef's Place, Pat's Place— places where the old-timers gather to "play the dozens," "signify," and indulge in all their other volatile, hyperbolic word games. (Reed, "Shy Genius" 95)

A sense of place as sentient and organic pervades Wilson's drama-world. The playwright's omnipresent fascination with various communal enclaves—stages, really—piqued his interest in community, performance, and voicedness. Moreover, that the gambling dens and street corners were probably male-dominated venues elucidates the author's persistent concern with the black subjectivity–masculinity nexus. With disarming candor he admits that "I doubt seriously if I would make a woman the focus of my work simply because of the fact that I am a man, and I guess because of the ground on which I stand and the viewpoint from which I perceive the world" (Shannon, *Dramatic* 222). Though one might take umbrage with this sort of gender essentialism,[7] the playwright's point is crucial to demythologizing his concentration on black men. Ultimately, his plays are neither misogynistic nor phallocentric, but they are male-centered. Wilson dismantles hackneyed definitions of maleness, for clusters of male characters dramatize the arduous internal excavation that must be undertaken in negotiating individual and collective identity.

When one begins to consider Wilson's representations of black men within the context of black drama in the second half of the century, comparisons with archetypal protagonists such as Hansberry's Walter Lee Younger and Baraka's Clay Williams are inevitable.[8] What resurfaces throughout the canon is a concern with black men's valiant though often misguided efforts to situate themselves into a fiction of archetypal masculinity—attempts that are often derailed by a virulently hostile hegemonic culture. Baraka spells out the ideological basis of black male dramatic representation in "The Revolutionary Theatre": "The Revolutionary Theatre must Accuse and Attack anything that can be accused and attacked. It must Accuse and Attack because it is a *theatre of Victims*. It looks at the sky with the victims' eyes, and moves the victims to look at the strength in their minds and their bodies. . . . Our theatre will show victims so that their *brothers* in the audience will be better able to understand that they are the *brothers of victims*, and that they themselves are victims if they are blood *brothers*" (211, 213; emphasis added). One could read these proclamations as cultural and artistic calls to arms that exhort the victims—"blood brothers"—to liberate and empower themselves. The repeated emphasis on "brothers" here is telling as well: all the blacks are Victims; all the victims are men; and women are accorded neither status.

I return briefly to Wilson's most adamant critic, the former dean of the Yale school of drama, Robert Brustein, to illustrate a more contemporary variation on the notion that black drama can be simplistically relegated to "agit-prop" or "guilt" literature. Assailing *Fences* as an ersatz *Death of a Salesman* in blackface, Brustein concludes: "Yet, for all his sense of black uniqueness, his recurrent theme is the familiar American charge of victimization. What is remarkable is the way in which audiences sit still for their portion of guilt" (*Reimagining* 26). The patina of racial and critical chauvinism notwithstanding, the terms "victimization" and "guilt" deserve especial attention, for they exemplify the tendency of some critics to objectify black writing and consign it to the rubric of "victim literature," where it can be summarily dismissed.[9] Thus, Brustein and Baraka become strange bedfellows, for each critic's underlying assumption is that black art has as its primary object a white audience. In Barakan discourse, this cruel theater of victims should flay said audience; in Brustein's, the audience masochistically accepts the lashings.

I concur instead with Wilson's assertion that "I try not to portray any of my characters as victims" (Shannon, *Dramatic Vision* 222). Plays with black protagonists do not necessarily present a bifurcated view, with irredeemable white victimizers and infallible black victims. Wilson does not repudiate protest inasmuch as he depicts characters that may have experienced crushing racism. But while these experiences may spawn the dramatic action, the author is not obsessed with redress. I would take issue with the notion that Wilson's plays "continue and deepen the motif of facing the white man which Baraka developed so fully" (Rocha, "Four B's" 7). Instead, one might conclude that his works contain shreds of protest but are not subsumed by it; "facing" the ubiquitous "Man" is by no means their raison d'être.

To this end, Wilson decenters singular characters by dramatizing communities of black men in order to depict their various phases of identity formation. As Shannon argues, "Often depicted on the verge of an emotional breakdown, Levee [*Ma Rainey*], Herald Loomis [*Joe Turner's Come and Gone*], Troy Maxson [*Fences*], and Boy Willie [*The Piano Lesson*] dominate center stage and become Wilson's primary spokesmen" ("Good Christian's" 127). While some characters do maintain more crucial roles in the hierarchy of dramatic action, Wilson resists the discursive tendency to represent any singular figure as *the* sociocultural incarnation of the long-suffering black man. Seldom does he heap the burden of "spokesvictim" upon any singular protagonist, though inevitably certain characters, such as Troy Maxson in *Fences*, who experiences the insidious racism that pervades professional athletics, reflect the author's social sentiments.

In situating a panoply of black male voices in central roles, Wilson envelops his plays with multiple perspectives to convey the multifaceted nature of post-1960s black male dramatic subjectivity, a discursive figuration far more complex than a simple replication of Anglo-American patriarchal subjectivity. Robert Vorlicky speaks to this shift in dramatic representations of the masculine in *Act Like a Man: Challenging Masculinities in American Drama*: "several contemporary American playwrights are confronting the assumptions that underlie the representation of male subjectivity. They are embracing the notion that the *asymmetries of gender affect the construction of male subjectivity*, resulting in a varied range of male identities when dramatizing men alone together" (3; emphasis added). Wilson's plays foreground multiple conceptions of gender that are often contradictory and conflicting. However, the Baldwinian "ritual of intercourse" becomes his strategic blueprint for dramatic writing, and his primarily—though not exclusively—male communities become sites where the terms of subjectivity can be negotiated and redefined. His characters cannot be categorized binarily as whole or psychically fragmented; there exist too many "asymmetries," too broad a range of masculinities. His characters' interactions reflect black men in the process of resituating themselves as individual and as communal subjects, in the process of "trying to find their songs."

Taken cumulatively, Wilson's men embark upon spiritual journeys into unexplored parts of themselves as well as their counterparts. Schematizing the melange of voices that populate his mise-en-scène, I offer the following paradigm of the Wilson subject:

1. The *mimetic* subject: This figure is physically present in his community but has misguidedly inculcated values that preclude emotional and spiritual bonds. This character often valorizes some aspect of a patriarchal masculinity: an obsession with economic independence and capitalistic values, an anachronistic, extramasculinized conceptualization of malehood rooted in violence and the objectification of women, or a debilitating belief that his subjectivity depends upon disproving/abrogating whites' depreciative master-narrative of black masculinity. Characters such as Levee in *Ma Rainey* and Floyd Barton in *Seven Guitars* (as well as Troy Maxson in *Fences*) exemplify this discursive formation.

2. The *aggregate* subject: This character lays claim to subject status through communal ties—the psychological and emotional connection to people with whom he shares geographic space. This fusing of psychic space and physical place allows these protagonists to achieve a sense of community that traverses temporal or spatial boundaries. Connecting with other blacks across time and space is an essential part of these characters' understanding of their subjectivity. Men such as Cutler and Slow Drag in *Ma Rainey* and Canewell in *Seven Guitars* exemplify many of these traits.

3. The *inchoate* subject: This liminal character is betwixt and between the previous configurations. Characters who fall under this category include Hedley in *Seven Guitars*. Such figures are often on the cusp of regeneration—or degeneration—and undergo some experience that alters their identities in the course of the play.

Of course, some characters may not be confined to the above categories or may embody characteristics of each, and the categories are not mutually exclusive; there is often overlap. But most significant is the scope of Wilson's depictions and his attempts to provide a panoramic representation of black men.

In effect, *Ma Rainey* and *Seven Guitars* (as well as *Joe Turner* and *Fences*, to which I will allude here but not discuss in depth) are structured around an imbrication of stories, intricately woven and related. At the vortex of Wilson's plays lies the performance principle, his deeply ingrained belief in the inspiriting and empowering possibilities of African and African-American vernacular, oral, and musical traditions in the reformation of the black male subject. Olaniyan's delineation of a "performative" identity illustrates why black vernacular culture is the sine qua non in investigations of Wilson's representation of black male subjectivity: "The performative . . . stresses the historicity of culture, that is, its 'made-ness' in space and time. . . . Identity in the performative conception is a *process* marked by endless negotiations. It is never closed or positive but always vulnerable, fragile" (30–31). Wilson depicts how the performative, in addition to being an organic process, requires a psychic and spiritual intermingling of self and others. To this end, musical performance, storytelling, story-listening, witnessing, and testifying represent authentic acts of cultural preservation, empowering acts of self-representation, and vehicles for collapsing emotional barriers black men erect between each other. These complex negotiations represent blues acts, the constant statement and restatement, articulation and signification that governs the characters' interactions and articulations of identity. Thus, the self's ability to "perform identity" in order to access its myriad possibilities becomes the cornerstone of Wilson's dramaturgy. Foremost, this mandatory act is a prerequisite for achieving communitas, which emblematizes male intimacy and connectedness. These performances become Wilson's recurrent formal strategy, one fashioned not around a series of linearly constructed events but around the sentient and multirhythmic blues voices that inhabit his drama-world.

THE "SPOOKED" BLUESMEN: THE THWARTED QUEST FOR COMMUNITY IN *MA RAINEY'S BLACK BOTTOM*

Wilson's first Broadway play, *Ma Rainey's Black Bottom*, is emblematic, for he will continually return to the male artistic community to interrogate various facets of male subjectivity. This play presents a range of black men, encompassing all of the stages in my schematization of the Wilsonian subject. *Ma Rainey* chronicles the life of the 1920s blues icon and the recording industry's pandemic economic racism. *Ma Rainey* "dramatizes the production of blues race-records as a critique of commercial and racial exploitation of blacks by whites" (Smith, "*Ma Rainey's*" 177). When Ma Rainey expresses this exploitation as artistic and sexual defilement "As soon as they [the white men conducting the recording session] get my voice down on them recording machines, then it's just like if I'd be some whore and they roll over and put their pants on" (64)—she speaks not only for Wilson but also for generations of black performers who were similarly bamboozled. But this seeming "protest" situation, which pits the fiercely independent Ma against the rapacious white record producers Sturdyvant and Irvin, is of less dramatic cogency than the play's rigorous examination of the internecine struggles among a cadre of African-American artists irrespective of white avarice. We must look beyond the dramatic scaffolding—the blatant critique of the recording industry—to locate the play's foundation: the male band members' tortured attempts to achieve spiritual and psychological connections among themselves.

The artists who make up Ma's band, Cutler, Levee, Toledo, and Slow Drag, are deformed to varying degrees and for myriad reasons: the inculcation of patriarchal masculinity; a preoccupation with hegemonic, market-based values; and the sanctioning of a hypermasculine ethos that locates violence and competition as part of men's genetic makeup. *Ma Rainey* evolves as a series of vignettes in which the male characters perform episodes from their lives. The play's multiple voicings and responses suggest a free jazz composition, where statements are made, reacted to, revised, reversed, and restated. Wilson departs from his usual dramatic strategy, given that *Ma Rainey* is not divided into scenes. His decision to use only act demarcations—the play consists of two acts—gives the work a jazz ambiance because the characters' voices respond emotively to each other. Wilson organizes the play around the layered telling and hearing of stories. As he points out, "What I tried to do in *Ma Rainey*, and in all my work, is to reveal the richness of the lives of the people, who show that the largest ideas are contained by their lives, and that there is a nobility to their lives" (Powers 52). The revelations of personal histories become the play's locus and central organizing device, more so than the overworked dramatic conceit of black victims versus white perpetrators.

Ma Rainey's quartet consists of Cutler, the group's leader, Toledo, a quasi Black Nationalist, Levee, a mercurial young artist manqué, and Slow Drag, the convivial pianist. The play, as Paul Carter Harrison notes, depicts "itinerant blues musicians in a rehearsal room engaged in the male ritual aggression of 'lyin' and signifyin'" while exchanging survival tales about coming and going in a hostile world, taunting each other with a contrapuntal—call 'n' response—choral configuration which presses them to the edge of physical confrontation" (306–7). Through the ceremonial process of testifying and witnessing, the bluesmen attempt to dismantle the barriers—whether erected by themselves or the larger society—that preclude community and contribute to black men's disaffection. And though the climactic violence would seem to place the play within the rubric of protest, the author's insistence on the curative and regenerative power of voicing history makes racial retribution more ancillary. Though physical violence punctuates the play, it cannot abrogate the insurmountable power of even a single voice in this gathering of male artists.

The title is both rhetorical and metaphorical. "Bottom" could be interpreted as an addendum to Clay's climactic aria in *Dutchman*, where he interprets Bessie Smith's coded admonition to whites to "kiss my black ass." "Bottom" has multiple connotations in the black literary canon. In the context of this play, the bottom is concretized by the "band room," the space the musicians most frequently occupy, "in the basement of the building" below the recording studio. Though this room may symbolize the band members' low rank on the socioeconomic totem pole, space takes on a metaphorical meaning, representing a potentially regenerative realm, a site that inaugurates the storytelling rituals. In terms of the gender-space nexus, Vorlicky raises a salient point about what he labels "male-cast" plays:

> It is precisely when American men are in institutional settings of confinement, and to a lesser extent in workplaces, that the likelihood of their self-expression—or their self-disclosure— increases. By self-disclosure I mean something almost wholly contained within the realm of language: an individualization that overcomes the restrictions of cultural coding, in particular the powerful masculine ethos, but an individualization wholly manifested in the characters' articulation of personal truths. (6–7)

This comment speaks to the tropic function of setting, where speech acts potentially animate healing and communion. Just as the prison in *A Lesson Before Dying* stimulated Grant's and Jefferson's self-disclosures and their subsequent emotional-spiritual union, so too does the band room stimulate the interior psychic and historical journeys upon which the characters embark. The black male stories Wilson creates are alternatively comical, scatological, and tragic. Collectively, they bespeak the vastness of black male interiority, and the telling and hearing of them dramatizes the valuable though tenuous nature of community.

Storytelling in the play catalyzes spiritual connections and exposes the gulf that often separates black men who share common physical places but not psychic space. One story-performance that marks the constructive and reformative potential of voice is Cutler's rendition of the way Slow Drag acquired his name. Though Slow Drag refuses the invitation to recite the story himself, Cutler becomes his surrogate and weaves for the other men a ribald anecdote steeped in the blues, replete with music, sex, competition, violence, and survival.

According to Cutler, Slow Drag earned his name at a competition for the "best slow draggers." He "looked over the competition, got down off the bandstand, grabbed hold of one of them gals, and stuck to her like a fly to jelly" (45). When the woman's knife-wielding lover threatened him, "Slow Drag just looked over the gal's shoulder at the man and said, 'Mister, if you'd quit hollering and wait a minute . . . you'll see I'm doing you a favor. I'm helping this gal win ten dollars so she can buy you a gold watch.' The man just stood there and looked at him, all the while stroking that knife. Told Slow Drag, say, 'Alright, then, nigger. You just better make damn sure you win.' That's when folks started calling him Slow Drag" (45; author's ellipsis). This humorous episode is also a microcosm of the play: the dance, like the storytelling ritual, is an authentic cultural practice that potentially fosters communal ties; simultaneously, however, it portends doom when the specters of financial and sexual competition are introduced. Cutler doesn't tell a complete, self-contained story, because the resolution of his blues riff is much less significant than the act of performing it. The retelling of this story marks the blossoming of a speech community, a site where black men's voices are not bound by the strictures imposed by Anglo-American culture. Wilson conjures the image of Zora Neale Hurston's Janie Crawford, who entrusts her story to her "kissin' friend," Phoebe: " 'You can tel 'em what Ah say if you wants to. Dat's just de same as me 'cause mah tongue is in mah friend's mouf' " (9). Through the ritual retelling of his story, Slow Drag's tongue, like Janie's, is figuratively in Cutler's "mouf" his story metamorphosing into blues literally and metaphorically. Just as Hurston casts black women's speech acts as a celebratory form of sisterhood and as an act of resistance, Wilson depicts black men as brothers who are experientially, psychically, and historically bound. This ritualistic story-performance, as a tale told, retold, and recreated, embodies the play's overall jazz contours and sensibilities.

Cutler's centrality as a griotic figure is borne out not only in his insouciant recollection of Slow Drag's naming but also during his bracing tale about "Reverend Gates," a figure not present in the play but whose dehumanizing experience Cutler vividly re-creates. At this moment, he becomes a cultural custodian and conduit, for he presides over the stories about black men's lives irrespective of geographic or temporal boundaries. Reminiscent of Reverend Homer Barbee's resonant sermon and the Invisible Man's address on the dispossessed,[10] Cutler's "invocation" recalls the black preacher, who establishes a call-and-response relationship with his audience: "I'm gonna tell you something. Reverend Gates . . . you know Reverend Gates? . . . Slow

Drag know who I'm talking about. Reverend Gates . . . now I'm gonna show you how this go where the white man don't care a thing about who you is" (78–79; author's ellipses). This prelude links Cutler to a black sermonic tradition, where the speaker piques the congregation's interest by delaying information and employing certain rhetorical flourishes.[11] In setting the stage for his performance, Cutler satisfies what the story theorist Livia Polanyi deems the "burden of making the relevance of the telling clear" (21). Unlike Toledo, Cutler intuitively gauges his audience because he is culturally and cosmically embedded in its vernacular and customs.

Though he embroiders a disquieting tale of how a group of white men forced Reverend Gates to dance for their sadistic pleasure (a stark reversal of his comic "Slow Drag" anecdote), most crucial is the reception of Cutler's story by men who share his emotional space. Slow Drag offers intermittent affirmative responses, while Toledo "witnesses" by adding, "You don't even have to tell me no more. I know the facts of it. I done heard the same story a hundred times. It happened to me too. Same thing" (80). While Eileen Crawford argues that the men "discuss in their many moving stories their suffering and tribulations, these narratives, in essence, must be seen as rituals of complaint directed primarily *at* the white man" (42), it is significant that the bonds forged here are not based solely on common discriminatory experiences. Instead, they are produced by the amalgam of men telling stories, listening to, inspiring, and affirming each other's voices. When Cutler asserts the tale's veracity—"Reverend Gates sat right in my house and told me that story from his own mouth" (81)—we get a vivid idea of what Wilson himself envisioned when he articulated the organic power of storytelling: "If you're going to tell someone a story, and if you want to keep information alive, you have to make it memorable so that the person hearing it will go tell someone else. This is how it stays alive" (Moyers 168). The stories Wilson's black men impart transmit their mutual histories, as the playwright demonstrates that these narratives are integral to the ritual process of reconstructing black male subjectivity.

Given the layered story-voicings that constitute the play's central action, I take issue with the notion that Toledo represents the play's "singular choral figure, an unofficial griot or chronicler of the collective history" (Harrison 308). He represents the unmediated Black Nationalist voice, evinced by his Clay-esque soliloquy on why blacks are the "leftovers" of an oppressive white history (47). But whereas Toledo's pseudointellectual culinary analogy puts him at odds with the other band members—he derides them for misinterpreting his esoteric racial analyses—Cutler's stories speak definitively to the experiences the men share in a language they comprehend. Hence, he closely resembles what I have delineated as the aggregate subject, a figure who valorizes and immortalizes black men's past and present individual life-stories and re-creates them within a communal, affirming milieu.

However, the relationship between speakers and hearers isn't completely harmonious, for Levee represents a disruptive presence throughout the play. For instance, when Cutler is preparing his audience for his "Reverend Gates" story, Levee constantly challenges him over picayune details such as a train's itinerary: "You can stop telling that right there! That train don't stop in Sigsbee" (79). Unlike the other men, Levee is antagonistic throughout the storytelling event, foreshadowing his murder of Toledo and the psychological implosion that follows. By contesting minute facts of Cutler's tale, Levee fails to grasp the larger truths, not merely the repugnant treatment meted out to Reverend Gates but the importance of hearing and affirming the voices of other black men. He discounts their words, thereby replicating the white record producers' protracted devaluation of the black musicians; Levee and Sturdyvant patronizingly refer to them as "boys" throughout the recording session. Wilson casts Levee as an inveterately discordant voice that undermines the liberating potential of the burgeoning speech community, thereby portending the character's psychic degeneration at the play's conclusion.

As Levee's central role in the storytelling and listening evinces, there exists no hierarchy of voices and stories in the play. On the contrary, Wilson democratically grants each character an opportunity to speak his own reality. Though openly contemptuous of his fellow musicians' stories, Levee also has the opportunity to relate a life-altering experience, one that might explain his volatile and subsequently anticommunal behavior. At the conclusion of the first act, he delivers a Wrightian southern gothic story that not only demonstrates whites' searing hatred of blacks but the scars that such hatred leaves on the black body and psyche. Recalling an experience in Natchez, Mississippi, when he was only eight years old, Levee reveals the sexual and economic violence whites perpetrated in response to his father's business acumen. After his father declares young Levee "man of the house" before departing to buy farming supplies, Levee witnesses the barbarous gang rape of his mother by white men. Despite his futile attempts to defend her, one of the men "reached back and grabbed hold of that knife and whacked me across the chest with it" (57). Afterwards, his father devises a plan in which he resettles his family while feigning acceptance of his wife's violation. Refusing to go quietly, he embarks on a reconnaissance mission: he returns to avenge the rape by hiding in the woods and waiting for the perpetrators. Though his father is lynched in the ensuing battle, Levee divulges that he "got four of 'em before they got him" (58). While the attempt to defend his mother leaves a scar across his chest, the emotional wounds traumatize Levee as an adult. To make whites pay for his irreparable psychic scars, he vows to sell his songs to white record producers by engaging in obsequious behavior. Levee apparently hopes to parlay the mask that grins and lies into a monetary reward borne from his parents' blood.[12]

However, his means of salving his pain and avenging a racially violent childhood are severely wrongheaded, rendering him a mimetic subject— one determined to define himself within the constricting construct of patriarchal masculinity. Levee's childhood is a potential hotbed of Freudian hermeneutics: his psychological castration, the unresolved Oedipal complex, his lingering distrust of black men. Almost inevitably, his adulthood is burdened by the sins of fathers, both white and black. Thus his blues becomes not the jagged grain that sustains but a weight that encumbers his reconnection to other black people. Peter Middleton's comments on the role of oppression in male subject formation shed further light on Levee's psychosocial trauma: "Oppression confers an identity. For members of an oppressed group to recognize that they are oppressed is crucial, because that is the moment when they perceive that their experience is not the result of their own specific nature or the nature of the world, but the result of an alterable state of things (however difficult change might be in practical terms)" (146). Hence, Levee's life is subsumed by an inviolable narrative of oppression—his perpetual view of himself as a victim of an insurmountable white patriarchy. However, he does not view his situation as "alterable"; instead of challenging the pathological patriarchal masculinity that led to his mother's rape and father's lynching, Levee inculcates that pathology, which contributes to his devaluation of self.

Moreover, his adoption of a hypermasculine mindset leads him to view women as conquests, perhaps a reaction to his childhood psychological emasculation. Though Cutler warns him that she is "Ma's gal," Levee pursues Dussie Mae, claiming that the projected windfall from his songwriting will allow him to provide gifts far more lavish than those she receives from Ma. This becomes the most perverted form of mediated desire, since Levee's pursuit of Dussie Mae is fueled by competition. In addition to seeing Ma as a sexual opponent, Levee views her as an ersatz white male who thwarts his artistic endeavors (e.g., when Ma proclaims that the band will perform her version of "Black Bottom," not Levee's). Incarnating the mimetic subject, Levee harbors a distorted conceptualization of subjectivity, one garnered through material accoutrements and sexual spoils.

Throughout the play, Levee's relationship with Ma Rainey amplifies his conflicted definition of masculinity. Because she maintains a limited degree of power in her dealings with white men, he casts her as an adversary. Whether it be his insistence that the band play his version of "Black Bottom" or his pursuit of Dussie Mae, Levee views Ma as an obstacle on his road to self-elevation. In a modified form of plantation politics, he envisions Ma as a Mammy figure, an operative of the white power structure. For Levee to gain access to culturally sanctioned definitions of masculinity, her authority and voice must be neutralized. A fictive descendent of Bigger Thomas, Levee elevates black women to the position of faux white men, the gatekeepers of masculine privilege. In a bizarre conflation, he simultaneously loathes and emulates black women because they wield power even within the white patriarchy—evinced by Ma's behavior. Simultaneously, however, he devalues women by reducing them to objects of male sexual domination—hence his objectification of Dussie Mae. Deposing and possessing the ersatz white men, black women, enables Levee to revise and correct the childhood tragedy that reduced him to an invisible, powerless spectator and object-victim.

Though I have focused primarily on Wilson's representations of black men and the tenuous nature of community, Levee's interactions with Ma emphasize her essential role in the play. Wilson immerses her within the black male community through her masculine persona: she brazenly loud-talks and curses white men (record producers and policemen alike), she flaunts her lesbianism, and she freely interacts with the men in the band. In a memorable scene with Cutler, she castigates white producers for "raping" her economically and claims the blues as blacks' cultural and epistemological property whose true meaning, she insists, will forever elude whites. Wilson's fictive reincarnation of the blues legend blurs and subsequently shatters gender boundaries and constructions. In fact, the men would have done well to emulate her behavior instead of confining themselves to provincial notions of male subjectivity. The most conspicuous examples of this include Levee's frequent challenges to others' voices, his fight with Cutler over religion (in the latter portion of act two), and, most catastrophically, his murder of Toledo at the play's end.

Only during the instances of storytelling or musical performance do the male musicians begin to break out of their debilitating notions of masculinity. One particularly effusive example occurs early in the play. Waiting for the ever-tardy Ma to arrive at the recording session, the men dispute whether they will record her or Levee's version of "Ma Rainey's Black Bottom." Cutler then decides to have the band practice "Hear Me Talking to You" and instructs Slow Drag to "sing Ma's part," which opens thusly:

Rambling man makes no change in me
I'm gonna ramble back to my used-to-be
Ah, you hear me talking to you
I don't bite my tongue
You wants to be my man
You got to fetch it with you when you come. (27)

The title and lyrics of this blues abound with gendered connotations. The title underscores the play's concern not merely with the importance of speaking one's self but the necessity of having an audience participate in the "talking" by actively listening; Wilson considers this dynamic a fundamental dimension of the blues. This cultural performance is made more valuable and instructive by the performer himself. Wilson's substitution of Slow Drag for Ma blurs the gender boundaries that the men otherwise hold unimpeachable; the name Slow Drag comically corroborates this.[13] Slow Drag's performance of the song alters its meaning substantially. No longer a woman's assertion of verbal and sexual dominance, Slow Drag's rendition of "Hear Me Talking to You" restates the play's central concern: the conditions and difficulties surrounding black male intimacy and community. The performative realm thus represents a potentially transgendering space where black men can flout the dictates of normative masculinity that forbid even nonsexual intimacy among men, race notwithstanding.

Given the paucity of "blues moments" like Slow Drag's performance or Cutler's tragic-comic tales, *Ma Rainey* might leave the impression that black men are perpetually relegated to lives of abuse and oppression; the denouement ostensibly seems to corroborate such a conclusion. Like *Dutchman*, the play ends with an act of paroxysmal violence: Levee stabs Toledo because Toledo "stepped on my shoe with them raggedy-ass clodhoppers!" (92). However, the source of Levee's discontent is not the soiling of his cherished shoes but another crushing defeat: Sturdyvant, the more hostile of the two white record producers, refuses to listen to several songs he has composed and "takes them off [Levee's] hands" for a paltry five dollars. But Wilson moves beyond defining black male subjectivity as being overdetermined by economic exploitation. The predominantly white recording industry irrefutably has a long and shameful history of defrauding black artists; thus, Wilson does not have to dwell on this point. From a sociological standpoint, what has putatively come to be known as "black-on-black violence" would offer one plausible though facile explanation for the murder. Such an interpretation would situate the play securely in the shopworn category of protest drama, the requisite thesis being that whites are incorrigibly evil and that blacks are the powerless objects of their diabolical maneuvers who respond by mutilating each other.

However, in terms of the play's emphasis on black men's communal rituals and interactions, the murder is a part of a wider anthropological context that goes beyond a parochially racial one. René Girard has examined the etiology of violence, concluding that "When unappeased, violence seeks and always finds a *surrogate victim*. The creature that excited its fury is abruptly replaced by another, chosen only because it is vulnerable and close at hand" (2; emphasis added). In this context, violence involves a series of displacements and replacements that are not inherently racial. Perhaps Levee murders Toledo not premeditatedly but because he hastily finds in Toledo a substitute for Sturdyvant. Levee's action may therefore be as much the result of transference and convenience as the result of any racial animus. Thus Wilson's conclusion invites alternatives to jejune discussions of black male "pathology," a popular calumny at a moment when warehousing black men has become a lucrative practice and is seen as a necessary remedy to stem the black male "menace."

Because Levee's murder of Toledo engenders his own spiritual and emotional death,[14] it is significant that Cutler and Slow Drag survive and will likely perpetuate the vernacular rituals that promote communal intercourse. Unlike Levee and Toledo, who are haunted by and obsessed with white male hegemony, Slow Drag and Cutler embody the power of storytelling and blues as liberating rituals in black men's attempts to define or negotiate alternative vehicles for subjectivity. The play's violent conclusion does not undermine its central point: black men maintain the ability to deliver each other from a state of deformation, an asphyxiating realm where so many have perished. Though *Ma Rainey's Black Bottom* may appear to be a treatise on the wages of economic and racial violence as well as black men's destructive responses to oppression, it traverses the tradition of black masculinist protest literature. Its tiered[15] structure allows Wilson to subvert the requirements of realistic and protest drama by centering not how whites "pimp" black art but by interlarding the play with black men "performing self" in ways that are potentially regenerative and healing. Though Cutler and Slow Drag do not represent a thriving male artistic or vernacular community, they embody black men's potential to locate within each other their nascent blues voices.

As is his dramatic signature, Wilson presents an array of subjectivities in *Ma Rainey's Black Bottom*. Levee, the mimetic subject who wrongheadedly adopts the same values that led to his parents' deaths, may haunt us as an irremediably tragic figure. Aggregate subjects like Cutler and Slow Drag survive him, however. Their voices, linking black men's experiences through time and space, reverberate as the invaluable "bottom" that moors blues people like Ma Rainey. The often devalued internal lives of black men may appear ancillary, but they are invariably essential—the blackness of blackness. In *Seven Guitars*, Wilson returns to the male artistic community to probe black men's arduous struggle to reposition themselves as subjects.

"YOU DON'T NEVER GET THE FULL STORY"?: THE PERILS AND PLEASURES OF COMMUNAL LIVING IN *SEVEN GUITARS*

Despite the twelve-year gap between the Broadway premieres of *Ma Rainey's Black Bottom* and *Seven Guitars*, one can easily discern why they might be considered companion pieces. Like its predecessor, *Seven Guitars* foregrounds an assemblage of musicians who work tirelessly to forge spiritual and emotional ties. Another quartet of men engages in myriad performances attempting to voice individual and collective experiences. As is his common dramatic strategy, Wilson locates music as the lens through which he explores black male subjectivity. Moreover, racial oppression and black victimology are not the play's driving forces, underscored by the fact that Wilson uses basically the same agon: a black blues artist is shamelessly commodified, though the perpetrators of this exploitation are not a part of the play's dramatic action. The dramatist underplays protest and instead utilizes his dramatic space to probe the inner lives of his protagonists, who struggle to define their subjectivity. Contrary to one character's declaration that "you don't never get the full story," Wilson attempts to sketch a composite story-portrait of black men in *Seven Guitars*.

Like the spooked bluesmen of *Ma Rainey*, the artistic collective in *Guitars* is marked by its communal impulses and marred by an adherence to paralyzing and anachronistic constructions of subjectivity. Especially noteworthy is the sense of a cosmological male community, as Wilson's characters frequently invoke historical, artistic, and mythic icons, thereby illustrating that black men's attempts to commune transcend time and space. The play poses several trenchant questions: Why are black men's relationships governed by an adherence to hegemonic values and mores? Can confining constructions of gender be vanquished? Or are black men who inhabit common physical ground doomed by a sort of collective entropy, an inexplicable but inexorable predilection for self-destructive behavior? And finally, how do cultural performances become modes of resistance that empower black men to move from a subjectivity that is mimetic (Levee) to one that is more expansive, inclusive, and collective? *Seven Guitars* becomes the dramatic countersign for *Ma Rainey*, for it reiterates the revivifying effects of male camaraderie as well as the self-destructive impulses that hasten the implosion of scores of black men.

Seven Guitars opens with six friends of the blues singer Floyd Barton returning from his funeral and commemorating his life through stories and music. While the details surrounding Floyd's death are withheld until the play's end, its hows and whys are of less importance than the internecine conflicts between Floyd and those closest to him: his former lover Vera, the band members Red Carter and Canewell, and his friend Hedley, who is originally from Haiti. The play retrospectively explores Floyd's life in relation to these three men and three women. Though Wilson deemed *Seven Guitars* a "murder mystery" (Shannon, *Dramatic* 229), this is somewhat a misnomer. The author himself hints at this when he states, "you then have to look at Floyd in whatever relations he is having with anybody in the play" (229).

I interpret *Seven Guitars* less as a prototypical whodunit than as a drama charting men's attempts to connect and the seemingly insurmountable obstacles that hinder them. The play unfurls as an examination of competing ideologies, spawned by Floyd's ill-conceived idea of subjectivity and the conflicting attitudes of those around him. An array of different types of performances, *Seven Guitars* more closely resembles a Bearden collage than a murder mystery. The mystery genre, with its requisite plot convolutions and emphasis on action and suspense, is far too prescriptive and confining given the play's multidiscursive framework.

As one of the play's two strongly ideological figures, Floyd "Schoolboy" Barton has internalized the mythological narrative of Anglo-American male selfhood: the ardent belief that any man can parlay hard work and individual talent into success. Like Ben Franklin's black fictive heirs Invisible Man and Walter Lee Younger, he espouses a Panglossian belief in "opportunity," a word he frequently invokes to describe why he must return to Chicago by any means necessary to record another "hit" for a white recording label. A distinctly masculinized ethos informs Floyd's ontology and epistemology: he has served time in prison and the armed services, two institutions historically entrenched in oppressive constructions of black maleness.[16] Think for instance of the conclusion of Chester Himes's *If He Hollers Let Him Go*, in which Bob Jones is given two "choices": to serve jail time because of a white woman's spurious rape charge or to enlist in the army during the Second World War. Hence, as confining spaces within a fiercely hegemonic culture, these institutions reify black men's psychic imprisonment and devitalization.

Through these male-dominated venues, Wilson emphasizes Floyd's self-deluding belief in the American Dream. In fact, this may elucidate Wilson's choice of name: "Schoolboy" suggests a naive adherence to America's hollow promise that material prosperity is available to all. His insatiable desire for material accoutrements mediates all of his relationships. Floyd expresses these sentiments frequently, first when he recalls meeting Vera, whom he spurned but still desires:

> I had just got out the army. They give me forty-seven dollars. Adjustment allowance or something like that. I come on up Logan Street and I seen you. That's why I always say I had a pocket full of money when I met you. I seen you and said, "there go a woman." . . . My hands got to itching and seem like I didn't know what to do with them. I put them in my pocket and felt them forty-seven dollars . . . that thirty-eight under my coat . . . and I got up my nerve to say something to you. You remember that? Seem like that was a long time ago. (12; author's ellipses)

Floyd's recollections suggest a tainted conception of masculinity, one that objectifies women while fetishizing money and guns. This fetishism and objectification epitomize the supreme patrinarrative, a fiction that black men have willingly inherited from their white counterparts. In a subsequent paean to Chicago, he tells Canewell:

> I'm going there to take advantage of the opportunity. I'm gonna put out some more records. I know what will make a hit record. I leave here on the Greyhound and I bet you in one year's time I be back driving a Buick. Might even have a Cadillac. If you come visit me you be able to use my telephone. I'm gonna have everything. Some nice furniture. The white man ain't the only one can have a car and nice furniture. Nice clothes. It take a fool to sit around and don't want nothing. I ain't no fool. It's out there for somebody it may as well be out there for me. If Vera go up there with me and she don't like it, I'll send her back. But at least she will have the chance to see the opportunities. (80)

In Floyd's value system, the urban North becomes the black Mecca that offers material if not spiritual fulfillment. Using white American men's markers for success as his benchmark, he desires these possessions primarily because they have ascribed them value. In his schematization, Vera becomes another adornment who can be transported or discarded at will. In essence, Floyd adopts a patriarchal black masculinity that is as pernicious as its white counterpart. Like his dramatic predecessor Levee, Schoolboy represents the mimetic subject, for he privileges similar conceptions of masculinity that will induce his psychic and physical demise.

Consistent with his proclivity toward commodification, Floyd's attitudes about art reflect his distorted notions of manhood. The modus operandi of Floyd's predecessor, Ma Rainey, is worth revisiting. Though one could argue that she allows herself to be compromised and exploited, she nevertheless understands her devaluation. As if she were heeding Dr. Bledsoe's advice to the neophyte Invisible Man, Ma becomes a distaff version of the trickster who knowingly plays the game and manipulates the rules in order to exercise at least nominal agency. By controlling the conditions under which her voice will be recorded, and by also employing sass and invective as modes of resistance, Ma Rainey wields a substantial amount of power in the art–commodity nexus. Floyd, however, gullibly assumes that a sort of laissez-faire capitalism will reward him while also allowing him to maintain economic autonomy. Wilson aptly names him: as "Barton" euphonically suggests, he barters his voice, maniacally attempting to parlay his talents into profits for Savoy Records.[17] Though Wilson's symbolism here is somewhat turgid, the fact that Floyd's guitar remains "in pawn" for the play's duration emblematizes Floyd's role in the compromising and objectifying of his artistic voice. His obsessive attempt to peddle his talents leads ultimately to his psychic implosion, for he will subsequently rob a bank and physically threaten Canewell. He, like many male protagonists, willingly swallows the argot of the American Dream and the attendant mythic Anglo-American male self-creation story.

Wilson foregrounds an array of male characters who serve as countervoices to Floyd's hopelessly credulous one. Throughout *Seven Guitars*, Canewell represents one such voice. As his name suggests, he personifies a Toomerian southern ethos that Wilson insists must remain an abiding part of black life regardless of one's geographic location. The perils of northern exposure are painfully illuminated when Canewell recalls his imprisonment in Chicago's Cook County jail for singing and playing his harmonica on the street: "I said, 'If I'm gonna stand here and play I may as well throw my hat down . . . somebody might put something in it.' The police said I was disturbing the peace. Soliciting without a license. Loitering. Resisting arrest and disrespecting the law. They rolled all that together and charged me with laziness and give me thirty days. I ain't going back up there" (23; author's ellipsis). In Canewell's dissenting opinion, Chicago becomes a black man's no-man's-land, a place that criminalizes not merely the black man's artistic voice but his very being. His subsequent sequestration and silencing lay bare the risks black men undertake when attempting to convert their art into profit without the backing of the puissant white recording industry.

Wilson's depiction of Chicago as inimical to black subjectivity is a discursive pattern in black literature. The city represents the spiritual, emotional, or actual sepulchre for countless protagonists—Bigger Thomas, Lutie Johnson, and Walter Younger Jr. and Sr. come immediately to mind. Throughout the play it is metamorphosed into more than a physical environment. Characters superimpose their most cherished desires upon it until it represents a psychic as much as a geographic space their psychological Canada. Though his plays are not pastorals in which the city emblematizes social and personal disintegration, Wilson's representation of Chicago as the black man's dystopia dovetails with other black dramatists' portrayals of the urban milieu. As Robert Tener observes, "One of the major views of the fictive city to emerge in the decade of the sixties in African-American drama is that it is no place to be somebody. For those fictional blacks who appear in the plays of Ed Bullins, Amiri Baraka (LeRoi Jones), Charles Gordone, Adrienne Kennedy, and Lorraine Hansberry, the soul has apparently gone out of the city, its structures, and even its streets, producing a demonic world" (236). Canewell's denunciation has its antecedents, as his voice and experiences contradict Floyd's halcyon vision of the city. Thus,

Canewell functions as Wilson's spokesman, voicing the playwright's ardent belief that "if we [African Americans] had stayed in the South, we would have been a stronger people" (Rothstein 8).[18]

An even more prominent countervoice, Hedley is simultaneously Floyd's nemesis and doppelgänger; their relationship clearly parallels Toledo and Levee's. As a vendor who hawks everything from cigarettes to chicken sandwiches, Hedley ostensibly possesses an economic autonomy that eludes Floyd. Though Wilson does not specify the character's birthplace, his speech patterns and dialect suggest a Haitian origin; this is supported later in the play by his reverential memories of the Haitian revolutionary Touissaint L'Ouverture. Hedley's identity is a veritable callaloo: a Haitian who embodies the mythic, self-made Anglo-American male in economic terms, he castigates the West generally and white men specifically. Fiercely oppositional, he practices a syncretic religion that encompasses Rastafarianism, voodoo, and a distinctly Afrocentric form of Christianity. Hedley melds his polytheism with an impassioned, Diasporan nationalism, fervently exalting the legacies of Marcus Garvey and L'Ouverture. On the surface, at least, his is a corrective voice, one that punctures the shibboleths of Western/American male subjectivity to which Floyd adheres.

Despite these differences, both characters are bound because they imbue white men with the power and authority they so passionately crave. In Toledo's words, they are "spooked up with the white men" (*Ma Rainey* 55). Haunted by memories of dispossession and powerlessness, Hedley seeks redress for whites' colonization of his homeland. For instance, he rhapsodizes about owning a plantation, a place where "the white man not going to tell me what to do" (24). His "white man's disease," perhaps symbolized by the tuberculosis that afflicts him, becomes more chronic as the play progresses; hence, there is a tangible connection between his physical deterioration and his psychic obsession with avenging a multitude of white transgressions. Hedley's ruminations recall other psychically maimed men in Wilson's oeuvre—for instance, Gabriel in *Fences* and Hambone in *Two Trains Running*—whose life-altering encounters with whites prove catastrophic:

> Everybody say Hedley crazy cause he black. Because he know the place of the black man is not at the foot of the white man's boot. Maybe it is not all right in my head sometimes. Because I don't like the world. I don't like what I see from the people. The people is too small. *I always want to be a big man. Like Jesus Christ was a big man. He was the Son of the Father.* I too. I am the son of my father. Maybe Hedley never going to be big like that. But for himself inside ... that place where you live your own special life ... I would be happy to be big there. And maybe my

child, if it be a boy, *he would be big like Moses*. I think about that. *Somebody have to be the father of the man to lead the black man out of bondage*. Marcus Garvey have a father. Maybe if I could not be like Marcus Garvey then I could be the father of someone who would not bow down to the white man. Maybe I could be the father of the messiah. I am fifty-nine years old and my time is running out. Hedley is looking for a woman to lie down with and make his first baby. Maybe . . . Maybe you [Ruby] be that woman for me. Maybe we both be blessed. (67–68; emphasis added)

This eruption buttresses the notion that Hedley functions as the play's "slightly deranged and misunderstood conscience" (Shannon, "Transplant" 663) and renders Hedley what I delineated as a mimetic and inchoate subject.

However, aside from the mental disorientation suggested by his copious second-person references, Hedley's belief system is deeply flawed. Envisioning whites as the incarnation of evil, he fashions himself as a neo-Garveyite. That he cannot effect change, however, makes him a quasi race man and thereby compounds his frustration and psychic disintegration. As a result, a sort of race neurosis sets in because he ascribes to whites such impenetrable power and authority. Moreover, by invoking Moses and Christ, Hedley emulates venerated icons of Anglo-male religious authority—a glaring contradiction in his conceptualization of whites as evil that recalls Gabriel Grimes's infelicitous preachments in Baldwin's *Go Tell It on the Mountain*. His biblical desire for a line of heirs is the zenith of hegemonic male privilege. Stated another way, Hedley's inculcation of archetypal forms of patriarchal masculinity is exposed by his obsession with fathering a race as a bulwark against white oppression. Wilson foregrounds the shortcomings in Hedley's Sutpenian design, one glaring problem being the ecclesiastical preference for male children and the belief that women exist merely as the vessels through which this royal line is sired. Like Floyd Barton, Hedley envisions black male subjectivity as an inverted form of its white counterpart, a replication of a historically and categorically malignant construct.

Wilson's characterization of Hedley dramatizes the pitfalls of and links between cultural domination and identity formation: the sociopolitical colonization of his Caribbean homeland leaves him mentally colonized, reified in his fixation on white male hegemonic privilege as the foundation of black subjectivity. Not surprisingly, this fixation begets not only a sense of alienation among his compatriots but, more profoundly, a cosmological disconnection. Throughout this study, I have argued that the communal resituation of black men physically and emotionally has a curative effect; "Sonny's Blues" and *A Lesson before Dying* attest to the empowering and liberating potential of community. Conversely, however, Hedley's psychohistorical and multiethnic male triumvirate, consisting of Jesus, Moses, and Marcus Garvey, paralyzes him and impedes his psychological development—his attempt to become an aggregate subject. Despite their veneration and historical import, all of these figures personify a masculine power and privilege that Hedley mistakenly valorizes and emulates.

Though teetering on the precipice of psychic decomposition, Hedley reveres male historical figures who form a personal, cultural, and religious godhead. Recalling a boyhood experience in Haiti in which his teacher berated him for being a "black-as-sin nigger" who will never live up to L'Ouverture's legacy, he ruminates:

> I go home and my daddy he sitting there and he big and black and tired taking care of the white man's horses, and I say, "How come you not like Toussaint L'Ouverture, why you do nothing?" *And he kick me with him boot in my mouth. I shut up that day*, you know, and then when Marcus Garvey come *he give me back my voice to speak.* It was on my father's deathbed, with Death standing there, I say to him, "Father, I sorry about Toussaint L'Ouverture, Miss Manning say nobody ever amount to nothing and I never did again try. Then Marcus Garvey come and say that it was not true and that she lied and I forgive you kick me and I hope as God is with us now but a short time more that you forgive me my tongue." It was hard to say these things, but I confess my love for my father and Death standing there say, "I already took him a half hour ago." . . . So I dragged him with me these years across an ocean. Then my father come to me in a dream and he say he was sorry he died without forgiving me my tongue and that he would send Buddy Bolden [a blues singer to whom he refers throughout the course of the play] with some money for me to buy a plantation. *Then I get the letter from the white man* who come to take me away. So I say, "Hedley, be smart, go and see Joe Roberts." We sat and talked man to man. Joe Roberts is a nice man. I told him about Toussaint L'Ouverture and my father and Joe Roberts smile and he say he had something to give me. And he give to me this (*He takes out a machete that is wrapped in his burlap apron, crosses over, and sits on his stool*). (86–87; emphasis added)

Hedley becomes part of a coterie of Wilson tragic heroes for whom community remains a desired but elusive goal. Reminiscent of Troy Maxson (*Fences*) and Herald Loomis (*Joe Turner's Come and Gone*), he is burdened by the sins of biological and historical black fathers and omnipotent, vindictive white ones. And like Schoolboy Barton, he invests white men's words (his reception of the letter marking a repetition of an earlier scene in which Floyd received a patronizing letter from the president of Savoy Records) with the power to transform him into a sovereign, empowered subject. After Hedley happens upon some money that Floyd has stolen, he assumes it is the same money he dreamed that his father would bequeath him. That he slashes Floyd's throat is a sadly logical conclusion: the two men most enamored with the emblems of patriarchal privilege—money, property, women, male heirs—in effect suffer the same fate. While Floyd's death is a physical one, Hedley's is emotional and spiritual. In Wilson's dramatic configuration, Hedley and Floyd are Levee's descendants: they apotheosize distorted forms of male subjectivity, thereby doing irreparable damage to themselves and other black men.

SEVEN GUITARS AS INTERTEXTUAL BLUES

Though *Ma Rainey* and *Seven Guitars* end violently, Wilson is not validating the culturally sanctioned image of the feral black male. To counter his depiction of maimed black men, the dramatist often portrays ritualized performance to display alternative forms of black manhood. He often employs music and sports as "performances" that enable black men to move beyond cramping constructions of masculinity. *Seven Guitars* maintains a distinct intertextual dimension as Wilson recasts, reverses, and revises crucial scenes from Baldwin and Ellison. This artistic signifying accentuates the work's self-reflexivity, for the dramatist's aesthetic practices reiterate the play's core concerns about the power of black men's interactions. In other words, the curative potential of the gender-specific male community that these performances demonstrate is evidenced by Wilson's invocation of his literary forefathers' legacies. Their inspiriting voices reverberate throughout his artistic production, though he expands and iterates the centrality of performance in black men's identity formation.

Unlike the linearly configured well-made play, *Seven Guitars* contains multiple types of verbal and musical utterances that go beyond dialogue and the development of plot. At the literal center of the play lie two primarily (but not exclusively) masculinized performances—an impromptu blues/gospel sing-along and a boxing match. In the first, Wilson uses "Sonny's Blues" as an intertext to convey the value of gendered cultural performance and the ancestral wisdom available to black men willing to take the journey back. This performance precedes a re-enactment of a Joe Louis fight that centers not the fight itself but the characters' responses to it. Just as Ishmael Reed formally and thematically "tropes" *Invisible Man* in *Mumbo Jumbo*, Wilson revises the "Battle Royal" by dramatizing the potentially regenerative aspects of a historically dehumanizing ritual. That characters such as Hedley recall

Ellison's redoubtable Ras the Exhorter subtly suggests that *Seven Guitars* is a tour de force in signifying.

Wilson's revisiting and revising of these two male literary ancestors' texts, where he repositions himself discursively, recalls the different forms of signifying that Henry Louis Gates Jr. labels a "ritual of close reading":

> Reed's use of parody would seem to be fittingly described as motivated Signifyin(g), in which the text Signifies upon other black texts, in the manner of the vernacular ritual of "close reading." [Alice] Walker's use of pastiche, on the other hand, corresponds to unmotivated Signifyin(g), by which I mean to suggest not the absence of a profound intention but the absence of a negative critique.... Whereas Reed seems to be about the clearing of a space of narration, Walker seems to be intent on underscoring the relation of her text to Hurston's, in a joyous proclamation of antecedent and descendant texts. (xxvi–xxvii)

While Gates's rubric posits a distinctly gendered signifying, in which male writers critique and distinguish themselves from literary forefathers while Walker and other women authors venerate their foremothers' voices, it does help to situate Wilson among his male predecessors. Though I would not go as far as to say that Wilson's critique of Ellison amounts to a clearing of literary space, the playwright—consciously or unconsciously—tropes what Gerald Early calls "one of the most famous fictional boxing depictions in all of American literature" (25). Wilson recalls Baldwin's use of musical performance to facilitate male bonding and intimacy. That he literally centers these blues moments—they occur at the play's midpoint—underscores the notion that black subjectivity is grounded in cultural practice and ritual, buttressing the link between individual and collective performance and wholeness. The extemporaneous musical performance precedes the boxing match as a kind of invocation. After the "official" members of Floyd's band begin to play, Hedley pieces together an instrument made with a "two-by-four, a hammer, a nail, and a piece of chicken wire" (49). What commences is the quintessence of black vernacular/oral performance, replete with call and response, witnessing and testifying, and the cadences and rhythms of gospel and blues—a laying on of sacred and secular voices:

> HEDLEY: Now. When I was a little boy I asked my grandfather where his mother was. He say she was long gone far away. Say when he play this he could hear her pray. I asked him, "How?" He say, "Listen."

(*He plucks the string*)
>   I didn't hear her. But I learned it and I used to sit and play
>   and try to hear her. Once. Maybe. Almost.

(*Hedley begins to play the instrument. It is a simple tune for a simple instrument: really not much more than a piece of wire vibrating. The men listen hard.*)

FLOYD: *If I could hear my mother pray again,* I believe I'd
>   pray with her. I'd be happy just to hear her voice again. I
>   wouldn't care if she was cussing me out. They say you don't
>   miss your water till your well run dry. *If I could hear my
>   mother's voice again* I never would say nothing back to her.
>   I wouldn't mind hearing her singing either. She used to do
>   that sometime. *Used to sing "Old Ship of Zion."* I believe that
>   was her favorite. Though sometime she used to sing "The
>   Lord's Prayer." I can still hear her singing . . .

(*He sings* [the Lord's Prayer]) (49–50; emphasis added)

That Wilson interpolates the two central spirituals from "Sonny's Blues" grounds the play in the polyphonic tradition of Baldwin. Recall that the songs "If I Could Only Hear My Mother Pray Again" and "Tis the Old Ship of Zion" serve as the musical bridges for Sonny's reconnection to his narrator-brother. These spirituals spark the narrator's memory of his mother's injunction that he watch over the younger Sonny and lay the groundwork for the cathartic rendition of "Am I Blue," which catalyzes the final reconciliation of the prodigal Sonny and his solipsistic narrator-brother.

Similarly, Hedley's call elicits Floyd's response, in which he summons the regenerative and healing power of his dead mother's voice. As a result, Floyd spends most of the play raising money for her headstone; Wilson may as well be engaging in a bit of what Gates calls "joyous" signifying, since Walker's marking of Hurston's grave has been documented in Robert Hemenway's biography of Hurston. Moreover, since gospel music in black literature is often associated with women or homosexual men (think of Rose Maxson singing "Jesus, be a fence all around me every day" in *Fences*, or the professional gospel singer Arthur Montana in *Just Above My Head*), Floyd, at least temporarily, overcomes the limitations of hegemonic masculinity by invoking a *female* ancestral voice as a source of empowerment and spiritual renewal. His singing of his mother's song represents an inversion of the major leitmotif in *Joe Turner's Come and Gone*, where the healer-conjurer Bynum extols the knowledge that his father taught him how to recognize and claim his own "song," which allows him to assist others in resuscitating their voices. The improvised gospel-blues performances thus mark self-reflexive or metadramatic moments in the play. Wilson, anchored in African and African-American traditions, invokes the voice of his literary ancestor Baldwin to sanctify his artistic expression.

The sacred gives way to the secular in the following scene, in which the characters listen to the broadcast of the 1939 Joe Louis–Billy Conn bout. Wilson's insertion of this "social text" echoes a discursive feature of Toni Morrison's fiction in that historical events are interwoven to highlight not the events themselves but the role they play in the development of self and community.[19] Many male authors employ boxing metaphorically, and comparisons between its representation here and in *Invisible Man* are inevitable. However, like Reed, Wilson signifies on Ellison by using boxing as a unifying and almost sacred ritual that crystallizes the community of black men *and* women. Recall in *Invisible Man* how the battle functions as both cultural spectacle and symbol: it exemplifies sexism and racism, black myopia and self-erasure, and a general barbarism hidden beneath the patina of American puritanism.

More reminiscent of Gaines's portrayal of it in *A Lesson before Dying*, the fight, like the singing it follows, has a transformative and invigorating effect on those who hear it. An event that ostensibly ennobles an archaic and destructive conception of maleness, one predicated on pugilism and competition, has an almost holy effect on those who experience it. As is often the case in African-American literature, the line between sacred and secular performance is not only blurred but obliterated. After Louis knocks Conn out, the characters engage in another impromptu, cathartic expression: "The men celebrate. They begin to circle the yard chanting 'The Brown Bomber.' Red Carter grabs Louise and starts to dance with her. He pulls her into the center of the yard. Red Carter begins to dance. Canewell and Louise imitate him. Canewell stops and watches Red Carter admiringly. Canewell begins playing his harmonica" (53). The black fighter represents what Early calls a "conundrum" for both blacks and whites, a "symbol, political and social, and as a kind of running commentary, critical and complimentary, in the whole matter of what it means to be a black American" (33). Nevertheless, instead of inciting a race/class riot or so-called black-on-black violence, boxing in *Seven Guitars* inaugurates more culturally galvanizing rituals such as dance, another discursive element Wilson often employs to dramatize the liberating potential of African cultural practices.[20] Wilson transforms and represents a heretofore exclusively masculinized ritual as the basis of renewed communal ties; boxing becomes inclusive, abrogating the rigid gender boundaries that it traditionally reinforces. The musical and boxing spectacles together form a verbal and transverbal call and response, each performance complementing the other.

Wilson's reverence for black fighters dates back to the poetry he composed in the early 1960s. He asserts that his poem "Muhammad Ali" is "modeled after an African praise song in which you give praises of any kind" (Shannon, *Dramatic* 202). It is not surprising, then, that he deconstructs a ritual so commonly equated with male barbarism, imbuing it with restorative and cathartic qualities. However, it is rather ironic and a bit misleading that Joe Louis is such a looming historic presence in *Seven Guitars*. The boxer's life was fraught with the same contradictions, shortcomings, and tragedies that befall the men in this play. Nevertheless, the life of another boxer sheds further light on Wilson's tropological use of the sport.

Earlier, I pondered the euphonic salience of Floyd's last name, Barton, as a derivative of "barter." However, his first name carries equal significance, for it conjures memories of another famous black prizefighter, Floyd Patterson; the character's persistent concern with scoring a musical "hit" ironically bolsters this connection. In his pioneering work on literary and cultural figurations of boxing, Early comments on the enigmatic life of Patterson, a man who claimed John Wayne as his "favorite movie actor" and also declared that " 'I am a Negro and I'm proud to be one, but I'm also an American' " (33, 38).[21] In this context Floyd Barton's life becomes a gloss on the boxer with whom he shares a first name. The fictionalized blues singer's naive and misguided inculcation of the discourse of American success and masculinity echoes Patterson's own misplaced hero worship and his dual/ dueling identities. That he emulated Wayne, whose films and personal life exalted the excesses of white patriarchal masculinity and xenophobia, is both confounding and pitiable—but not shocking, considering the degree to which black men have modeled their behavior on abhorrent constructions of male subjectivity. Wilson uses the prizefighter's biography as an urtext for his portrayal of Floyd Barton: the latter becomes the mimetic double of the former, both men psychically consumed by their desire to include themselves within a narrative of American masculinity that has historically stymied black male liberation.

If one accepts that Floyd's is a warping and deforming conception of black subjectivity, then his murder might be seen as a constructive act. In this light, the health of the community might depend on expunging the materially crazed Floyd, who physically threatens Canewell after he accidentally finds Floyd's stolen money. However, the denouement, in which the characters are returning from Floyd's funeral, is much more ambiguous on this point. Instead of tying up the action in the tradition of the mystery or realistic play, the conclusion of *Seven Guitars* perhaps poses more questions than it answers, thereby resisting what Olaniyan calls the "hegemonic tradition of the 'well-made play' " (21). By revealing Hedley's murder of Floyd to the audience while withholding this information from the other characters, Wilson jettisons the structures and strictures of Western dramatic idioms, instead privileging black men's relationships and their perpetual search for different forms of community. Like Gaines, the playwright de-emphasizes violence by focusing on the destructive and constructive ways in which black men attempt to define their subjectivity. Wilson charts the devolution and disintegration of a character wedded to what Du Bois derided as America's "gospel of work and money" through Floyd Barton. Conversely, however, by centering homosocial and heterosocial rituals such as boxing, musical performance, dancing, and signifying, Wilson offers alternative vehicles for black male selfhood.

That August Wilson steeps his plays in the performative evokes comparisons to the Nigerian dramatist and Nobel Laureate Wole Soyinka, who similarly interfuses his plays with ritual. Dramas such as *Death and the King's Horseman* demonstrate that "For him, ritual is not only a cultural anchor but also a creative ideal for the representation of experience and phenomena that resist simplistic rationalism or socioeconomic calculation" (Olaniyan 62). When thinking of Wilson's performative aesthetic, rituals, especially masculinized ones, are the matrix of his forays into black men's psyches. *Seven Guitars*, like all of his works, problematizes putative and sacrosanct definitions of American manhood, evidenced by the persistent liberating potential of community that allows the remaining characters to sing Floyd Barton's aptly titled song, "That's All Right," in the wake of his emotional and physical evisceration. Though not all of Wilson's men can survive their encounters with the jagged grain, characters such as Red Carter, Canewell, Slow Drag, and Cutler remain resilient and indestructible black blues people who make a way out of no way. Complementing the centrality of ritual is the artistic legacy of Baldwin, whose griotic voice resonates throughout the playwright's oeuvre. Wilson's communal voice is ultimately part of a larger black male artistic landscape, for he painstakingly razes the figurative fences that separate generations of African-American men, be they writers, singers, blues musicians, or history's leftovers.

NOTES

1. Wilson reiterated how the Black Power movement of the 1960s nurtured his personal and artistic flowering at the eleventh biennial national conference of the Theatre Communications Group at Princeton in June 1996: "I find it curious but no small accident that I seldom hear those words 'Black Power' spoken, and when mention is made of that part of black history in America, whether in the press or in conversation, reference is made to the Civil Rights Movement as though the Black Power movement—an important social movement by America's ex-slaves—had in fact never happened. But the Black Power movement of the '60s was a reality; it was the kiln in which I was fired, and has much to do with the person I am today and the ideas and attitudes that I carry as part of my consciousness" ("Ground" 14–15).

2. The verbal jousting between Brustein and Wilson has surfaced in public and print. Wilson named names in his Princeton address (printed in the September 1996 edition of *American Theatre*), calling Brustein's criticism of grant-awarding procedures that benefit

some minority artists "sophomoric" ("Ground" 71). Brustein offered an acerbic rebuttal: "For me, Wilson's speech, not to mention his letter [in *American Theatre*, October 1996], resounds with separatist and exclusive demands. As a 'race man,' dedicated to 'Black Power,' he would force us into extreme color consciousness. Yet, he continues to refer to 'white' culture as if it were a monolithic entity without its own shades of color and varieties of difference" ("Forum" 63, 81).

3. I am riffing here on Eleanor W. Traylor's eloquent description of Baldwin's *Just Above My Head*, which she calls "a gospel tale told in the blues mode" (95).

4. Paul Carter Harrison makes this point when he articulates the shortcomings of Hansberry's dramatic poetics of the late 1950s: "The missing ingredient was style, some form of particularized presentation—more textual in its orientation than the highly esoteric kinetic rituals of Barbara Ann Teer's National Black Theatre—resourceful enough to reveal mythic layers of folk culture without becoming burdened with the familiar sociological formulations on the black experience that had constrained the *blues voice* of Lorraine Hansberry's *Raisin in the Sun*, subordinating her dramaturgy to the structural limitations of social realism popularized in the traditional American theater" (Harrison 298–99).

5. See Artaud's classic 1958 drama manifesto *The Theater and Its Double*, where he provides a theory and context for what he delineates as the theatre of cruelty.

6. The term "polyrhythmic" appears in Werner's essay on Wilson, "The Burden and the Binding Son: August Wilson's Neo-Classical Jazz," in *Playing the Changes*. Werner notes that Antonio Benitez-Rojo uses the phrase "polyrhythmic literature" in discussing the "interaction of European binary systems with Native American, Asian, and African traditions" (278).

7. One particularly problematic reading of Wilson is Kim Marra's "Ma Rainey and the Boyz": "Like most of his canonized predecessors, Wilson writes in a predominately realistic mode whose narrative structure posits a male protagonist and constructs female characters as Other" (123).

8. Darwin T. Turner's "Visions of Love and Manliness in a Blackening World" remains an informative exploration of how male representation in African-American drama has evolved. More recent studies include Carla J. McDonough's *Staging Masculinity*. In her chapter "August Wilson: Performing Black Masculinity," she provides an overview of social constructions of gender and uses Hansberry's Walter Lee Younger as a prototype for black male dramatic protagonists. She asserts that "Wilson's work is affected by and responds to a broad theatrical tradition: it encompasses the white fathers of American drama and the dramatic predecessors who helped to establish a theatrical tradition for African American dramatists" (140).

9. Along the same lines of Brustein's generally dismissive attitude toward black artistic production, David Littlejohn's *Black on White* remains one of the most execrable "studies" on black writing. This book is, with few exceptions, a protracted homily on black literature's failure to be "universal" and "positive." It opens thusly: "It may one day be different, but a white American today will find it an exhausting and depressing enterprise to immerse himself for long in the recent literature of the American Negro—for a number of reasons. Much of the writing, like much of the writing of any race, is simply poor, the product of small minds that happen to be Negro" (3).

10. For an insightful critical investigation of the sermonic tradition in black literature, see Dolan Hubbard's *The Sermon and the African American Literary Imagination*.

11. See Sandra G. Shannon's "The Long Wait" and Sandra Adell's "Speaking of Ma Rainey/Talking about the Blues" for discussions of the rhetorical and strategic function of "waiting" in the play.

12. Levee's violence-riddled past evokes comparisons with Wright's autobiography *Black Boy* and short story "Long Black Song." In the former, Wright's Uncle Silas Hoskins is killed by whites who are jealous of his thriving business; in the latter, another entrepreneur, also named Silas, is murdered by a gang of white men after he kills a white salesman with whom his wife has slept. Finally, Levee's birthplace, Natchez, is about twenty miles from Wright's birthplace in Mississippi.

13. Harry Elam makes a similar point about the significance of Slow Drag's "female impersonation": he contends that it "suggests a critique of restrictive gender roles and potentially symbolizes the artificiality of gender." However, I disagree with his assertion that Slow Drag's rendition "emphasizes principally the song's humor and cynically mocks the theme of female empowerment" (172). Slow Drag's version seems not to mock female empowerment but to expose the limitations of masculinity that are challenged only because of Ma's tardiness and not in the men's daily lives.

14. Harrison insightfully concludes that in murdering Toledo, "Levee has not only desecrated a natural life, but also cut himself off from ontological continuity, a sort of cosmic suicide" (311).

15. Victor Turner's work on ritual drama and performance is instructive in thinking about the myriad ways of interpreting the play's conclusion: "The many-leveled or tiered structure of a major ritual or drama, each level having many sectors, makes of these genres flexible and nuanced instruments capable of carrying and communicating many messages at once, even of subverting on one level what it appears to be 'saying' on another" (*Anthropology* 24).

16. For a sustained discussion of the intersections between race, masculinity, and war, see Greene's chapter "The Wars of Eden" in *Blacks in Eden*.

17. One cannot help but note a similar aural connection from *A Raisin in the Sun*: the character Murchison—"merchant's son"—who upheld his father's mercantilistic and classist values during his courtship of Beneatha Younger.

18. Shannon's "A Transplant That Did Not Take" elaborates on Chicago's thematic salience in the play specifically and in black history generally.

19. For a comprehensive discussion of the fight itself, see Jeffrey T. Sammons's *Beyond the Ring*, especially the section "Lull before the Storm" (120–22).

20. Mary L. Bogumil and Kim Periera discuss the role of the West African Juba as well as other African cultural practices alluded to in *Joe Turner's Come and Gone*.

21. Quoted from Floyd Patterson's 1962 autobiography *Victory over Myself*.

WILLIAM W. COOK

Members and Lames:
Language in the Plays of August Wilson

To be lame means to be outside of the central group and its culture; it is a negative characterization. . . . What all lames have in common is that they lack the knowledge which is necessary to run any kind of a game in the vernacular culture.

—William Labov, *Language in the Inner City*

lame: n. adj. (1950s–1990s) to be unaware of street culture.

—Clarence Major, *Juba to Jive*

The recent Oakland Schools case on black English (1996) and its precedent in Wayne County, Michigan (1979), have drawn public attention to a long-contested issue in African American letters. What is at stake is the nature and status of that particular version of American English spoken by some members of the African American community, and the function of that language in public discourse, particularly in those arts that purport to be part of an African American aesthetic.

James Weldon Johnson, writing in 1921, commented on his view of the limitation of that special form of American speech: "Negro dialect is . . . an instrument with but two full stops, humor and pathos. So that even when he confines himself to purely racial themes, the Aframerican poet realizes that there are phases of Negro life in the United States which cannot be treated

From *Black Theatre: Ritual Performance in the African Diaspora*, edited by Paul Carter Harrison, Victor Leo Walker II, Gus Edwards, pp. 388–396. © 2002 by Paul Carter Harrison, Victor Leo Walker II, and Gus Edwards.

in the dialect either adequately or artistically" (Johnson: 880). He pointed favorably to the writers of the Irish Renaissance as models for a new poetry, one not tied to the plantation tradition, which he saw inextricably embedded in "Negro" dialect. Johnson also inveighed against the "eye dialect" (the use of aberrant spelling to indicate black speech sounds), which he charged was borrowed from the local colorists of the turn of the century and the plantation school of poets:

> What the colored poet in the United States needs to do is something like what Synge did for the Irish; he needs to find a form that will express the racial spirit by symbols from within rather than by symbols from without, such as the mere mutilation of English spelling and pronunciation. He needs a form that is freer and larger than dialect.... Negro dialect is at present a medium that is not capable of giving expression to the varied conditions of Negro life in America, and much less is it capable of giving the fullest interpretation of Negro character and psychology. (Johnson: 881)

Johnson's criticism must be seen in the context of his own career. Dialect poems like "Sence You Went Away" (1900) are traditional products of the dialect school and, as such, stand in contrast to *God's Trombones* (1927), with its abandonment of "eye dialect" for a focus on the rhythms and cadences of black speech, an emphasis on what Johnson would call "symbols from within."

Johnson sees Paul Laurence Dunbar as a gifted poet victimized by the craze for dialect poetry. Dunbar said on more than one occasion that he was forced to write dialect poetry because it was the only language the public would listen to from a "Negro" writer. Dunbar is more eloquent on the subject in the 1903 poem "The Poet" than he is in any prose statement.

> He sang of life, serenely sweet,
> With now and then, a deeper note;
> From some high peak, nigh yet remote,
> He voiced the world's absorbing beat.
>
> He sang of love when earth was young,
> And Love, itself, was in his lays.
> But ah, the world, it turned to praise
> A jingle in a broken tongue. (Dunbar: 191)

I cite Johnson and Dunbar early in this discussion because August Wilson began as a poet and both Dunbar and Johnson played major roles in the development of twentieth-century black theatre, but we can trace the argument over black English in art through the New Negro Renaissance, through the black arts movement, and into our own day. The principal poets of the black arts movement, Leroi Jones (later Imamu Amiri Baraka), Sonia Sanchez, and Don Lee (later Haki Madhubuti) among them, opted for a language closer to northern urban black speech than to the rural southern dialect of the earlier plantation school. They were nevertheless clear in their insistence that the new black poetry could not be written in standard English. Geneva Smitherman, in her groundbreaking study *Talkin and Testifyin* (1977), argues that for the black arts artists, "an individual's language is intricately bound up with his or her sense of identity and group consciousness." She cites Fanon's argument for home dialect over the dominant discourse of the metropole: "Every dialect is a way of thinking." Smitherman sees the revolution as manifested in language for the black arts movement and a continuing issue for our own day. (Smitherman was one of the expert witnesses in the Wayne County suit, which insisted that teachers' ignorance of the home dialect of their students impeded their efforts to teach those students the dominant discourse of the nation. A similar court test of the nature of black English [ebonics] took place later, in an action brought in Oakland, California.)

> It continues to be the painful and trying task of the black consciousness movement to destroy the ambivalence about black language and culture and replace the old pejorative associations with new positive ones. Throughout the 1960s and on into the seventies, the clarion call of black politicians, artists, leaders, and intellectuals has been ethnic, their role revolutionary, the language black. Undoubtedly this has been in recognition of the fact that language is interwoven with culture and psychic being. Thus to deny the legitimacy of Africanized English is to deny the legitimacy of black culture and the black experience. (Smitherman: 174–75)

Frantz Fanon makes a similar point. "To speak means . . . to assume a culture. . . . In school the children . . . are taught to scorn the dialect. . . . The educated Negro adopts such a position with respect to European languages . . . because he wants to emphasize the rupture that has now occurred. He is incarnating a new type of man that he imposes on his associates and family" (Frantz Fanon, *Black Skins, White Masks*, cited in Smitherman: 171).

As a playwright, August Wilson seeks a way through the dialect/language briar patch that is linked to but different from those of his predecessors. Wilson is not much interested in the phonological or syntactical particularities of black speech; what interests him are the affective forms of the language. Narrative sequencing—the telling of the self through stories—is a central feature of black speech and of Wilson's characters. As Geneva Smitherman puts it,

> Black English speakers will render their general, abstract observations about life, love, people in the form of a concrete narrative. . . . They are not content just to sit back and rattle off the words to a story. . . . If the story is in response to an actual comment or question in a real-life situation, the storyteller comes on with a dramatic narration. . . . Subject matter includes . . . not plain and simple commentary but a dramatic narration and a communal reenactment of one's feelings and experiences. Thus one's humanity is reaffirmed. (Smitherman: 147–51)

Wilson's characters are ghost haunted. They bear with them memories and experiences they have either suppressed or dare not share. Their ghosts, the central subject of the blues, are the psychological baggage we bear, baggage that accrues as a result of the disruptions and disjunctions that have been our experience of life. Frequently we choose to suppress such ghosts, to deny their reality. The Great Migration was the first and greatest disruption. We entered a new world still carrying with us the operative responses of the spaces and cultures we were forced to leave behind. In our determination to be new or "born again," we too quickly discarded the wisdom of the home space and the ancestors who preside over it; we disdained the "safe spaces" in our new home, those cultural sites that retain a vital connection with the ancestral home. Note the way in which Wilson alerts his readers to this experience of cultural disjunction and its effects:

> For the immigrants of Europe, [immigration to America was] a dream dared and won true. . . . The descendants of African slaves were offered no such welcome or participation. . . . The city rejected them. . . . By 1957, the hard-won victories of the European immigrants had solidified the industrial might of America. War had been confronted and won with new energies that used loyalty and patriotism as its fuel . . . and the hot winds of change that would make the sixties a turbulent, racing, dangerous, and provocative decade had not yet begun to blow full. (*Fences*, preface, xvii–xviii)

Joe Turner's Come and Gone repeats the theme of the Great Migration and its losses and challenges.

From the deep and the near South the sons and daughters of newly freed African slaves wander into the city. Isolated, cut off from memory, having forgotten the names of the gods and only guessing at their faces, they arrive dazed and stunned, their hearts kicking in their chests with a song worth singing. They arrive . . . seeking . . . a way of bludgeoning and shaping the malleable parts of themselves into a new identity as free men of definite and sincere worth.

Foreigners in a strange land, they carry as part and parcel of their baggage a long line of separation and dispersement which informs their sensibilities and marks their conduct. (*Joe Turner's Come and Gone*, preface)

Although narrative sequencing can be used to deceive (for example, we embellish our worth in the community and conceal our ghosts from ourselves and others), self-deception does not succeed in Wilson's world. Other characters, refusing to believe the subterfuge, pressure the prevaricator into honest confession. The need to achieve a vital connection to our past is linked to a desire to be free of that past. Freedom to move toward self-construction and cultural wholeness is predicated on making peace with our ghosts. We cannot hide behind deceptive verbal masks forever. We must reveal and be revealed. It is on just such episodes of confrontation and revelation that Wilson builds his dramas. As Robert Frost wrote, "The best way out is always through."

The confrontations in Wilson's plays can be studied within a structural framework elaborated by Andrew K. Kennedy in his book *Dramatic Dialogue: The Duologue of Personal Encounter*. This structure or rhetorical unit, which Kennedy calls the "confessional duologue," frequently has the effect of reestablishing the confessor within the community. Kennedy defines the "confessional duologue" as "the dialogue of personal encounter whereby the characters compel essential self-disclosures from one another through interlinked sessions of talk" (Kennedy: 167). In order to certify our humanity and to escape the weight of the ghosts that haunt us, we go to the people; we tell how we did or did not get over. A kind of prose blues, narrative sequencing, or testifying marks the climactic moments in Wilson's plays. Kennedy calls this a kind of logotherapy.

To apply Kennedy's structural design is not to attribute to him a direct influence on Wilson but to note that Wilson, through his immersion in black culture, has arrived at a series of those "universals" too frequently marked off as the exclusive domain of white artists. It is to account in some way for the contradictions found in "mainstream" commentary on his work. The same critics who praise the dramatic power of his work fault that same work for what they see as verbal excess and lack of tidy, linear structure. But their notions of structure and language are alien to the cultural roots from which Wilson draws strength—and alien, too, one might add, to the white dramatists of the "confessional duologue," among them Eugene O'Neill, Tennessee Williams, and Edward Albee.

The following scheme, adapted from Kennedy's book, provides a structure within which to consider language encounters in Wilson's plays, one that moves beyond "eye dialect" and its phonological and lexical vagaries and beyond the mere surface features of black speech. Wilson is more interested in the deep structure of that speech, and in its communal and ritual powers. The confessional duologue is triggered by drink, frustration, or other "loss-of-control" experiences, and its intensity is heightened by evasion, repudiation, and denial. The more violent the rejection of the confession, the more violent that confession becomes. During such encounters, characters are asked (but more frequently forced) to confront the ghosts they have refused to acknowledge. The boundaries they have erected between reality and fantasy, between mask and face, between past and present are erased. Such encounters are an expression of the need for communication and companionship; yet they often lead to accusation and counteraccusation. In the comic mode, they result in understanding and empathy; in the tragic, in increased isolation and alienation. Linguistic markers of such moments are the frequent instances of code shifting. Dialogue leading up to the confession is marked by short, partial lines, a kind of modern stichomythia, but when the confession itself occurs, the language shifts to the poetic discourse of the people and is marked by the musicality of that discourse. This is the language of dream, of aspiration, of memory; it is the language of vision (Kennedy labels it "the dialect of the tribe"). This is the language of those moments that constitute a kind of verbal reconnection and ritual healing.

Note the sequence of testifying (counter-confession) that marks the syllogistic refutations of Wilson's first Broadway success, "Ma Rainey's Black Bottom." Act 1 ends with Levee telling the story of the rape of his mother and the lynching of his father. He is goaded into this narrative by charges that he is "spooked by the white man." The purpose of the narrative, then, is not to reveal the experience of his parents but to define himself as a formidable adversary, one who even as an eight-year-old is not to be trifled with. His testifying is underscored by Slow Drag's song "If I Had My Way," as the act closes. Slow Drag's song is not a mockery of Levee's confession; rather, it serves as a musical equivalent, an underscoring of that confession. This narrative explosion prepares the audience for Levee's extreme response to Cutler's admonitory tale of the experience of Reverend Gates. Having witnessed Levee's rage in the narrative of his parents' fate, we are not surprised when he reads that narrative into the one Cutler is telling. Just as he will do in another deadly scene, Levee directs the ghost of his rage not against the God he believes to be the guilty party, but against the spinner of a tale. That Cutler's story is the experience of all blacks is shown in the call-and-response of the group as they "bear him up" as any good congregation would. (To "bear up" a speaker is to encourage that speaker, by verbal, musical or kinetic response, to tell more and thereby to affirm the truth of what is told.) Levee refuses to believe that he shares a common fate with the others or that he is powerless in the hands of forces beyond his control. Each of the central characters in *Ma Rainey* has a moment of confession, a moment when he or she confronts those memories, those experiences, those ghosts that will not be ignored. The confession is rarely voluntary but is usually provoked by others.

We see this pattern repeated in *Joe Turner's Come and Gone*. Characters use narrative sequencing to convey a theme that, to the uninitiated, might seem extraneous to the main plot but that is in fact a central structuring device in Wilson's plays, and a form of the "home language." The first act of *Joe Turner* closes with Herald Loomis's vision of the walking bones of the ancestors, his recovery of the many thousand gone. Here the call-and-response pattern is more in the foreground than was the case in Cutler's narrative, thanks to Bynum's attempt to move Loomis to confront the full implications of his tale, to get Loomis to move beyond the tragedy and loss of his story to the empowering force of this connection with his past. He must go through this suppressed memory if he is to live beyond its song of death and isolation to a "song of self-sufficiency, fully resurrected, cleansed and given breath, free from any encumbrance other than the workings of his own heart and the bonds of the flesh, having accepted the responsibility for his own presence in the world, he is free to soar above the environs that weighted and pushed his spirit into terrifying contractions" (*Joe Turner*, 94–95). Levee's tragedy is that he directs his knife not at his horrors and exploiters but at Cutler and God, with ultimately fatal consequences. The very language rituals that Loomis finds redemptive do not empower Levee. Unable or unwilling to exorcise his ghosts, he is doomed to yet another unconscious reenactment of their deadly scenario. If Loomis is free to soar, "all the weight in the world suddenly falls" on Levee. If Loomis in *Joe Turner* can move from a song of death and isolation to one of self-sufficiency, the trumpet at the end of *Ma Rainey* is "blowing pain and warning."

The closing image of painful and admonitory trumpeting at the end of *Ma Rainey* echoes Gabriel's trumpeting and atavistic dance at the end of *Fences*. This ritual, which effects the apotheosis of Troy, like the other closing dramatic moments described above, provides a cap to previous moments of narrative sequencing. The question with which we should approach such a linguistic device in Wilson's plays always implicates us in the success or failure of the confessional moment. Does it find support in the community? Is the speaker borne up? Does the confession succeed in laying to rest those ghosts of the past that have incapacitated their host? Does the confession open up greater possibilities for its having been shared? Does the speaker come to conscious appreciation of the burden of living with ghosts?

Clearly such questions are a part of our attention to Troy's confessional narrative of life with his father and his own painful coming of age. Troy is very conscious that he, like his father, is incapable of love. His resurrection of the ghost of his father—which occurs at the end of the scene following his rejection of love as a part of his duty to his son—clarifies for us and for him the constraints (the fences?) within which he has been forced to live his life. Rose, too, has her moment of full confrontation with her past and the shaping effect of that past on her present. Here counter-confession is a mark of her rejection of the Troy structured for her sympathy in a moment of confession. Here, as in the later *Joe Turner*, Wilson provides us with a confessional narrative that results in an enlarged rather than a diminished life. Rose, who at first used language as a weapon to wound Troy, recovers a very different Troy in the closing scene of the play. Just as Raynell and Cory can now sing Troy's song, accepting and forgiving the past, so too Gabriel and Lyons are back in the yard. Gabriel is ready for the sacred ritual. The fences that closed them in, supposedly for their protection, that served as resistance to change, have come down. They prepare to go out of the yard freed of the burdens of a past that, unacknowledged, severely limited their ability to live fully.

Yet one more demonstration of the power of narrative sequencing, the power of "confessional duologue" to assert personality and to inscribe a desired self in the community, can be found in two extended speeches by Memphis in *Two Trains Running*. In his bitter denunciation of "Black power niggers," Memphis angrily denies the reality of justice, the power of protest to achieve any worthwhile goal, and the self-hatred of those who adopt "black-is-beautiful as a slogan." This explosion, which occurs in act 1, scene 2, seems at first dramatically disproportionate to the words and actions that trigger it. A second narrative closes the act and places Memphis in the dangerously free category of those who have lost their loved ones and thus their source of comfort and possibly even of redemption. "Everything had changed. I felt like I had been cut loose. All them years something had a hold of me and I didn't know it. I didn't find out till it cut me loose" (*Two Trains Running*, act 1, scene 2).

We discover the deeper sources of his early explosion when he responds to West's attempt to profit from Memphis's sale of his building. Memphis is still living the desired rather than the actual end of a past horror. This is the ghost he reveals in act 2. His is a bitter, hard-won wisdom. "I say, 'Okay.

I know the rules now. If you do that to something that ain't never done nothing to you . . . then I know what you would do to me. So I tell you what. You go on and get your laugh now. Cause if I get out of this alive I know how to play as good as anyone.' Once I know the rules, whatever they are, I can play by them" (*Two Trains*: act 2, scene 1). Memphis loses this time, but the story is not over. He lives with the ghost of the dead mule, Stovall, and the lost land, just as other ghost-haunted Wilson characters live with lynching, rape, murder, and betrayal. Memphis, like Hambone, is determined to get his ham and no substitute will do. In fact, the echoing of Hambone's quest extends what might otherwise be an individual, eccentric memory into the experience of a people. The ghost-haunted tell and retell their stories using that art by which the powerless reveal who they are. In reenacting their moments of greatest tragedy they accomplish a twofold task: they are borne up by the community and partially sustained by its soul force; and they keep those shaping moments alive and open to narrative refashioning. They seek new endings.

While Wilson avoids eye dialect in its most overt forms, he does re-create for his audience the linguistic world of black Americans. While narrative sequencing or the "confessional duologue" serve as major structuring devices in his works, he employs a range of verbal signs far more numerous and varied. His characters talk trash, they deliver self-aggrandizing monikas, they indulge in fine talk. They are experts at the dozens, joning, or ranking, geniuses at signifying; they are skilled tellers of tall tales about superbloods; they have an inexhaustible supply of the cautionary tales so necessary to the education of the marginalized. If Sterling sees himself as a sweet-talking player, he reflects that self in his language play. "That's all a man need is a pocketful of money, a Cadillac, and a good woman. That's all he need on the surface. I ain't gonna talk about that other part of satisfaction. But I got sense enough to know it's there. I know if you get the surface it don't mean nothing unless you got the other" (*Two Trains*: act 2, scene 3).

In her 1995 study *The Dramatic Vision of August Wilson*, Sandra Shannon offers an excellent review of those critics who fail to appreciate the positive uses of Wilson's "confessional dialogue." Where I have argued that this dialogue is a powerful structuring device for revelation, self-affirmation, and cultural recovery, critics unfamiliar with the language devices of Wilson's dramas see lack of structure. Michael Marshall, for example, in a review of *Joe Turner's Come and Gone*, wonders if Wilson "has yet been able to create a form that can contain his volcanic subject matter, or whether the breaking, spillover effect is what he intended" (Shannon: 128). Another critic, David Richards, observes that "Wilson's elemental power continues to overwhelm the basic structure of his drama. His efforts remind you of a large man trying to squeeze into a suit two sizes too small. Every now and then, you hear the fabric ripping" (Shannon: 128). But the very excess to which these critics point is the heart of Wilson's project. Critics enamored of the spare, well-made play cannot be expected to appreciate the power and rightness of Wilson's eruption of words. These words are a "purgation that will banish the obsessive ghosts of the past" (Pereira: 101). In short, they are possessed of the verbal skills that distinguish the members from the lames.

This self-certifying language was a hedge against the not spoken, the repressed, the ghosts who have haunted these characters' lives. In keeping with the earliest African rituals and drama, they are freed by giving voice to the ghosts they have carried with them. In this way they are able to find their song and enter the crucible of self-creation. The language of Wilson's drama is not excessive. It is both apt and efficacious and scholars need to give it the same careful attention that Paul Carter Harrison, Sandra Adell, and Craig Werner have given to blues and jazz.

References

Dunbar, Paul Laurence. *The Complete Poems of Paul Laurence Dunbar*. New York: Dodd, Mead and Company, 1980.

Hurston, Zora Neale. *Their Eyes Were Watching God*. Urbana: University of Illinois Press, 1978.

Johnson, James Weldon. "Preface to The Book of American Negro Poetry." In *The Norton Anthology of African American Literature*, ed. Henry Louis Gates Jr. and Nellie Y. McKay. New York: W. W. Norton, 1997.

Jones, LeRoi. *Home*. New York: William Morrow, 1966.

Kennedy, Andrew K. *Dramatic Dialogue: The Duologue of Personal Encounter*. New York: Cambridge University Press, 1983.

Labov, William. *Language in the Inner City: Studies in the Black English Vernacular*. Philadelphia: University of Pennsylvania Press, 1972.

Major, Clarence. *Juba to Jive: A Dictionary of African-American Slang*. New York: Penguin, 1994.

Pereira, Kim. *August Wilson and the African American Odyssey*. Urbana: University of Illinois Press, 1995.

Shannon, Sandra. *The Dramatic Vision of August Wilson*. Washington, D.C.: Howard University Press, 1995.

Smitherman, Geneva. *Talkin and Testifyin*. Boston: Houghton Mifflin, 1977.

Wilson, August. *Ma Rainey's Black Bottom*. New York: New American Library/Plume, 1985.

———. *Fences*. New York: New American Library/Plume, 1986.

———. *Joe Turner's Come and Gone*. New York: New American Library/Plume, 1988.

———. *The Piano Lesson*. New York: New American Library/Plume, 1990.

———. *Two Trains Running*. New York: New American Library/Plume, 1992.

ÇIĞDEM ÜSEKES

"We's the Leftovers": Whiteness as Economic Power and Exploitation in August Wilson's Twentieth-Century Cycle of Plays

The widespread critical attention August Wilson's work has enjoyed has helped establish his stature as *the* African American playwright of the late twentieth century. In particular, scholars have focused almost exclusively on Wilson's black portraits, concurring with the dramatist who, both in his plays and in his interviews, accentuates the struggles of his black characters. Consequently, whites have only been regarded as secondary actors in Wilson's drama, despite Wilson's observation that white society is the main antagonist in his plays (Grant 114). Wilson's white characters have appeared time and again in Wilson scholarship; however, they have been treated as peripheral, rather than central, to his plays.[1] Because the lives of Wilson's black characters are inseparable from those of white Americans, we need to pay more deliberate attention to images of whiteness in Wilson's work. For these reasons, in this essay I would like to reconsider his plays through the lens of whiteness. My goal in doing so is not to further privilege the already-prevalent concept of whiteness in American society and literature but to disclose its focal position in African American art and to initiate a better understanding of its connotations in Wilson's drama.

Admittedly, there are few on-stage white characters in Wilson's plays: Irvin, Sturdyvant, and the policeman in *Ma Rainey's Black Bottom*; Rutherford Selig in *Joe Turner's Come and Gone*; and the unseen yet present ghost of

From *African American Review* 37, no. 1 (Spring 2003): 115–125. © 2003 by Çiğdem Üsekes.

James Sutter in *The Piano Lesson*.[2] Wilson's fictive black world, however, is peopled with many whites; if they do not appear on stage, they materialize in the lives, stories, and conversations of his black characters. As early as in *Ma Rainey*, the playwright began reflecting on the external white world bearing down upon African Americans by employing off-stage characters. Wilson's tendency seemingly to marginalize whiteness by restricting it, for the most part, to an off-stage presence serves an important purpose: The dramatic focus can thus remain on the black characters while also implying that whites, even in their absence, are very much present, since they clearly circumscribe and govern the lives and potentialities of the black characters. Thus, Wilson's dramatic work, whose emotional center lies with his African American characters, also consistently draws attention to the pervasive and negative impact of Euro-Americans in the black community. Henry Louis Gates, Jr., makes the same point: ". . . one of Wilson's accomplishments is to register the ambiguous presence of white folks in a segregated black world— the way you see them nowhere and feel them everywhere" (55).

Considered as a whole, Wilson's twentieth-century cycle of plays underscores the economic, social, and judicial dominance of white Americans.[3] In this essay, I will address the first and foremost part of this equation: Wilson's emphasis on how property or capital bestows power on whites in American society so that they can make decisions which determine the course of other people's lives and, in so doing, often disrupt and destroy those lives for their own economic survival.[4] Although Wilson's cycle of plays proposes to rewrite the white version of American history in the twentieth century (with a play dedicated to each decade), it also looks back in time to slavery, the era when whiteness became associated with the most abominable ownership imaginable: that of human flesh.

Wilson first began to inspect the nature and source of Euro-Americans' economic power in *Ma Rainey's Black Bottom* (1984). Set in Chicago in 1927, the play exposes the exploitation of blues musicians by the white moguls of the recording industry. *Ma Rainey's Black Bottom* opens with Sturdyvant and Irvin, white characters modeled after these businessmen. "*Preoccupied with money*," according to Wilson's character notes, Sturdyvant "*is insensitive to black performers and prefers to deal with them at arm's length*" (17). He owns the record company where Ma Rainey and her band are preparing to make a new record, and as Sandra Adell suggests, he "finds it particularly irritating to have to put up with one who comports herself as if she were a queen" (58). Sturdyvant has a firm grip on the band, if not Ma Rainey, because of his economic privilege. Whereas the musicians obey him almost sheepishly, Ma combats his control over her, but her resistance results in a more adamant power struggle between the two:

STURDYVANT. I'm not putting up with any shenanigans. You
   hear, Irv? . . . She's your responsibility. I'm not putting up
   with any Royal Highness . . . Queen of the Blues bullshit!
IRVIN. Mother of the Blues, Mel. Mother of the Blues.
STURDYVANT. I don't care what she calls herself. I'm not
   putting up with it. I just want to get her in here . . . record
   those songs on that list . . . and get her out. Just like
   clockwork, huh? (18)

Presumably having been crossed in the past by Ma Rainey, Sturdyvant passes
the responsibility of "handling" her to Irvin, Ma Rainey's manager, who is
entrusted with the role of negotiator. Irvin, Wilson says, *"prides himself on
his knowledge of blacks and his ability to deal with them"* (17). Thus, while
Sturdyvant remains aloof from the black musicians, Irvin, the go-between,
carries out his orders. But the power struggle in the studio, even in the
absence of the Mother of the Blues, takes its toll on the musicians, who soon
clash with each other about which songs to practice for the recording session:
Ma's selection or that of Sturdyvant? While Ma's longtime band members
Cutler and Slow Drag champion her, Levee endorses Sturdyvant's choices
in his hope to win the white man's favor and thus to be associated with his
power, the power that Sturdyvant does not hesitate to exercise relentlessly
over those like Levee. To his disappointment, however, Levee will, by the
end of the play, discover his role to be merely that of a pawn in the game
determined by whites.

   When Ma finally makes her appearance on stage, she refuses to go along
with Sturdyvant's selection for the record. Her hostility toward the white men
she works with has more to do with her reaction to her disempowerment as a
black woman artist than with the songs per se, although the record becomes
the site of their conflict:

   You decided, huh? I'm just a bump on the log. I'm gonna go
   which ever way the river drift. Is that it? You and Sturdyvant
   decided. . . . I'm gonna tell you something, Irvin . . . and you go
   on up there and tell Sturdyvant. What you all say don't count
   with me. You understand? Ma listens to her heart. Ma listens to
   the voice inside her. That's what counts with Ma. . . . Now, if that
   don't set right with you and Sturdyvant . . . then I can carry my
   black bottom on back down South to my tour, 'cause I don't like
   it up here no ways. (63)

Because she can rely on her Southern fans for her financial survival, Ma
Rainey can defy Sturdyvant, and the power she derives from having an

alternative provides her with the unwavering tenacity she needs in her dealings with Sturdyvant and Irvin. And maybe most importantly, Ma Rainey recognizes that her record offers a lucrative business deal for Sturdyvant. In the end, the triumph is hers, at least to a certain extent: According to Sandra Shannon, "Despite her acknowledged degradation, Ma's victory seems to be in maintaining her dignity in the face of the apparent 'prostitution' of her talents and in exercising as much control as possible over the rights to her music" ("Ground" 152). Ma Rainey's triumph can best be understood in terms of her familiarity with the rules of the game, which enables her to remain in control and to negotiate with the men on her own terms. Therefore, even when most of her wishes are fulfilled, she leaves the studio without signing the release forms, the last site of her power over Sturdyvant. In *Ma Rainey*, August Wilson raises questions about who "owns" and "decides" the blues: the black artist or the white producer. The play ends on an ambiguous note when Ma departs from the studio without having given Sturdyvant the rights to her music.

But the white producer's economic exploitation extends far beyond Ma Rainey to her musicians. Having commissioned Levee to write songs for him, Sturdyvant later rejects them and offers a pittance as compensation for Levee's time. Enraged by this turn of events, Levee takes out his anger on Toledo, stabbing to death his fellow musician who, ironically, had earlier warned him about what to expect from white folks like Sturdyvant:

> See, we's the leftovers. The colored man is the leftovers. Now, what's the colored man gonna do with himself? That's what we waiting to find out. But first we gotta know we the leftovers. Now, who knows that? You find me a nigger that knows that and I'll turn any whichaway you want me to. . . . And that's what the problem is. The problem ain't with the white man. The white man knows you just a leftover. 'Cause he the one who done the eating and he know what he done ate. But we don't know that we been took and made history out of. Done went and filled the white man's belly and now he's full and tired and wants you to get out the way and let him be by himself. . . . you just ask Mr. Irvin what he had for supper yesterday. And if he's an honest white man . . . which is asking for a whole heap of a lot . . . he'll tell you he done ate your black ass and if you please I'm full up with you . . . so go on and get off the plate and let me eat something else. (57–58)

Toledo's rather long monologue, one of the most vital passages in *Ma Rainey*, articulates Wilson's concise version of African American history, a long history of abuse, impotence, passivity, and muteness. Furthermore, it introduces "the white man" as an off-stage character whose influence is severely felt among blacks. It is this generic off-stage presence that Wilson will consistently summon in his later work.

Wilson resumes his critique of the white man's economic power over and exploitation of blacks in *Joe Turner's Come and Gone* (1986). The play examines the lives of African Americans in the 1910s in a Pittsburgh boarding house while reminding its audience that slavery is neither a forgotten memory nor a thing of the past. In fact, *Joe Turner* is as much interested in the era of slavery as it is in that of post-Reconstruction, when the children of the freed slaves were migrating north in search of a better life. Their quest, however, which led them to new horizons, also placed them in an unfamiliar landscape, sometimes without friends or family to support them.

Among these displaced black characters that *Joe Turner* brings to life dwells one white man, Rutherford Selig, but the most significant emblem of whiteness in *Joe Turner's Come and Gone* is the off-stage eponymous white character who looms over the black characters.

The historical Turner was the brother of the Governor of Tennessee and installed a quasi-slavery system in the South long after the Emancipation. Because of his privileged status, Joe Turner could secure free labor for himself without having to suffer any consequences. In an interview, Wilson elaborates on the historical background of his character: "Joe Turner would press Blacks into peonage. He would send out decoys who would lure Blacks into crap games and then he would swoop down and grab them. He had a chain with forty links to it, and he would take Blacks off to his plantation and work them" (Powers 53). The play's protagonist, Herald Loomis, is one of these enslaved African American men, and because of the seven years he has spent in bondage, he has been estranged from his wife and his family as well as his sense of self. Merely witnessing Loomis's suffering is sufficient to recognize the compelling symbolic presence of the white man on stage: "He represents the evil that takes away all the potential identified with black men, whether that evil historically took the form of slavery, sharecropping, or convict labor as a result of being jailed without any semblance of due process" (Harris 56). The destructive history Joe Turner epitomizes in this play is the haunting history white America has imprinted on black Americans. Turner is the most prominent symbol, in August Wilson's twentieth-century cycle of plays, of the economic exploitation and abuse African Americans have experienced at the hands of whites. In fact, the playwright has noted that the seven years Herald Loomis spent in peonage can "represent the four hundred years of slavery, of being taken out of Africa and brought to America" (Powers 54).

Reminiscent of the same history in some ways, Selig, the only on-stage white character of *Joe Turner*, is the closest August Wilson has come to creating a multi-dimensional white character. He is, for example, clearly welcome in the black boarding house where Seth's wife Bertha wants him to feel at home: "Sit on down there, Selig. Get you a cup of coffee and a biscuit" (7), and "You know you welcome anytime, Selig" (11). What distinguishes Selig from Wilson's other white characters is his sense of belonging in the black community. But even this more or less positive emblem of whiteness is not without defects. Known as the People Finder among blacks, according to one perspective in the play, he keeps records of his customers in order to locate them for others in the future. Yet Selig, because of African American history, inhabits a problematic role as the People Finder:

> I can't promise anything but we been finders in my family for a long time. Bringers and finders. My great-granddaddy used to bring Nigras across the ocean on ships.... You're in good hands, mister. Me and my daddy have found plenty Nigras. My daddy, rest his soul, used to find runaway slaves for the plantation bosses. He was the best there was at it. Jonas B. Selig. Had him a reputation stretched clean across the country. After Abraham Lincoln give you all Nigras your freedom papers and with you all looking all over for each other ... we started finding Nigras for Nigras. Of course, it don't pay as much. But the People Finding business ain't so bad. (41)

Rutherford Selig comes from a long tradition of "People Finders," a euphemism in this case for those in the slave-trading business or for runaway-slave hunters. Selig does not conceal the fact that members of his family have been the arch-enemies of Africans and later African Americans, although he appears to overlook the hostility which has historically existed between his ancestors and the ancestors of the blacks in the community where he works. Selig now employs his skills in a legitimate and clean trade, yet it still is a business and his source of livelihood. Its history is far from being untainted, stretching back in time to slavery. As people with African origins were objects for material gain for Selig's ancestors, his black customers are objects for Selig to locate for money. In this regard, his business carries a strong resonance of his family's past encounters with blacks.

Bertha further challenges the decency of Selig's trade, claiming that the white man only finds folks he has already taken away: "Then he charge folks a dollar to tell them where he took them. Now, that's the truth of Rutherford Selig. This old People Finding business is for the birds. He ain't never found nobody he ain't took away" (42). Like Bertha, who remains skeptical of Selig's business and its ethics, critic Kim Pereira, too, refuses to interpret Selig's role in the black community as benevolent: "... Rutherford Selig has found an innovative way to continue the family tradition by finding black people separated as a consequence of slavery and sharecropping" (59). Selig's history overlaps those of his black customers and workers, and it is in this history, in the absent off-stage white characters whom Selig himself names, his father and grandfather, that we find the missing pieces of the puzzle of white–black interaction in America.

The People Finder stands for the economic power and exploitation associated with whiteness in more ways than one. A peddler, he provides Seth with raw materials and then sells the end products to other blacks in the community. Selig does not exploit Seth in quite the same way that Sturdyvant exploits the black musicians in *Ma Rainey's Black Bottom*, but Selig's relationship with Seth is still mainly one in which the white man symbolizes the capital, and the black man the labor. Selig is the employer and Seth the employee. Alan Nadel observes the racially charged aspect of Selig and Seth's business relationship by stating that the former "controls the economy in which [Seth] Holly's labor is traded" ("Boundaries" 99). This business relationship is not the "happy fusion of black and white traditions," as Peter Wolfe would have it (94).

Joe Turner's Come and Gone also advances the dramatist's agenda on whiteness via other off-stage white characters, such as the rapacious white man who extorts fifty cents a week from black laborers at Jeremy's workplace by threatening them with the loss of their jobs. Jeremy refuses to comply: "It didn't make no sense to me. I don't make but eight dollars. Why I got to give him fifty cents of it? He go around to all the colored and he got ten dollars extra. That's more than I make for a whole week" (64). Jeremy is aware of the injustice of the situation, but his courage in standing up to the white man costs him his job, thereby disclosing the vulnerability of black Americans in the business world.

Jeremy's story also exemplifies the importance of oral narratives for African Americans. While the dramatic genre more than likely demands that at least some events take place off-stage, thus requiring the related information to be distributed by some other means, Wilson's plays rely extensively on storytelling. His black men communicate their experiences and the lessons therein through oral narratives.[5] August Wilson has confirmed the essential character of the oral tradition in black culture:

> So anytime you have five black characters on stage, it's very natural for them to tell stories, because the stories are the only way that cultural information, ideas and attitudes, community sanctions, ways of conduct, et cetera, are revealed. If I tell you a story, I'm telling you how you are supposed to act in the world.

I don't just tell you a story to entertain you. There is information
in there for your benefit. (Goldman 15)

One of the benefits of this dramatic device is that, while information is
circulated with the help of stories, the whites, who are crucial to the plays
themselves, are relegated to an off-stage presence in order to reserve the
limelight for the black characters.

In *The Piano Lesson* (1987), Euro-Americans lurk behind the scenes,
too. Situated in 1936, the play deliberately looks back once again at the
historical and personal significance of slavery. The dramatic conflict at
the heart of *The Piano Lesson* revolves around the two options available
to Boy Willie and his sister Berniece regarding their family's heirloom
piano. Whereas Berniece wants to hold onto this symbol of her heritage,
Boy Willie claims it would be put to better use if they sell it and with
the money buy the land on which their ancestors have toiled as slaves.
Another pivotal actor in this family drama is the ghost of a white man,
James Sutter, whose ancestors have claimed proprietorship over both the
black family and the piano. In fact, the piano becomes the site of conflict
among these three characters as they, at different points and for different
reasons, lay claim to the piano.

    Since it represents the ancestors of the black family and evokes their
white masters, too, the piano is the single most important prop on stage.
Originally, it belonged to Robert Sutter, the grandfather of James Sutter,
who had bought it for his wife in exchange for two of his slaves. When
Miss Ophelia found the absence of her former slaves too much to bear, her
husband had Boy Willie, the great-grandfather of Boy Willie and Berniece,
carve on the piano images of his wife and their son, the two Sutter slaves
who had been sold. However, Boy Willie brings to life on the piano more than
what his master asks for; his extended family and the landmarks of their lives
also find their way on to the piano, which, thus, serves not only as a reminder
of the black family's history of bondage but also of African American cultural
history. Boy Willie's carvings transform the piano into more than a musical
instrument; it becomes a catalyst in the interactions of the black and the white
families. Until then, the piano has belonged to the Sutters. However, Boy
Willie, by carving his family history on it, has also claimed it as his property.
The new value the piano assumes—it has been bought, in the first place, at
the price of Boy Willie's family, and it artistically tells their story—results in
friction between the two families and their future generations. Boy Willie's
grandson Boy Charles associates the piano with his own family: According
to him, whoever owns the piano also owns the black family. Therefore, it has
to be removed from the Sutter household. Not surprisingly, this information

is once again presented via the stories black characters tell each other on stage. These narratives unveil the past that has shaped the present in which the ghost of James Sutter "refuses to relinquish his claim on the piano as well as an unspoken related claim on these descendants of slaves once owned by the Sutter clan" (Shannon, *Dramatic* 160). The late Sutter haunts the black family and asserts his ownership of the piano with his unrelenting presence on stage.

Ownership remains a source of contention among the present-day members of the black family, too. Whereas Berniece insists on keeping the piano (thus, her family history and the ghosts from her past) in her possession, Boy Willie wants to buy land with it because he believes, as does August Wilson, that whites are privileged because of what they own. According to this reasoning, African Americans with land will enjoy equal rights as Euro-Americans, an advantageous position denied to Boy Willie's father, who had no option but to sharecrop for the white man:

> See now . . . if he had his own land he wouldn't have felt that way. If he had something under his feet that belonged to him he could stand up taller. . . . If you got a piece of land you'll find everything else fall right into place. You can stand right up next to the white man and talk about the price of cotton . . . the weather, and anything else you want to talk about. (92)

Boy Willie (much like Hedley in *Seven Guitars*) sees the white man's property as the main source of his power over the black man. African Americans in the past lacked prestige because they could only serve as laborers on the white man's land, first as slaves, later as sharecroppers. Once these roles are upset, Boy Willie believes the white man's authority will end. Wilson has voiced his agreement with Boy Willie's position in an interview with Nathan Grant, declaring land the "basis of independence" (104).

Nevertheless, Berniece refuses to acquiesce to Boy Willie's plan, and the siblings remain at odds with each other until the very end, when the ghost of Sutter poses a more dangerous threat to the black family, and they need to unite forces in order to defeat him. Anne Fleche maintains that the dramatic conflict shifts in the course of the play from that between the brother and the sister to that between "their family and Sutter" (10). The ghost with whom Boy Willie wrestles in the end in "*a life-and-death struggle fraught with perils and faultless terror*" can only be exorcised by Berniece, who summons help from the spirits of her ancestors by playing the piano for the first time in years (106). The ending affirms that the piano rightfully belongs to the black family, who have not only conceived it as a work of art but also earned it, over many generations, with their blood.[6]

August Wilson's next play, *Two Trains Running* (1990), reinforces yet again the economic power of whiteness and Euro-Americans' exploitation of African Americans. The play takes place in 1969 in a Pittsburgh restaurant where its characters are working hard to ensure their economic survival in a white-dominated world. Many years ago, one of its focal off-stage white characters, Lutz, hired Hambone, a black man, to paint the fence around his store. They struck a deal according to which Hambone would receive a chicken for his labor or a ham if the job were done well. When Hambone finishes his painting job, he expects a ham, believing he has done a satisfactory job, but since it is up to Lutz to determine the merit of the black man's labor, Hambone feels cheated out of his ham. He has protested this injustice by standing outside Lutz's store every day for nine years and demanding his ham in the few phrases he can now utter: "I want my ham. He gonna give me my ham." Hambone is a symbol in the play (as is Lutz), a man who would not just take anything but what he thinks he deserves. Holloway, "*a man who all his life has voiced his outrage at injustice with little effect*" (5), admires and supports Hambone's position: "[H]e ain't willing to accept whatever the white man throw at him" (30).

Regardless of what the conflict between Hambone and Lutz might portend, *Two Trains Running* ends with a somewhat promising outlook on an African American economic future. In a battle of his own with city hall, which is trying to buy out his restaurant, Memphis finally receives more from them than what he has bargained for. Yet the underlying message remains hopeless: The blacks' money ends up in the pockets of the dominant group:

> The money go from you to me to you and then—bingo, it's gone.... You give it to the white man. Pay your rent, pay your telephone, buy your groceries, see the doctor—bingo, it's gone. Just circulate it around till it find that hole, then—bingo. Like trying to haul sand in a bucket with a hole in it. (34)

Because the economic system is in the hands of the majority, African Americans cannot retain the money they earn, and they have to rely on illegal operations like playing numbers, which is once again controlled by whites. When Sterling hits the numbers and discovers his share has been cut by the Alberts—a regular occurrence whenever "thirty or forty niggers get lucky enough to hit the numbers the same day," according to Holloway—he protests furiously (84). Sterling's calling off the bet with Old Man Albert and asking for his two dollars back without returning the white man's six hundred, marks an attempt, albeit feeble, at retaliation.

Discussing the historical background for his play, Wilson has drawn attention to the inequity in the American economic and social setup, even as late as the sixties:

In 1968, the relationship of blacks to white Americans was not that much different than the relationship of slaves to their masters. It was like a day off on the plantation. Nobody was working. There were no jobs. There were all these people with families but no means of support, because society didn't have any use for them. (Dworkin, "Blood" 8)

Holloway's "stacking niggers" speech (34–35) confirms Wilson's observation above. That the socioeconomic system in America has from the outset weighed on the shoulders of its black citizens, holding them down, is one of the points Wilson revisits in his work. Without black workers both during and after slavery, America would not be the America that it is today. Whites have used blacks to attain their goals and to build an optimal society for themselves, but having accomplished their objectives, they have no further use for blacks, who in the end are discarded by those who have exploited them and their labor to the fullest extent. Moreover, Euro-Americans have managed to take credit for the products of black labor and do not hesitate to disparage these workers now for their "laziness," a handy excuse to explain away their unemployment in the sixties, the historical backdrop for *Two Trains Running*.

Seven Guitars (1995) returns to a world similar to that of *Ma Rainey's Black Bottom*. Both plays, although set in different eras, the former in the 1940s and the latter in the 1920s, explore how record companies owned by whites take advantage of black musicians. Floyd Barton, like Ma Rainey, has to work with the white moguls on unequal terms. Not until he has a hit record does his manager, Mr. T. L. Hall, another off-stage white character, invest in Floyd, and does Savoy Records invite him to Chicago for another recording session. Though now famous, Floyd and his musician friends are as hard up as ever. In this capitalistic setup, the whites are only interested in making a profit off Floyd's music, and not in his or his band's financial welfare. Canewell and Red Carter, for instance, complain about their past experiences with white producers, especially about having been cheated out of their wages:

FLOYD. This time it's gonna be different. We gonna get the money up front.
CANEWELL. It wasn't all about the money. He treat me like he didn't care nothing about me.
FLOYD. He don't have to care nothing about you. You all doing business. He ain't got to like you. Tell him, Red, you got to take advantage of the opportunity. It don't matter if he

> like you or not. You got to take the opportunity while it's
> there.
> CANEWELL. Just cause I was there on an opportunity don't
> mean he got to treat me bad. He on an opportunity too.
> You creating an opportunity for him. (47)

The black musicians in the recording business have no value as human beings for the white businessmen. Thus, *Seven Guitars* posits that blues musicians like Ma Rainey have not made much, if any, progress in the two decades between the twenties and the forties. Artists like Floyd are as expendable as they were twenty years earlier, and American society and businesses are not likely to be transformed in favor of their black workers.

Arguably, Mr. T. L. Hall is the least attractive off-stage white in *Seven Guitars*: He has sold fake insurance in the poor black neighborhoods. Canewell remains the only character, though, to perceive Mr. T. L. Hall's thievery through a Darwinian lens: "There's lots of poor people. Mr. T. L. Hall say he didn't want to be one. Selling that fake insurance might have been his only chance not to be poor" (85). Approached from this perspective, the exploitation of blacks by whites, no longer synonymous with inequity, might merely illustrate nature's principle of the survival of the fittest.

Given the recurrence of negative white portraits in Wilson's twentieth-century cycle, we are left with a difficult question about the playwright's stance on whiteness: Does August Wilson regard Euro-Americans as immoral individuals who have been exploiting their black fellow countrymen for centuries? I think the answer to this question is not so easy as it seems. Wilson has denied that he aims to depict whites as depraved souls. For instance, in response to a question about Selig's intentions, Wilson has defended his white character: "... he's not evil at all. In fact, he's performing a very valuable service for the community" (Powers 53). Some of Wilson's black characters appear to share this assessment of white America. Like Canewell, who doesn't castigate Mr. T. L. Hall, Memphis in *Two Trains Running* excuses Lutz's treatment of Hambone, saying he would have done the same himself, and underscores instead the foolishness of leaving it up to someone else to determine the value of one's own labor.

I believe that Wilson's target is instead the American capitalist system, which allows the strong to be stronger and the weak to be exploited. No one can deny, though, that this system was established by whites who have reaped its benefits. Whites, since their initial contact with blacks, have approached them as free or cheap labor and have capitalized on their labor. Thus, even after the Emancipation, the American history of the twentieth century remains one of abuse and bondage for African Americans. Black Americans, now free, can still not enjoy sovereignty, economic independence, or cultural equality and are unfortunately still within the tight grasp of the white majority. Mary Bogumil comments on the stasis in American racial relations that Wilson depicts: "Wilson's strategy of writing a play for each decade of the twentieth century focuses attention on this long journey with little progress and change, one that so many African Americans have taken" (9).

Wilson's foremost critic, Robert Brustein, takes issue with the adverse representations of whiteness that Wilson projects in his twentieth-century cycle:

> Presumably Wilson is preparing to cover ... more theatrical decades of white culpability and black martyrdom. This single-minded documentation of American racism is a worthy if familiar social agenda, and no enlightened person would deny its premise, but as an ongoing artistic program it is monotonous, limited, locked in a perception of victimization. (28)

Has Wilson invested too much in narratives of victimization as Brustein claims, or does he use the story of whites' exploitation and abuse of blacks to convey a sense of black victory and hope for the future? Wilson maintains that his goal is the latter. In an interview with Bonnie Lyons, he has spoken up for his black characters who, he argues, "don't respond as victims. No matter what society does to them, they are engaged with life, wrestling with it, trying to make sense out of it. Nobody is sitting around saying, 'Woe is me'" (11). Likewise, C. W. E. Bigsby perceives a celebratory tone in these plays but also warns us: "This is not to say that . . . [Wilson] deals with victories but that he chooses to focus on the often losing battle of individuals placed under the kind of pressure which makes personal meaning so difficult to sustain" (287). By placing his black characters under such pressure, Wilson often exalts his drama to the level of tragedy, in (unconscious) accordance with Arthur Miller's redefinition of the Greek concept in his essay "Tragedy and the Common Man":

> ... the tragic feeling is evoked in us when we are in the presence of a character who is ready to lay down his life, if need be, to secure one thing—his sense of personal dignity. From Orestes to Hamlet, Medea to Macbeth, the underlying struggle is that of the individual attempting to gain his "rightful" position in his society. (4)

Even though Wilson has made a point of distancing himself from the Western literary tradition, his writings observe the dramatic principle Miller discusses above. In Wilson's plays, black characters find themselves in an ongoing struggle with a hostile social and economic structure and its white representatives. Whether they fight may be more important than whether they win or lose in the end.

August Wilson's plays honor the "warrior spirits" among African Americans, those who are not afraid to put up a fight with white society and with whatever or whoever else may stand in their way. The "warrior spirits" are those, Wilson explains, "who look around to see what the society has cut out for them, who see the limits of their participation, and are willing to say, 'No, I refuse to accept this limitation that you're imposing on me . . .'" (Moyers 179). Most of Wilson's plays end by celebrating the success of such warriors: Boy Willie wrestles with the ghost and exorcises it with the help of Berniece; Herald Loomis breaks free of his past; Memphis receives a large sum from city hall for his restaurant. Of the few who lose in the end, Levee and Floyd, for example, their lives attain more meaning as a direct result of their doomed battles. And as August Wilson suggests, we should be extolling these individuals and their lives rather than merely condemning the antagonistic forces in their way because the latter response, after all, would diminish them to the position of objects rather than acknowledge their full subject status. A better understanding of Wilson's delineation of whiteness gives us a more complete sense of the struggles and achievements of these black warriors.

NOTES

1. While a number of scholars have been perceptive regarding the crucial presence of white society on Wilson's otherwise black stage—see, for example, Bogumil; Wolfe; Rocha; Harris—a systematic and comprehensive analysis of August Wilson's white portraiture is yet to be undertaken.

2. Like Sandra Shannon, I consider the ghost to play a significant and tangible role on stage. He is, without any doubt, a palpable force for both the black characters and the audience.

3. See Üsekes.

4. For my discussion, I draw from Wilson's cycle of plays with the exception of *Jitney!* and *King Hedley II*, the yet-unpublished accompanying pieces to the cycle, and *Fences*, a play which foregrounds the social privileges of white Americans more so than their economic privilege.

5. As Norine Dworkin has remarked, storytelling is central to Wilson's work, as it is to African American literature in general ("Chronicle" F5).

6. Boy Willie and Berniece's ancestors have worked as slaves for the Sutters; in addition, Boy Charles has paid with his life for stealing the piano from the Sutter household.

WORKS CITED

Adell, Sandra. "Speaking of Ma Rainey/Talking about the Blues." Nadel, *May* 51–66.
Bigsby, C. W. E. *Modern American Drama, 1945–1990*. 1992. Cambridge: Cambridge UP, 1994.

Bogumil, Mary L. *Understanding August Wilson*. Columbia: U of South Carolina P, 1999.

Brustein, Robert. "The Lesson of *The Piano Lesson.*" *New Republic* 21 May 1990: 28–30.

Dworkin, Norine. "Blood on the Tracks." *American Theatre* May 1990: 8–9.

———. "The Wilson Chronicles." *Sun-Sentinel* 22 Apr. 1990: F1+.

Fleche, Anne. "The History Lesson: Authenticity and Anachronism in August Wilson's Plays." Nadel, *May* 9–20.

Gates, Henry Louis, Jr. "The Chitlin Circuit." *New Yorker* 3 Feb. 1997: 44+.

Goldman, Jeffrey. "Think of History as One Long Blues Tune: August Wilson." *Dramatics* Apr. 1990: 12–17.

Grant, Nathan L. "Men, Women, and Culture: A Conversation with August Wilson." *American Drama* 5.2 (1996): 100–22.

Harris, Trudier. "August Wilson's Folk Traditions." 1994. *August Wilson: A Casebook*. Ed. Marilyn Elkins. New York: Garland, 2000. 49–67.

Lyons, Bonnie. "An Interview with August Wilson." *Contemporary Literature* 40.1 (1999): 1–21.

Miller, Arthur. "Tragedy and the Common Man." 1978. *The Theater Essays of Arthur Miller*. Rev. ed. Ed. Robert A. Martin and Steven R. Centola. New York: Da Capo, 1996. 3–7.

Moyers, Bill. "August Wilson." *A World of Ideas: Conversations with Thoughtful Men and Women about American Life Today and the Ideas Shaping Our Future*. Ed. Betty Sue Flowers. New York: Doubleday, 1989. 167–80.

Nadel, Alan. "Boundaries, Logistics, and Identity: The Property of Metaphor in *Fences* and *Joe Turner's Come and Gone*." Nadel, *May* 86–104.

Nadel, Alan, ed. *May All Your Fences Have Gates: Essays on the Drama of August Wilson*. Iowa City: U of Iowa P, 1994.

Pereira, Kim. *August Wilson and the African-American Odyssey*. Urbana: U of Illinois P, 1995.

Powers, Kim. "An Interview with August Wilson." *Theater* 16.1 (1984): 50–55.

Rocha, Mark William. "American History as 'Loud Talking' in *Two Trains Running*." Nadel, *May* 116–32.

Shannon, Sandra G. *The Dramatic Vision of August Wilson*. Washington, DC: Howard UP, 1995.

———. "The Ground on Which I Stand: August Wilson's Perspective on African American Women." Nadel, *May* 150–64.

Üsekes, Çiğdem. "'You Always Under Attack': Whiteness as Law and Terror in August Wilson's Twentieth-Century Cycle of Plays." *American Drama* 10.2 (2001): 48–68.

Wilson, August. *Joe Turner's Come and Gone*. New York: Plume, 1988.

———. *Ma Rainey's Black Bottom*. New York: Plume, 1985.

———. *The Piano Lesson*. New York: Plume, 1990.

———. *Seven Guitars*. New York: Plume, 1997.

———. *Two Trains Running*. New York: Plume, 1993.

Wolfe, Peter. *August Wilson*. New York: Twayne, 1999.

AMANDA M. RUDOLPH

Images of African Traditional Religions and Christianity in Joe Turner's Come and Gone and The Piano Lesson

Throughout August Wilson's plays, characters are struggling with and wrestling over their ideas of religion and God. In *Ma Rainey's Black Bottom* (Wilson, 1984), Levee says, "If he's a man of God, then where the hell was God when all of this was going on? Why wasn't God looking out for him?" (p. 81). In *Joe Turner's Come and Gone* (Wilson, 1984), Loomis speaks out: "You all sitting up here singing about the Holy Ghost. What's so holy about the Holy Ghost? You singing and singing. You think the Holy Ghost coming? . . . What he gonna do, huh?" (p. 250). In *The Piano Lesson* (Wilson, 1990), Avery tells Berniece about the ways of God: "With the strength of God you can put the past behind you, Berniece. With the strength of God you can do anything!" (p. 71). All these characters question the role of God in their lives or in the lives of the people around them. How does a Christian God help the Black person? Why would God let these terrible things happen to Blacks? Will God help the Black person attain what he or she deserves? Wilson explored these questions in two of his plays.

Wilson sets up a dichotomy between the role of Christianity and the African traditional religion (ATR) (defined by belief in ancestors, belief in spirits, and the practice of magic and ritual) in two of his plays, *Joe Turner's Come and Gone* and *The Piano Lesson*. In fact, although these same concepts may be used in other plays by Wilson, they are an integral part of the structure

From *Journal of Black Studies* 33, no. 5 (May 2003): pp. 562–575. © 2003 Sage Publications.

of these two pieces. The plays are structured so that, in the end, one religion must be accepted to resolve the conflict in each play. Wilson illustrated these two polarized religions by creating images that reflect the tenets of ATR and Christianity in *Joe Turner* and *The Piano Lesson*.

To see the dichotomy, we must first look at the tenets of ATR and Christianity and the way Wilson interprets both of them. ATRs encompass many different types of belief systems. One definition of ATR is

> the observance of rules of conduct in the way the individual conducts his or her daily life, the practice of rituals, and the recognition of the ever presence of the living–dead (ancestors) to allow the person to coexist in harmony with other members of the community and nature. (Kamara, 2000, p. 503)

This definition is very broad; it does not narrow the scope of the belief system, as does Christianity, by focusing on acceptance of a specific savior, Jesus Christ. Gibreel M. Kamara (2000) stated that ATRs are the religion of Black people, native Africans or not, due to connections in history. He continued by saying that Black people become torn between the ATR and the religion of the U.S. majority, Christianity. We see this same dichotomy in Wilson's plays. Aylwald Shorter (1977) compared ATR to Christianity and stated: "Christianity is a 'Religion of the Book,' a highly literate religion with a long history of theological expositions, written and oral. . . . African Traditional Religion, on the other hand, is not only historically preliterate, it is by choice not even always orally articulate" (p. 7). ATR is a more symbolic and abstract religion than Christianity. Kamara included five components of ATR based on the delineation in *African Traditional Religion* by E. B. Idowu: "belief in God, belief in the divinities, belief in spirits, belief in the ancestors, and the practice of magic and medicine" (as cited in Kamara, 2000, p. 508). For the scope of this article, belief in God will be assumed for both ATR and Christianity.

To explore the dichotomy found in these two plays, we must also define what constitutes African Christianity. When the slaves were brought to America from Africa, some of their religious artifacts were lost. As these people began living in America, the religion from Africa was somewhat regained as slaves began worshipping. The White slave owners refused to share Christianity with the slaves at first, as they were afraid it might bring equality. Soon they were convinced that Christianity would make the slaves more docile. The slaves rejected Christianity on the basis that any religion that participated in slavery was not valid. Eventually, the slaves embraced part of Christianity because of the telling of the exodus story (Paris, 1994). Paris (1994) stated that the exodus story is critical to the change in the slaves' beliefs because "it connotes a living and caring God who not only sees, hears, and knows about human suffering but willingly chooses to become actively engaged in a liberating activity" (p. 73). The Black people then used the church as a way to embrace freedom and overcome racism. The history of Christianity for the American Black differs greatly from the history of Christianity for the American majority and even other minorities. ATRs tend to view all people as messengers of religion, whereas Christianity maintains a hierarchy of divine leaders. Christianity is a word-based religion. The power of Christianity would dissipate without the Bible. Therefore, for the comparison in this article, organization and reliance on the words will characterize Christianity.

Finally, before we look to the plays themselves, we must look into August Wilson's background. Wilson was born in Pittsburgh in 1945 to a Black mother and White father (Lyons, 1999). His mother raised him after his father left. He began writing poetry and eventually turned to playwriting. His goal was to write one play for each decade in the 20th century; he has published six (Lyons, 1999). The focus of this article deals with the play for the 1910s, *Joe Turner's Come and Gone*, and the play for the 1930s, *The Piano Lesson*. These plays deal with the problems facing Black people during those time periods in America. Some of the problems are recurrent, like the role of religions. Wilson said,

> Today I would say that the conflict in black America is between the middle class and the so-called underclass, and that conflict goes back to those who deny themselves and those who aren't willing to. America offers blacks a contract that says, "If you leave all that African stuff over there and adopt the values of the dominant culture, you can participate." . . . The ones who accept go on to become part of the growing black middle class and some areas even acquire some power and participation in society, but when they finally arrive where they arrive, they are no longer the same people. . . . They've acculturated and adopted white values. (Lyons, 1999, p. 2)

Wilson's ideas are applicable to the religious struggle going on in America and in his plays. Wilson also talked about Christianity and stated: "The Christianity that blacks have embraced, they have transformed with aspects of African religion, African style, and certainly African celebration. The church is the only stable organization in the black community, and the community is organized around the church" (Lyons, 1999, p. 5). On the other hand, Wilson contended that churches have been the source of the Ku Klux Klan and still promote inequality today (Lyons, 1999). Wilson seems to have a contradictory nature that is not so pronounced in his plays. Not only is the philosophy behind the religious dichotomy important, but the intended audience of the plays influences the interpretation. According to Wilson,

> I don't write for any particular audience, but the idea of audience is built into the craft of playwrighting. In terms of what that audience may specifically look like, it looks like me. I have to satisfy the audience that is myself. I don't write for a black or white audience beyond that. (Carroll, 1994, p. 249)

As we look to the plays and the images of religion, it is important to keep in mind the author's ideology behind his work.

As the lights come up on the first scene of *Joe Turner*, the audience is immediately introduced to magic, part of ATRs. Wilson included a strong theme of spirituality in *Joe Turner*. Because the play is set in 1911, the environment and society are not far removed from slavery, Africa, and the religions of those times and places. Wilson said *Joe Turner* was his favorite play of the ones he has written (Lyons, 1999). One could argue the favoritism comes with the deep African religious practices in the play. The play is full of examples of ATR. Specifically, the play includes a story of a Shiny Man, rituals, ghosts, a *juba* or rhythmic dance, and a self-inflicted cutting, all of which relate to the tenets of ATR.

As the play begins, the first character the audience hears about is Bynum, the root worker. Roughly, the first three pages of the play are focused on Seth and Bertha (the owner of the boarding house and his wife) discussing Bynum (a resident) and his ritualistic killings of the pigeons. After the discussion, Bynum enters and, within five pages of his entrance, the audience hears the story of Bynum and the Shiny Man. Bynum explains his story to Rutherford Selig, a traveling salesman. Bynum says that he met a Shiny Man in the road. The Shiny Man and Bynum walked down the road around the bend. Bynum says,

> I turned around to look at this fellow and he had this light coming out of him. I had to cover up my eyes from being blinded. He shining like new money with that light. He shined until all the light seemed like it seeped out of him and then he was gone. (p. 212)

As the Shiny Man disappeared, Bynum saw his father. Bynum's father came to help him find his song that Wilson uses as a metaphor to represent what is in the heart of the person that makes him or her different and special. "I had the Binding Song. I chose that song because that's what I seen most when I was traveling. . . . So I takes the power of my song and binds them together" (p. 213). Later in the narrative, Bynum asks his father about the Shiny Man, and his father says he is "One Who Goes Before and Shows the Way" (p. 213). Sandra Richards (1999) said, "The story of a 'shiny man' [is] suggestive of the Yoruba gods Ogun and Esu—who encourages fellow travelers to claim their predestined 'song' in life" (p. 92). She went on to say Ogun is the god who first made a tool, an iron sword, and the shininess the Bynum sees may be the iron of Ogun (Richards, 1999). Whether Wilson is consciously making a comparison of the Shiny Man to Ogun and/or Esu, it is obvious the Shiny Man is god and a higher power influencing Bynum and others.

Wilson also uses ATRs in more subtle ways. Another example in *Joe Turner* is the rituals of Bynum. As stated previously, the play opens with Bertha and Seth talking about Bynum's (the very epitome of ATR) actions with the pigeons. The text does not actually state the purpose behind Bynum's actions. Basically, Bynum performs a type of ritual killing of the pigeon that concludes with Bynum pouring the pigeon's blood over its grave. The blood consecrates and seals the grave. Whatever the purpose of the ritual, the pigeon is laid to rest in clean, protected ground. Bynum's rituals set him up as the clearest example of ATR.

> Through Bynum, he [Wilson] hoped to show the continuing role of African mysticism in the lives of his characters and the potential of what Wilson terms "African retentions," which, in his view, can serve as both a source of strength and a kind of psychic balm for the twentieth-century African Americans. (Herrington, 1998, p. 81)

Another example that illustrates a tenet of ATR is the appearance of Miss Mabel, a ghost. Reuben, who lives next door to the boarding house, lost his best friend Eugene when he died. Eugene asked Reuben to release his pigeons after he died. Reuben kept the pigeons, breaking the promise to the dead boy. Miss Mabel returns from the afterworld to tell Reuben he must release the pigeons or Eugene will not be able to travel on to where he should be. Wilson uses the pigeons as a metaphor for Loomis's struggle. Loomis must let go of his rage to find his way just as Reuben must let go of his grief to free Eugene. The appearance of Miss Mabel exemplifies two tenets of ATR. First, Reuben immediately believes he has seen a ghost. Although Zonia is skeptical, he maintains he encountered a ghost. ATR asserts a belief in spirits, and Reuben automatically accepts the spirit in his world. Second, the ghost gives advice, which is one of the roles of ancestors. Sandra Shannon (1995), a Wilson scholar, states that

Loomis must acknowledge "that in order to go forward, they must revisit those pasts" (p. 125). The path that Reuben is on is a reflection of where Loomis is headed. Reuben opens up to the ancestors and accepts the past, the death of Eugene. Loomis will follow eventually. Again, the symbol is deeply entrenched in the ideas of ATR.

In *Joe Turner*, his most spiritual play, Wilson also incorporates the juba. According to the stage directions of *Joe Turner*, the juba

> is reminiscent of the ring shout of the African slaves. It is a call-and-response dance. Bynum sits at the table and drums. He calls the dance as others clap hands, shuffle, and stomp around the table. It should be as African as possible, with the performers working themselves up into a near frenzy. The words can be improvised but should include some mention of the Holy Ghost. (p. 249)

Richards (1999) referred to historian Sterling Stuckey's belief that the jubas were directed to gods and ancestors. Wilson uses the juba as a synthesis of Christianity and ATR. The tradition of the juba is in African practices, but the characters in *Joe Turner* shout about the Holy Ghost. This meshing of tradition forces Loomis into remembrance of ancestors and past places (Richards, 1999). This remembrance leads to the vision of Africa and builds to the end of act 1. Wilson sets up the battle between Christianity and ATR by the end of act 1. In act 2, only one religion will lead to salvation.

The play also includes images and tenets of Christianity. Basically, there are two instances that incorporate Christianity. The first, interestingly enough, is the appearance of the Shiny Man. The second strong proponent of Christianity is Martha. She is part of the church, and even her name, Martha Pentecost, reflects the dominant religion. These elements create the opposing force to ATR.

The Shiny Man can be interpreted as a direct connection to ATR, but he can also be interpreted as a link to Christianity. Kim Pereira (1995), scholar of Wilson's work, interprets the One Who Goes Before and Shows the Way as an allusion to John the Baptist, who went before Jesus. Pereira said the ultimate baptism was the blood of Christ the Lamb, and the blood appearing on Bynum's hands relates to those baptisms. The reference to the Shiny Man can be related to the Christian tradition because there are many paintings and passages that refer to Jesus as illuminating and the Light. Although Pereira made a good argument for the Christian interpretation of the Shiny Man, the character of Martha is a stronger Christian figure in the play.

Martha is the wife of Herald Loomis. In the play, Loomis is searching for his wife. He was taken by Joe Turner and forced to work for the man for 7 years. On his release, he begins to look for his wife. It is a long, hard search. Martha moves in with her mother after the landowner kicks her off the sharecropping property: "I stayed and waited there for five years before I woke up one morning and decided that you were dead. Even if you weren't, you was dead to me" (p. 285). She tells how she followed the church: "Reverend Tolliver wanted to move the church up North cause of all the trouble the colored folks was having down there" (p. 285). She stopped waiting for the return of Loomis and embraced the church. She even changed her name to Martha Pentecost. When she finds Loomis at the boarding house, she is the symbol of Christianity. As Loomis begins to struggle with his identity and ancestry, Martha begins to recite the 23rd Psalm. She relies on the words of Christianity to resolve the struggle within Loomis. In the end of the play, Martha is the total embodiment of Christianity.

Overall, *Joe Turner* depicts the very real struggle between Christianity and ATR. The final scene determines the winner of the battle. Loomis reaches a crisis; he must choose. Martha speaks the words of Christianity, and Loomis still struggles. As he begins to understand his song, he denies everyone who tried to bind him. Finally, he understands that he bound himself, and only he can set himself free. While Martha continues to speak the 23rd Psalm, Loomis saves himself from a life of misplaced binding and slashes his chest. In this final scene, blood is the ultimate cleanser. Loomis is made clean as well as whole again. "You want blood? Blood make you clean? You clean with blood? [Slashes himself] I'm standing! I'm standing! My legs stood up! I'm standing now!" (p. 288). Pereira (1995) agreed with Paul Carter Harrison's interpretation that the cutting is a "reenactment of the Osirian mythos, which invites the death of the body in order to allow for the resurrection of the spirit/body" (p. 80). If so, the bloodletting is firmly entrenched in ATR. Even if this interpretation is incorrect, it cannot be denied that ATR is the means to salvation for Loomis in *Joe Turner*. "Moreover, Loomis's sacrilegious gesture undermines the Christian belief in Jesus Christ's crucifixion as the ultimate sacrifice undertaken for all humanity" (Shannon, 1995, p. 131). Jesus has betrayed Loomis. And Loomis takes the responsibility of his life on himself. He needs no one else to bleed for him; he can do it himself. Wilson said, "Loomis is not only illustrating his willingness to bleed but saying that if salvation requires bloodshed, he doesn't need Christ to bleed for him on the cross. He's saying something like, 'Christ can do some stuff I can't, but if it is about bleeding, yeah, I can bleed for myself' " (Lyons, 1999, p. 5). Loomis will take the African way—take responsibility for his soul through his own ritual and magic. Throughout *Joe Turner*, Wilson used images related to ATRs. The rituals, the juba, the ghosts, and the Shiny Man all helped to define the African path. The Shiny Man and Martha also represented Christianity. As this dichotomy became clear, the triumph of one over the other was the only alternative for resolution. In *Joe Turner*, ATR won.

The second play to explore the religious dichotomy is *The Piano Lesson*. The action of the play centers on an old family piano. Berniece lives in Pittsburgh with her uncle and daughter, and the piano. Her brother, Boy Willy, comes up from the South to sell the piano to gather enough money to buy a piece of land. As Berniece and Boy Willy fight and argue, the ghost of Sutter, slave owner of the family's ancestors, begins to haunt the home. In the end, Berniece turns to her friend Avery, a self-proclaimed Christian minister, to exorcise the house. Avery begins the ceremony, but only Boy Willy and Berniece can finish it. Wilson focused on the same conflict in *The Piano Lesson* as he did in *Joe Turner*. The characters struggle to accept or deny the African heritage and religion and embrace Christianity. In *The Piano Lesson*, the conflict is not so obvious. Unlike the many examples of ATR in *Joe Turner*, *The Piano Lesson* contains one major symbol for ATR and one for Christianity. The ghost of a dead White slave owner, Sutter, oddly enough, represents ATR. Avery, the newly sanctioned Christian minister, represents Christianity. The piano is not tied to either religion; it is the vehicle for the conflict. Berniece could easily play the piano in Avery's church, and all ATR would be denied. Or she could play at home and celebrate her ancestors. The piano only creates a mean to develop the larger conflict. These two symbols, the ghost and Avery, meet in a violent death match at the end of the play where only one religion, ATR or Christianity, will prove worthy.

The image of ATR in *The Piano Lesson* is the appearance of the ghost of Sutter. One of the tenets of ATR is the belief in spirits. Sutter's ghost appears in the first scene of the play. Berniece immediately accepts the apparition as a ghost: "Sutter . . . Sutter's standing at the top of the steps. . . . He was standing there . . . had his hand on top of his head. . . . I told him to go away and he just stood there looking at me" (p. 13). There is no question as to what Berniece saw, and eventually, all members of the family will witness the ghost of Sutter. The support of ATR comes not from the fact that the ghost is the dead White slave owner, but that the characters of the play can openly accept the presence of a spirit. Shannon (1995) posited that Wilson intentionally included examples of Black culture into his work, and the ghost is one of those examples. Eventually, it is the ghost that brings the characters to a place where a decision must be made. The African heritage, represented by the White man, forces a battle.

The Christian image in *The Piano Lesson* is much clearer. Avery represents the force of Christianity in the Black world: Thirty-eight years old, honest and ambitious, he has taken to the city like a fish to water, finding in it opportunities for growth and advancement that did not exist for him in the

South. He is dressed in a suit and tie with a gold cross around his neck. He carries a small Bible. At Avery's first entrance, he epitomizes Christianity. As stated earlier, one of the main tenets of Christianity is the reliance on the written word. Avery carries the written word with him, which serves as the White man's god. "Avery faces the dilemma of deciding how much of himself he can compromise without 'selling out' to the white man" (Pereira, 1995, p. 92). Avery accepted the White man's god and became a preacher. He works as an elevator operator in the White man's business world. Pereira (1995) also described him as "honest, intelligent and compliant" (p. 92). How much of himself did he sacrifice for success in the city?

Avery represents the Christian way in the play. He is a minister and feels he has been "called." Avery has a dream in which the Lord speaks to him. He relates how he felt after awakening to the other characters:

> I had a peace about myself that was hard to explain. I knew right then that I had been filled with the Holy Ghost and called to be a servant of the Lord. It took me a while before I could accept that. But then a lot of little ways God showed me it was true. So I became a preacher. (p. 25)

Shannon (1995) supposed that the other men in the play reject the story of Avery's call and consider him a con man like themselves. In this sense, Avery is just making a living and getting by like the rest of them. This attitude of the other characters undermines the power of Christianity and sets up Avery and Christianity for defeat at the end of the play.

The conflict between ATR and Christianity reaches climax at the end of the play, not unlike *Joe Turner*. Berniece asks Avery to bless the house so that the ghost of Sutter will disappear. After reading his Bible the previous night, Avery comes to the house and begins the ceremony.

> O Holy Father we gather here this evening in the Holy Name to cast out the spirit of one James Sutter. May this vial of water be empowered with thy spirit. May each drop of it be a weapon and a shield against the presence of all evil and may it be a cleansing and blessing of this humble abode. Just as Our Father taught us how to pray so He say, "I will prepare a table for you in the midst of mine enemies," and in His hands we place ourselves to come unto his presence. (p. 105)

The entire act of exorcism is reliant on the words in the Bible. Avery's blessing and exorcism do not work; Christian words are not enough for the demons of the past (Pereira, 1995). "Wilson believes that an all-out confrontation with this ghost is the essential point of the play" (Shannon, 1995, p. 161). Boy Willie has no investment in Christianity. He sees that the religion is useless against the ghost, and he takes on the ghost physically. Berniece realizes she cannot win by herself. She knows the power lies with the ancestors within the piano. She begins her own exorcism; she plays the piano and sings:

> I want you to help me
> I want you to help me
> I want you to help me
> I want you to help me
> I want you to help me
> I want you to help me
> Mama Berniece
> I want you to help me
> Mama Esther. (p. 107)

She helps Boy Willie and they begin to win. Wilson said,

> So it's when Berniece breaks her self-imposed taboo against touching the piano, when she calls on her ancestors, that something radical changes. The ghost Boy Willie was wrestling with upstairs gets off of Boy Willie, and Boy Willie knows something important has happened. (Lyons, 1999, p. 8)

Berniece accepted the past and her ancestors and drove away the ghost of Sutter. Berniece, by accepting tenets of ATR, was able to accomplish something Avery could not do with all his words and bibles. Wilson chose the African way to overcome in *The Piano Lesson* just as he did in *Joe Turner*.

In conclusion, Wilson used many different symbols and characters to represent Christianity and ATR in his plays. Wilson pulls from the very basic tenets of ATR to depict religion in his plays. He uses ritual, magic, spirits, and the ancestors. Wilson also incorporated Christianity. The basis of Christianity is in the Bible and the words contained therein. Many of the characters symbolizing Christianity recite the Scripture, and some, like Avery, actually carry the book around. These symbols set up a dichotomy in Wilson's work, especially *Joe Turner* and *The Piano Lesson*. In both plays, the two religions are set up to be in conflict, and only one of the religions can resolve this conflict. Wilson's characters choose ATR over Christianity repeatedly to overcome.

Interestingly, Wilson's doubt in the usefulness of White America's Christianity for Black people is not a new movement in literature. In

1968, Benjamin E. Mays included a chapter titled "Ideas of God Involving Frustration, Doubt, God's Impotence, and His Non-Existence" in his book, *The Negro's God as Reflected in His Literature* (1968, p. 218). He listed three ideas that recur in Black literature regarding God:

1. There is a strong tendency to doubt God's value to the Negro in his struggle to gain a stable economic, social and political foothold in America.
2. God is described as having outlived his usefulness. Historically, when gods have outlived their usefulness, either they have been abandoned or a new conception of God has been developed to meet the new experiences. The younger Negro writers seem to be inclined to abandon the idea rather than develop new concepts.
3. There is a denial of the existence of God.

Wilson's work reflects all these ideas. Character after character questions the role of God in his or her life. Will God help the Black person get ahead? Characters talk of God being obsolete. Will a Christian God help me? they ask. And characters deny the existence of a Christian God. If there is a God, why does He let bad things happen to the Black people? Wilson expanded on these ideas. He is beginning to develop a useful God and religion for Black Americans. His plays promote an acceptance of ATR, but he includes the Christian God as well.

As African people were brought to America, their religious ideas meshed with those of the multiple cultures they encountered to create a spirituality unique to them. Wilson wants to remind the African American audience of the spiritual roots of their ancestors. Not only did Wilson expertly weave the ideas into metaphors in the play, he used the ideas of African mysticism to provoke the African American audience to reconnect with spirituality from slavery and Africa. And from there, a new religion with old roots may begin.

WORKS CITED

Carroll, R. (1994). *Swing low*. New York: Carol Southern Books.

Herrington, J. (1998). *I ain't sorry for nothin' I done*. New York: Limelight Editions.

Kamara, G. M. (2000). Regaining our African aesthetics and essence through our African traditional religion. *Journal of Black Studies*, 30 (4), 502–514.

Lyons, B. (1999). An interview with August Wilson. *Contemporary Literature*, 40 (1), 1–2 1.

Mays, B. E. (1968). *The Negro's God as reflected in his literature*. New York: Russell and Russell.

Paris, P. J. (1994). The religious world of African Americans. In Jacob Neusner (Ed.), *World Religions in America* (pp. 69–91). Louisville, KY: Westminster/John Know Press.

Pereira, K. (1995). *August Wilson and the African-American odyssey*. Urbana: University of Illinois.

Richards, S. L. (1999). Yoruba gods on the American stage: August Wilson's *Joe Turner's Come and Gone*. *Research in African Literatures*, 30 (4), 92–105.

Shannon, S. G. (1995). *The dramatic vision of August Wilson*. Washington, DC: Howard University Press.

Shorter, A. (1977). *African Christian theology: adaptation or incarnation?* New York: Orbis Books.

Wilson, A. (1984). *Three plays*. Pittsburgh, PA: University of Pittsburgh.

Wilson, A. (1990). *The piano lesson*. New York: Penguin.

LADRICA MENSON-FURR

Booker T. Washington, August Wilson, and the Shadows in the Garden

> Whereas in Egypt the coming of the locust made desolation, in the farming South the departure of the Negro laid waste the agricultural industry—crops rotted, houses careened crazily in their utter desertion, and grass grew up in streets. On to the North! The land of promise.
>
> —Zora Neale Hurston, *Jonah's Gourd Vine*

Historically, the African American man has shared a connection with the American soil. Despite the chains of slavery, the binds of the sharecropping system, and the instability of landownership in the Jim Crow South, the black man has been able to establish a relationship with the soil of a nation that has been strengthened by his toil and irrigated by his blood. This idea has been discussed in both historical and literary texts. I contend, however, that nowhere does this symbiotic relationship between the black man and the soil resonate more significantly than in the twentieth century cycle dramas of playwright August Wilson. With the production of *Ma Rainey's Black Bottom*, August Wilson set out to compose a cycle of dramas that would chronicle the history of African American culture during each decade of the twentieth century. While scholars have discussed Wilson's works in numerous ways, I would like to contribute a more focused discussion, noting how Wilson has embedded the agrarian roots of the African American culture, specifically the black man's connection to the land, into the foundation of his dramatic

From *Mosaic* 38, no. 4 (December 2005): pp. 175–190. © 1996–2008 by ProQuest LLC.

texts and has challenged his audiences to consider his theory that "it was a transplant that did not take" (Rothstein, as qtd. in Shannon 659). He dramatizes how the migration of African Americans from the South to the North failed in its "promise" to reward the southern black severed from his home with a new life. Moreover, Wilson's theory suggests that the black male northern transplant will always, in memory or deed, carry the southern retention of farming in his blood, for it was in the blood of his father.

In *The Past is Present in the Dramas of August Wilson*, Harry Elam asserts that: "Wilson's cycle suggests that the tensions between father and son that contribute to anxieties of black masculinity must be addressed by confronting the past, finding room for forgiveness as well as resistance, remembering the 'father's story' in ways that allow one to hold on but also let go" (145). Drawing on Elam's reading of Wilson's cycle dramas, I argue that Wilson not only examines the tensions between father and son as explorations of black masculinity, but that these tensions also reflect the location of the "father's story." Usually for Wilson this story is set on a farm in the American South, and deals with the son's attempt to learn from or dismiss this stigmatized chapter and space in the annals of African American male history. What Wilson undertakes in his examination of this tension is similar to what Booker T. Washington accomplishes in the infamous "Atlanta Exposition Address" as he advocates that blacks should "cast down their buckets" into the trades learned in the school of American slavery. Wilson's dramas re-define and re-present the image of the black man on the farm, transforming him into a hero and his farm work into a noble profession through which he is given the power of creation, and the "green thumb" of life, to save his race and himself. This "green thumb" is located and illustrated in what I identify as both a hereditary and geographical connection to the southern soil. In *The Piano Lesson*, *Joe Turner's Come and Gone*, *Ma Rainey's Black Bottom*, *Two Trains Running*, and *King Hedley II*, August Wilson re-introduces the shadow in the garden—the black man—to the American literary imagination and uses his cycle series as a vehicle to educate his audiences about the black man and his desire to transform the southern gardens of slavery—the plantations and sharecropping fields—into his own Edenic, American Paradise.

In the controversial "Atlanta Exposition Address," Washington states: "No race can prosper 'til it learns that there is as much dignity in tilling a field as in writing a poem. It is at the bottom of life we must begin, and not at the top. Nor should we permit our grievances to overshadow our opportunities" (24–5). Although contested in the political writings of his contemporary, W.E.B. Du Bois, Washington's statements and the speech from which they were culled presented a socioeconomic theory for black uplift that would become for many persons a feasible means toward achieving the American promises of "life, liberty and the pursuit of happiness." Ninety years later, dramatist August Wilson revisits this socioeconomic theory in his twentieth-century series of dramas. Although avoiding the debatable accommodationist ideology of Washington's speech, Wilson's dramaturgy examines his contention that one of the worst things black people ever did was to leave the South. In "A Transplant that Did not Take: August Wilson's Views on the Great Migration," Sandra Shannon discusses Wilson's assessment of this issue and quotes Wilson's interview with Mervyn Rothstein: "We are a land-based agrarian people from Africa. We were uprooted from Africa, and we spent 200 years developing our culture as black Americans. And then we left the South. We uprooted ourselves and attempted to transplant this culture to the pavements of the industrialized North. And it was a transplant that did not take." Similar to the responses catalyzed by Washington's contention that blacks should utilize the skills learned during their tenure as slaves, Shannon notes how Wilson's pronouncement also caused outrage (659). However, Wilson has yet to retract or alter his position. Instead, he has augmented Washington's economic theory into his cycle dramas as an integral truth of black history, specifically for black men.

Through black male characters who have migrated by choice or by force from the agrarian soils of the South to the North, Wilson creates black men who find themselves historically, economically, and sociologically bound to the southern farms. Some, such as Levee, found in Wilson's *Ma Rainey's Black Bottom*, view this connection as destructive; thus, they transform it into fuel with which to ignite the funeral pyres of their traumatic pasts. Others, such as Memphis Lee of *Two Trains Running* and Boy Willie of *The Piano Lesson*, interpret this bind as their "inalienable right" to be American farmers and farm land owners; thus, they simultaneously support Washington's economic uplift plan for the African American culture and illuminate the "pride" that "tilling a field," especially a field that one owns, can instill within a man. Wilson's most recent character, King Hedley II (of the drama *King Hedley II*), brings Wilson's revision of Washington's economic theory full circle as he creates King, generations removed from the southern soil, but in search of a place to plant and harvest an identity for himself within the urban ghettos of the North. Wilson's men illustrate the economic and psychological paradoxes that face the black men who have a connection to the blood and pride soaked soil of the American South. However, these men also illustrate that fact that when black men attempt the "tilling of the soil," they are forced to confront and conquer economic, legal, and social hurdles in order to hold on to just a fraction of the promised "forty acres and a mule" of their pasts. I contend that through a revision of Washington's encouragement of twentieth-century African Americans to "cast down their buckets" in one of the trades learned in slavery, August Wilson's social and historical theories acknowledge and teach the historical importance of African American men's agrarian roots as a way of discussing the dangers of geographical and psychological migrations away from the land of the past.

Washington's socioeconomic theory suggests: "Cast it down in agriculture [. . .]. And in this connection it is well to bear in mind that whatever other sins the South may be called to bear, when it comes to business, pure and simple, it is in the south that the Negro is given a man's chance in the commercial world [. . .]" (24). Wilson includes this point in *The Piano Lesson*. This drama's plot reveals Washington's belief that the South would be the economic father of these black men through a heated debate on the value of landownership or a family heirloom. The participants in this debate—siblings Boy Willie and Berniece Charles—offer arguments that leave the audience to ask: "What would you do?" Although Boy Willie espouses a self-serving argument as to how the sale of the family's most precious heirloom, a piano carved with the pictorial history of Charles family from Africa to the slave plantation, will afford him the opportunity to become a landowner as "his daddy would have wanted," his desire to become a southern property owner is more complex than just an attempt to secure wealth. Rather, this opportunity will enable him to make a career in farming and, more importantly, to become equal to the white men of his father's past and of his present. Wilson writes Boy Willie's decision to become a farmer not as an acceptance of the fate that black men have been forced to follow, but rather as a choice to create something from the earth, something from the source that as Boy Willie states, "God ain't making no more of." This idea of choice is where Wilson's and Washington's economic uplift ideologies converge and prove that the black man (and black race) can, if willing, beneficially build upon the legacy of slavery and place himself (and itself) in a position of economic value and control.

Boy Willie's delivery of these passionate words of self-empowerment simultaneously acknowledges the forced enslaved history of the black man and illustrates his determination to prevent this past from making him ashamed of farming. In one of his most powerful arguments for landownership, Boy Willie says: "All that's in the past. If my daddy had seen where he could have traded that piano in for some land of his own, it wouldn't be sitting up here now. He spent his whole life farming on somebody else's land. I ain't gonna do that. See, he couldn't do no better" (863). This statement echoes Washington's contention that blacks should not "permit [their] grievances to overshadow [their] opportunities," and it further supports Boy Willie's choice to live a different life—professionally and geographically—from that of his family members and his friend, Lymon Jackson. As other African Americans who migrated to northern states to escape Jim Crow and for better economic and educational experiences, Doaker, Berniece, Wining

Boy, and now Lymon, do not deem Boy Willie's plan to purchase the land of their collective oppression as a valid reason to sell the piano. Moreover, Lymon does not understand why Boy Willie refuses to remain in Pittsburgh with his family and forgo his dream of farming. Boy Willie delivers a strong defence of his position: "You stay! I'm going back! That's what I'm gonna do with my life. Why I got to come up here and learn to do something I don't know how to do when I already know how to farm? You stay up here and make your own way if that's what you want to do. I'm going back and live my life the way I want to live it" (864).

The manner in which Boy Willie wishes to live his life is, ironically, connected to the same past that Berniece wishes to sequester in the "character" of the piano. Boy Willie, like the other Charles men (and Lymon), has learned to farm during forced periods of servitude on the plantation, on the plots of land that they sharecropped, and also as prisoners performing farm labour on the infamous Mississippi Parchman Prison Farm chain gang. It is this collective past that further solidifies the kinship between the Charles men and Lymon. It has helped to turn Doaker, the railroad cook; Wining Boy, the gambler and musician; Avery, the preacher and elevator operator; and Lymon away from the land and toward professions that will not remind them of their former ties to it.

Why does Wilson create Boy Willie, who is clearly the most vocal activist of this conglomerate of male characters, as the character with the most "farming pride"? It is because Wilson believes that one of the worst things that blacks did was to leave the South; for in leaving the South, they, in essence, aborted both the land and the trade of farming that they learned there and placed their hopes on the "pipe dreams" of the North. With their migration, not only did they rid themselves of the dust of the South, but they also began, generation by generation, to sever ties to that part of their history that Wilson seems to profess blacks should not be afraid or ashamed to claim. Boy Willie articulates this position as he responds to Berniece's statement to her daughter, Maretha: "Be still, Maretha. If you was a boy I wouldn't be going through this" (887). Although prefaced with retaliatory words to Berniece, Boy Willie's rebuttal clearly indicates his disdain for his sister's refusal to acknowledge the history of the piano and its value to the family: "[. . .] Sitting up there telling Maretha she wished she was a boy. What kind of thing is that to tell a child? If you want to tell her something tell her about the piano. You ain't even told her about the piano. Like that's something to be ashamed of. Like she supposed to go off and hide somewhere about that piano" (888). He, again, discusses why the piano should be sold and how its sale will enable him to build upon the controversial legacy that his father has left for him:

Many is the time that I looked at my daddy and seen him staring off at his hands. I got a little older I know what he was thinking. He sitting there saying, "I got these big old hands but what I'm gonna do with them? Best I can do is make a fifty-acre crop for Mr. Stovall [...]." See now ... if he had his own land he wouldn't have felt that way. If he had something under his feet that belonged to him he could stand up taller. That's what I'm talking about. Hell, the land is there for everybody. All you got to do is figure out how to get you a piece. Ain't no mystery to life. You just got to go out and meet it square on. If you got a piece of land you'll find everything else fall right into place. You can stand right up next to the white man and talk about the price of cotton ... the weather, and anything else you want to talk about. If you teach that girl she living at the bottom of life, she's gonna grow up and hate you. (888–89)

For Boy Willie, land becomes the Garden of Eden upon which he can firmly plant his feet and continue to create himself into a man. Similar to the Judeo-Christian God's act of creating Adam, Wilson has created Boy Willie, the character willing to complete the act of creation that was withheld from his father. In order to pay homage to his father, Boy Willie wishes to fulfill the dream that he believes his father had for his own life, for his family, and especially for his son.

Boy Willie's character is arguably selfish and immature. However, one cannot overlook his passion to obtain the land owned by the family that once owned his family, nor ignore his idea to change the land ownership from the Sutters' to his own. If he succeeds in his purchase of the land and successfully farms and reaps a profitable harvest, he can then feel more like the man he wants to become. Moreover, he can begin to balance the scales of the past. Elam states: "Boy Willie perceives himself as following in his father's footsteps, and sees farming as the family business. In addition, he imagines himself in a position to right the wrongs of racism that restricted his father's economic and social mobility." Thus, Elam continues, Boy Willie is "caught up in an agrarian vision of the American capitalist dream, and [he] associates the acquisition of wealth and property with masculinity" (132). Elam's equation of economic stability supports my contention that the farm for the black man is not only a symbol of American prosperity in the face of American racial adversity, but that it is also an assertion of manhood and homage to the paternal spirit. Moreover, it espouses the agenda of Washington's economic plan for black Americans and the belief that he shares with Wilson that "it is in the South that the Negro is given a man's chance in the commercial world" (24).

In *Two Trains Running*, set in 1960, Wilson situates the black man's tie to the land in the literal past life of bar and grill owner, Memphis Lee. Before becoming a successful entrepreneur, Lee was a proud landowner in the notoriously racist city of Jackson, Mississippi. Well into the drama we learn how Memphis was "run" out of Jackson and off of his land. Memphis's rendering of this traumatic experience softens his callously critical character, transforming him into a man who has turned the pains of his past into potent fuel for the man he has become since his arrival in the North. Like Boy Willie, Memphis does not take the first train rides out of the segregated South. He, instead, seeks to earn a living on the land that he owns and works with his own hands. Although the powers that be—the white landowners—allow Memphis to own the land, they include a clause in the land's deed that allows them to renege on their sale of the land to Memphis if water, a necessary irrigation source for plant life, is found. According to Memphis, "Jim Stovall, who I bought the land from, told me my deed say if I found any water the sale was null and void. Went down to the court to straighten it out and come to find out he had a bunch of these fellows get together to pick on me. He try to act like he ain't had nothing to do with it" (72). In *The Piano Lesson*, Boy Willie's uncle, Wining Boy, speaks a truth that is restated in Memphis's story of his lost land—"the black man can't fix nothing with the law" (859). Because Memphis cannot fight the white landowners on a balanced legal field, he relinquishes his power to them, especially after they castrate his mule:

> [...] They took and cut my mule's belly out while it standing there. Just took a knife and sliced it open. I stood there and watched them. They was laughing about it. I look and see where they got me covered. There's too many of them to fool around with. I don't want to die. But I loved that old mule. Me and him had been through a lot together. He was a good old mule. Remind me of myself ... I stood there and watched them cut his belly open. He kinda reared back, took a few steps, and fell over. One of them reached down, grabbed hold of his dick, and cut that off. I stood there looking at them. I say, "Okay. I know the rules now. If you do that to something that ain't never done nothing to you ... then I know what you would do to me." (72–3)

Memphis realizes that his fight would leave him both landless and physically emasculated. Thus, it would be best if he follows the road often travelled by both black men and women in the Jim Crow South—the train to the North. This train allows Memphis and his fellow travellers to escape the constant threat of physical and psychological trauma that the South offers.

Memphis's story also proves that his kinship with the land, though removed by force and time, is still an integral part of his identity. At the play's end we meet a Memphis who seeks to reclaim his land after his temporary exile from it. In his depiction of Memphis in *Two Trains Running*, Wilson pointedly states his contention that the South is the home of the black American experience; and, for the black man, the land that was once the bane of his existence is a vital component of his reality, his history, and his birthright. The loud gifts of urbanity—city life and the appearance of equality—are powerless against the powerful call of the soil, a call that is similar to the presence of the numerous African retentions prevalent in Wilson's black American cycle dramas. Instead, this retention is the southern retention of the black male experience. Shortly after we encounter Memphis Lee in act one, we hear this southern land owning retention as he responds to the numbers runner, Wolf: "I been here since '36. They ran me out of Jackson in '31. I hung around Natchez for three or four years, then I come up here. I was born in Jackson. I used to farm there. They ran me out in '31. Killed my mule and everything. One of these days I'm going back and get my land. I still got the deed" (31). Although Memphis's strong work ethic has enabled him to become a successful black American entrepreneur and landowner in the North, he still possesses his land deed and his connection to the southern soil and to his past. This bind, even thousands of miles away, is what allows the shadows of men such as Memphis Lee to be found in the gardens of the South. Memphis Lee's reclamation of his land is also his reclamation of the soul.

Kim Pereira suggests that as Wilson examines the lives of migrant blacks in his works, he "also raises questions about the rural South and the black American's place in it, and he explores the decisions that led them away from the familiarity of their farms into a strange industrial milieu" (3). *The Piano Lesson* and *Two Trains Running* illustrate the black man's decisions to participate in the northward migration and to re-migrate to the South. In Wilson's depiction of the re-migration of blacks to the South, his dramaturgy reflects the recent phenomena, particularly within the last twenty years, of African Americans who fled the South for the same reasons as Memphis Lee and the Charles family men, now returning to the South to reclaim the lands that their fathers once owned. These migrations reflect Washington's contention that "no race that has anything to contribute to the markets of the world is long in any degree ostracized. It is important and right that all privileges of the law be ours" (26). They also show Wilson's extension of the theory that the South is the place where the black man (and the black race) must first locate himself before he can (and it can) comfortably establish himself anywhere else.

Joe Turner's Come and Gone is the drama in which the rural and the urban collide and the hybrids of Washington and Wilson, and the northern soil and the agrarian descendant, are formed. The "feud" between urban entrepreneur Seth Holly and the mysterious visitor Herald Loomis results in a collision that not only allows Loomis, the migrant, to find his song and re-connect to his history, but also affords Seth the opportunity to understand the history of his southern boarders.

Loomis, a former sharecropper and prisoner on Joe Turner's Tennessee chain gang, has ventured North in search of his wife Martha Loomis (Pentecost). With Loomis comes not only his eleven-year-old daughter Zonia, but also the "old heavy coat" of his past as a black man-deacon-father-husband-chain gang detainee and the vision of bones walking on water. Carrying around this load, especially as a northern visitor, is burdensome both for Loomis and those persons he encounters. However, his story and history are illustrations of those memories Wilson contends numerous black men and women share as retentions of southern slavery. The garden-farm in this drama is symbolized by the clodhoppers Loomis wears and the stories he shares with Bynum, the conjure man, and Seth about his Tennessee past. Loomis also asserts that this garden-farm is both a place where most black people have worked, and a locale where the northern, southern, and African elements violently collide.

> BYNUM. You a farming man, Herald Loomis? You look like you done some farming.
> LOOMIS. Same as everybody. I done farmed some, yeah.
> BYNUM. I used to work at farming . . . picking cotton. I reckon everybody done picked some cotton.
> SETH. I ain't! I ain't never picked no cotton. I was born up here in the North. My daddy was a freed man. I ain't never seen no cotton.
> BYNUM. Mr. Loomis done picked some cotton. Ain't you Herald Loomis? You done picked a bunch of cotton. (267)

Joe Turner's Come and Gone begins with northern born Seth Holly observing the hoodoo practices of longtime tenant Bynum. Although Seth is disturbed by Bynum's pigeon sacrifices, he is equally disturbed about Bynum's planting of what he considers to be weeds in his vegetable garden: "Messing up my garden growing them things out there. I ought to go out there and pull up all them weeds" (208). These weeds are the roots that Bynum uses to bind people to one another and to assist people, particularly young women, in their attempts to resolve matters of the heart and soul. Because Seth is a northern born African American, he has no faith in nor understanding of Bynum's weeds and their powers. His questioning of their presence in his garden of cabbage and tomatoes is similar to his critique of the numerous southern migrants moving into cities like Pittsburgh in search of a better life for themselves: "These niggers coming up here with that old backward country style of living. It's hard enough now without all that ignorant kind of acting. Ever since slavery got over with there ain't been nothing but foolish-acting niggers. Word get out they need men to work in the mill and put in these roads . . . and niggers drop everything and head North looking for freedom" (209).

For Seth, his seemingly perfect garden (his northern world) is being attacked by the pollination of southern habits and a "backward style of living" that not only confirm his image of the southern Negro, but also causes him to incorrectly diminish the value of Bynum's "weeds" to his garden. It is from the "human weeds" present in his "respectable" boarding house that Seth is able to establish himself as an entrepreneur and self-sustained landowner in Pittsburgh. It is also because of the southern retentions that Seth's tenants bring that he is able to Juba (a communal dance "reminiscent of the ring shouts of African slaves" [249]) on Sundays and learn about the history of the black South and his African heritage.

Wilson introduces Seth's and Bynum's communal garden early in the drama to do more than demonstrate the agrarian abilities of northern soil. Rather, he creates a stage through which his audience can recall the significance and binding abilities of the soil, particularly when it is the soil of the black American experience. Although Seth boldly criticizes "southern niggers," he also willingly participates in a form of farming that all blacks in the country, particularly in the play's 1911 setting, had practiced. Whether in a cotton field or a simple vegetable garden, the seeds of the African American culture are sown within the same cultural soil of experience. Bynum and Loomis prove this, but Seth, a northern born black man, does not possess the innate ability to comprehend this connection. Just as Bynum believes that persons search for their songs, I suggest that the song of the American South is the song of farming, of gardening, of planting and harvesting, and everyone, even the Seths, know its melody, if not the words.

In "The Negro in the North: Are His Advantages as Great as in the South," Washington writes, "the Northern Negro who makes a success in business or in a profession must, in most instances, live beside and work for a people who have no special need of his talents. At best he can but perform for them a service that can be performed as well, if not better, by some one else" (63). This is one of the truths of the black migration that Wilson explores in his cycle dramas, especially in the blues inspired *Ma Rainey's Black Bottom*. Centred on the men who comprise the accompaniment band of famous blues songstress Ma Rainey, much of this drama, set in 1920, concerns itself with an illustrative clash between old music and new music similar to Alain Locke's contrasting of old Negro characteristics with new Negro characteristics in the essay and Harlem Renaissance manifesto, "The

New Negro." This drama hearkens back to the glory days of farming and landownership experienced by black men before they packed their guitars and moved themselves and their blues to northern cities.

Levee, the representative new Negro in this drama, is both agitator and agitated by the more seasoned and experienced Negro musicians in Ma's band. One would think that Levee was a northern born African American because of his extreme criticism of his elders and their old time music, but by the end of a full act of bantering between the naive Levee and the intellectual Toledo, we learn that Levee, too, has memories of this agrarian past: "We was living in Jefferson county, about eighty miles outside of Natchez. My daddy's name was Memphis . . . Memphis Lee Green . . . had him near fifty acres of good farming land. I'm talking about good land! Grow anything you want! He done gone off of shares and bought this land from Mr. Hallie's widow woman after he done passed on. Folks called him an uppity nigger cause he done saved and borrowed to where he can buy this land and be independent" (57). The rest of the story is traumatic and all too common, for the means by which the white men in the community attempt to emasculate and remind Levee's father of his "place" is by sexually assaulting his wife. As a child, Levee witnesses a black man's ability, his father's, to own and successfully farm land. Also during this formative stage in his life, he is forced to witness what success in the black man's garden-farm means to white southern society. I do not suggest that Levee turns away from the soil and toward the North and music as an escape from Jim Crow injustice, but I do assert that Levee's past and his attempt to "cloak" it in the new attitude of the North becomes his "overcoat" in the form of a southern retention that will not allow him to disassociate himself from his southern roots.

Wilson further complicates Levee's position as one who wishes to change the music to keep up with the times by creating a more jazzy sound out of the old backwoods blues sung by Ma Rainey. This change is both symbolic of the dawning of the Harlem Renaissance and its musical soundtrack of jazz music, and of the emergence of a new generation of black Americans—the children and grandchildren of sharecroppers and independent farmers—who migrated physically away from the farms, but who will always culturally—through acknowledgement or not—remain connected to the soils of the South. Shannon further supports my interpretation when she reads Levee as one of Wilson's most volatile examples of the failed transfer of the southern-agrarian man to the North:

> Abrasive, conniving, insecure, bitter, blatantly anti-Christian, and ultimately homicidal, Levee epitomizes the transplant that did not take [. . .]. Levee's potential to self-destruct because of his

severed ties with the South is also evident in his futile attempts
to replace Ma Rainey's "old jug band music" with his jazzed-up
arrangements. He scowls at his colleagues, and repeatedly taunts
them with insults stemming from his deep-seated loathing of
anything related to life in the South. His aversion to the South
surfaces in his instructions to fellow band members on how to
adopt his style of music: "Now we gonna dance it . . . but we ain't
gonna countrify it. This ain't no barn dance" (*Ma Rainey* 38). It
also appears in an early verbal jab at Toledo: "Nigger got them clod
hoppers! Old brogans! He ain't nothing but a sharecropper . . . Got
nerve to put on a suit and tie with them farming boots." (40)

Shannon's reading of the text contends that the blues music that
serves as the soundtrack for Wilson's dramas and their characters' lives is
an illustration of the southern retentions of the newly transplanted southern
agrarian black men. However, I interpret this blues experience, particularly
for Levee, as his attempt to eradicate the blues, the South, his father's land,
and the violation of his mother on his father's land as a failed attempt to
disconnect himself from the "brogans" worn by elders like Toledo. Shannon
also discusses Levee's reverence of his $11 Florsheim shoes. These shoes,
unlike Toledo's brogans, are appropriate for the shirt and tie image of the
North, and as Shannon notes: "Levee projects onto these shoes certain
aspects of his own subconscious struggle to succeed in the North and to
create as much geographic and cultural distance as he can between himself
and the South" (667). However, I suggest that Wilson proves through his
cycle dramas that this disconnection will always remain in the subconscious
of the southern black man.

While Wilson's *King Hedley II* brings his cycle dramas closer to
the conclusion of his cyclical goal, it is simultaneously contemporary
and historical, particularly because of the placement of a small garden in
an urban, ghetto backyard. The play opens with King planting seeds in
a small patch of earth in the yard. This action holds significance within
the borders of the plot, for not only do we have a seemingly odd farmer,
but we also have the act of planting as a physical metaphor for King's
desire to see the harvesting of his own biological seed so that others will
know that he has lived. This act of planting is not uncommon to American
or African American literature, especially in the case of black men who
desire to produce living testaments to their masculine presence and power
of creation. Interestingly, Wilson does not write King planting vegetables
or some other form of sustenance for his family, rather we encounter him
planting flowers for his wife, Tonya. Unlike Wilson's other farming men,
the planting of flowers enables King to present a sentimental side of the

black man who sees the earth as more than a place to grow food for survival or material wealth, but also as a place to sow and reap an age-old symbol of love and affection.

King's desire to plant is criticized by the soil from whence he sprang to life, his mother Ruby. Instead of encouraging her son's horticultural aspirations, Ruby offers advice that opposes King's actions:

> KING. These some seeds. I'm gonna grow Tonya some flowers.
> RUBY. You need some good dirt. Them seeds ain't gonna grow in that dirt.
> KING. Ain't nothing wrong with this dirt.
> RUBY. Get you some good dirt and put them seeds in it if you want them to grow. Your daddy knew what good dirt was. He'd tell you you need some good dirt. (184)

King, however, ignores Ruby's words and is found in the following scene watering the soil of his "urban garden," thus proving his belief that his seed can and will grow in any type of soil. Wilson writes King's gardening actions as movements that the character carries out while in dialogue with the other characters in the drama, and in doing so, the garden becomes his "evidence" and counterargument that his garden, as does his life, has potential for growth and change. For example, as King converses with his friend Mister about the whereabouts of the man who is seeking to avenge the death of his cousin, Pernell, killed by King, the garden becomes a significant point of reference:

> KING. I'm goin out there and look for him. When I find him, that'll be the last time we see each other. (*He points to a small, barely discernable spot of green growing where he planted the seeds.*) Look at that. See that growing. See that!
> MISTER. Yeah, I see.
> KING. Ruby tell me my dirt ain't worth nothing. It's mine. It's worth it to have. I ain't gonna let nobody take. Talking about I need some good dirt. Like my dirt ain't worth nothing. A seed is a seed. A seed will grow in dirt. Look at that!
> MISTER. Yeah, I see. (193)

King's trial with the garden and Ruby's words are reminiscent of Ruth Krauss's classic children's tale *The Carrot Seed* in that he, just as Krauss's protagonist, appears to be the only person who has faith that his flowers (seeds) will grow. Similar to the protagonist in Krauss's text, King assumes the role of the naive child whose faith conquers all the negative realities of his fate. King's garden may appear to be disconnected from Wilson's other shadows in the garden because of his distance from both the agrarian South and because of the contemporary setting of the play (video store, kung-fu movies, stolen refrigerators, etc.), but this contemporary garden is where Wilson and his dramaturgy demonstrate their ability to connect African American time and space. Because King is not privy to his true biological history, he is in a sense "miseducated" to follow the footsteps of his surrogate father King Hedley I, who lived his life aspiring to own the plantation (a place of farms and farming) that Hedley's father never owned during his lifetime. In reality, King's true father, the seed from which he has grown, was an Alabama man cut down during his prime by the bullet of his mother's wandering lover, Elmore.

Shortly before King learns the truth of his planting, he also learns that Tonya is pregnant and plans to abort the foetus rather than bring another child into a world that may force her to bury it before it becomes an adult. It is at this point that King's urban garden becomes symbolic of the decade that Wilson represents in *King Hedley II*: the 1980s, a period that witnessed an increase in gang violence, drive-by shootings, teenage pregnancies, AIDS, and HIV in the urban centres of America. King's garden, then, is not merely the space in which he attempts to grow flowers for his wife, but it is also the place where his name will continue to resonate throughout the world and within the garden of her womb. Again, using the garden that he has planted and is growing despite Ruby's critique of his "bad dirt," Elmore's trampling of his seedlings and, most importantly, despite his misinterpretation of the scar Pernell put on his face, King goes to the source, the soil, to argue that his seed deserves at least the chance to sprout into existence:

> Pernell put that scar on my face, but I put the bigger mark on myself. That's why I need this baby, not 'cause I took something out the world but because I wanna put something in it. Let everybody know I was here. You got King Hedley II and then you got King Hedley III. Got glass and bottles. But it still deserves to live. Even if you do have to call the undertaker. Even if somebody come along and pull it out by the root. It still deserve to live. It still deserve that chance. I'm here and I ain't going nowhere. I need to have that baby. Do you understand? (238)

King's flower garden and King as gardener are oddities within this contemporary setting, but his aspiration to create something from the earth and his soiled soul make this drama an illustration of the significance of knowing one's history, particularly when it concerns the agrarian South.

While it may be presumed that Leroy and Elmore had ties to the southern soil, we know that King's "father," King Hedley I, understood the soil, and that he and his father shared the same connection with the soil that most black men of the South did. However, once King learns the truth of his planting, he chooses to embrace both fathers and their respective histories, but at the expense of the garden that he has protected with his words and with a barbed wire fence. In the very last scene of the drama, King "picks up the barbed wire and throws it out of the way" and "stomps on his seeds and clears out the spot to play" Elmore in a game of craps. King hopes to beat Elmore and use the winnings to repay the loan that Elmore contends led to Leroy's death. Also, King prepares himself a "self-defense" motive by using the very weapon, a machete, that King Hedley I used to murder Floyd Barton in *Seven Guitars* (Wilson's play that *King Hedley II* sequels) (248). King's trampling and uprooting of his garden foreshadows the shedding of blood that will take place. This time the blood is King's. The savant character, Stool Pigeon (a.k.a. Canewell), very much like his dramatic cousin Bynum, predicts this turn of events in the prologue of the drama, and again at the play's end, as he pays homage to the ultimate farmer, the Judeo-Christian God to whom all of Wilson's farmers/gardeners must give credit for their harvest—good and bad:

> Thy Will! Not man's will! Thy Will!
> You Wrote the Beginning and the End!
> Bring down the Fire!
> Stir up the tempest!
> You got the wind in one hand
> and fire in the other!
> Riding on a black wind!
> The Alpha and the Omega!
> You a bad motherfucker! ... (251)

Wilson's continuation of this background theme in *King Hedley II* exemplifies yet another binding tie between his dramas. Although set within different decades of the twentieth century and featuring new characters with the exception of Aunt Esther, Ruby, Elmore and Stool Pigeon (Canewell), Wilson's cycle dramas demonstrate the changing face of black life in America against both the backdrops of race and class oppression, and against the historical background of African American agrarianism. Wilson, I suggest, uses the image of the black man as garden-farmer as a dramatic restatement of his belief in the ability of black culture, if it had remained largely in the South, to become self-sustaining farmers and landowners, and of the pride that black men should have for their agrarian past. Despite racism and their inabilities to "fix things with the law," Wilson's black farmers and landowners continue to view the soil and the South as their "promised land" where they can be men on their own terms and by their own standards. Thus the soil, the garden, for these shadows becomes not only a space of reclamation, but also a place of regeneration for their once soiled pasts.

WORKS CITED

Elam, Harry. "Men of August." *The Past as Present in the Drama of August Wilson*. Ann Arbor: U of Michigan P, 2004. 127–65.

Krauss, Ruth. *The Carrot Seed*. New York: Harper Collins, 1993.

Locke, Alain. "The New Negro." *The New Negro: Voices of the Harlem Renaissance*. New York: Touchstone, 1999. 3–18.

Pereira, Kim. Introduction. *August Wilson and the African American Odyssey*. Chicago: U of Illinois P, 1995. 1–12.

Shannon, Sandra. "A Transplant that did not Take: August Wilson's Views on the Great Migration." *African American Review* 31.4 (Winter 1997): 659–67.

Washington, Booker T. "The Atlanta Exposition Address." *African American Political Thought 1890–1930: Washington, Du Bois, Garvey and Randolph*. Ed. Cary D. Wintz. New York: M.E. Sharpe, 1996. 21–3.

———. "The Negro in the North: Are His Advantages as Great as in the South." *African American Political Thought 1890–1930: Washington, Du Bois, Garvey and Randolph*. Ed. Cary D. Wintz. New York: M.E. Sharpe, 1996. 60–4.

Wilson, August. *Joe Turner's Come and Gone*. *August Wilson Three Plays*. Pittsburgh: U of Pittsburgh P, 1991. 197–290.

———. *King Hedley II*. *The Fire This Time: African American plays for the 21st Century*. Eds. Harry Elam and Robert Alexander. New York: Theatre Communications Group, 2004. 173–251.

———. *Ma Rainey's Black Bottom*. *August Wilson Three Plays*. Pittsburgh: U of Pittsburgh P, 1991. 1–93.

———. *The Piano Lesson*. *The Prentice Hall Anthology of African American Literature*. Eds. Rochelle Smith and Sharon Jones. New Jersey: Prentice Hall, 2000. 838–98.

———. *Two Trains Running*. New York: Plume, 1993.

PHILIP D. BEIDLER

"King August":
August Wilson in His Time

For a long time, I had planned to call this essay "Me and My Shadow,
August Wilson." The title—intended to express the ironic conceit of parallel
lives—had come to me out of the memory of an old Al Jolson song that
must have still been around after World War II when Wilson and I were
growing up as contemporaries in Pennsylvania, he in the black Hill District
of Pittsburgh, and I in the white Quaker and German farmlands of Adams
County. In considering it, I obviously hadn't given much thought to the
ironies of popular music back in a world where the average American's idea
of a jazz singer was an old Jewish vaudeville guy performing in blackface.
August Wilson would have liked that, I believe.

I had begun writing the essay for a number of reasons, some
autobiographical and some literary. On the first count, I wanted to record
a rare experience of personal encounter, beginning with a September 2001
conference on writing and race at my university where August Wilson—a
bare two weeks after the 9/11 hijackings—had honored his commitment
to be the headline speaker, and where, as one of the organizers, I had
gotten to meet him and spend substantial time with him over several days.
As our acquaintance grew, we agreed to take a certain humorous pleasure
in discovering how many things we seemed to have in common: we were
the same age; we were both geriatric fathers, with young daughters almost

From *Michigan Quarterly Review* 45, no. 4 (Fall 2006): pp. 575–597. © 1996–2008 by
ProQuest LLC.

exactly the same age (and we were just sappy enough to go right to the wallet photos, my Katherine, his Azula); we both grew up in late 1940s and early 1950s Pennsylvania; we were both even half German. But then there was that other matter of race. The other half of my identity was also white, but the other half of his was black; and that small fact meant that we had also grown up and spent our lives in mutually alien universes. The idea of a shared history was a crazy falsehood.

So likewise, we both knew, was any conceit of shared cultural or artistic memory. Wilson's public lecture—the occasion proper of our meeting—elaborated his well-known vision of the unbridgeable abyss of difference, in life and art alike, separating Black America from White America. It was just that stark. And just that uncompromising. As he had done elsewhere, he asserted himself proudly, even belligerently as "a race man" in living and writing. He argued the unconditional necessity of a separatist black aesthetic and a black arts tradition, with black arts funding, black arts training, and black arts institutions. He unapologetically grounded his separatist artistic politics in the utterly bitter and alienating politics of being a person of African descent in American culture every day of his life.

During Wilson's visit, we had arranged performances of two of his plays. Those presented—one by our university and one by the local black college—were *The Piano Lesson* and *Ma Rainey's Black Bottom*. Wilson met with casts, looked in on rehearsals, and conducted student and faculty workshops. In these moments, as well as everywhere else, he honored his commitments with total generosity and attention. Near the end of his stay, I remember talking to him one last time, two hours into a hot, crowded, post-lecture reception at a faculty member's house, where I had assured him he was not at all obliged to go in the first place. I asked him if he wanted to go back to his hotel. No, he said. He was fine. When I left him, he was in conversation with a new group of people to whom he had just been introduced. You could tell he was listening carefully to some of them who were asking him questions. When he answered, he was talking quietly, smiling.

An equally important initial motive for me in trying to write "Me and My Shadow, August Wilson," however, lay in the transforming experience of cultural and artistic encounter I had found in the body of his work. After he left, I devoured all the print versions of the plays I could get my hands on, beginning again with *The Piano Lesson* and *Ma Rainey's Black Bottom*, then everything else. I plunged into the texts, reading and re-reading, sometimes silently and sometimes aloud; marking up the pages with underlines, stars, and brackets; scribbling my own words in the margins and on separate sheets. In my mind's eye, I tried to stage them, as *Piano Lesson* and *Ma Rainey* had been on stage; from summaries and reviews, I tried to envision the new ones coming into production—*King Hedley II, Gem of the Ocean,* and *Radio Golf.*

These would complete, as was eagerly anticipated, the great August Wilson cycle of ten dramas, one for each decade, chronicling African-American experience in this nation during the twentieth century.

King Hedley II moved from the stage into print. Reviews appeared of *Gem of the Ocean*—set in the first decade of the now previous century. In spring and summer of last year, notices appeared for *Radio Golf*, the 90s play completing the cycle. Reviews covered initial performances at the Yale Repertory Theater. Further announcements were awaited concerning the tryout process in other venues whereby the play, as had most of the others, would complete its odyssey to New York.

In late summer, I saw Wilson's photo again, accompanying a brief item in the *New York Times*. He was wearing, as he often did, what people sometimes called his "porter" or "newsboy" cap, but which always looked to me—given what I had seen personally of his tailoring—more like a fine English driving cap; and he also had that look he often does, quizzical, bemused, slightly startled, but meeting you right in the eye. The report concerned not his playwriting, however, but his health. August Wilson, it said, had liver cancer, with a few months to live. He was described as peaceful in spirit. "I've had a blessed life," he was quoted as saying. "I'm ready." Another, a few days later, announced that the Virginia Theater in New York would be renamed for him—the first such naming, it was pointed out, to honor an African American artist. The dedication was set for October 7. It was noted that Wilson might not live to see it.

He did not, of course. That is a shame. He would have especially liked the idea of renaming the "Virginia" theater. But he would have participated in the event mainly, I suspect, as part of being in production again, back in the city, back in the theater, wrestling with the final New York version of *Radio Golf*, right in the middle of the process to the end, watching, rewriting, restaging, totally reconceptualizing and reinventing, until he thought it was right. That is a shame. It is all a shame, because we are already coming to count his loss by the measure of his achievement, this American playwright who may be not simply the greatest dramatist, but also the greatest writer of our generation, and who became so by writing about the entire cultural sweep of American life in the twentieth century through a cycle of plays about black America predicated on its very incomprehensibility to white America.

So where do I—somebody from white America—get off saying these things about me and my shadow, August Wilson, who always described himself, at every opportunity, as a "race" man? Who announced at every turn what he was writing about—"black life presented on its own terms, on a grand and epic scale, in all its richness and fullness"? Who knew what kind of artistic medium he was trying to create—a black theater, centered on a black aesthetic, opening new doors to black artists, including playwrights, directors, and actors? And who knew exactly why? As he said in his famous 1996 essay, "The Ground on which I Stand," "there is no idea that cannot be contained by black life." Or, as he posited with an unassailable logic of both cultural and aesthetic authority—"Never is it suggested that playwrights such as Terence McNally or David Mamet are limiting themselves to white life." Accordingly, though I make certain claims of engagement, am I thus any different from the patronizing cocktail-party acquaintance described by Wilson at an otherwise all-white gathering who proudly announced to the playwright that when looking at Wilson, "he didn't see race"? That might be so, Wilson replied, but he didn't notice the guy saying that to anyone else in the group.

Well Wilson *was* writing about race. But he also knew he was really writing about history and cultural memory, because he knew—no, he insisted—that in America the two things were one thing and could not be pulled out of each other. Likewise, in the deepest understandings of art, he knew that he was writing for the theater. And *as an artist*—indeed with a single-minded dedication possibly unparalleled by that of any other major figure in our time—he knew in his deepest soul that the theater belonged to everybody. Anyone who doubts either point need only read the plays.

What they will find, I am convinced, is a cycle of dramas now likely to stand as the closest thing we will have to a twentieth-century African American world picture—in the sense that criticism once talked about the Renaissance world picture; or, yes, since the term has been out there crowding Wilson for years, the Shakespearean world picture. It recalls fully the world of the tragedies, comedies, histories, and romances, an imaginative world in which it becomes possible to envision black life in America in the twentieth century through a transforming totality of theatrical experience.

At the same time, if the world created in Wilson's plays is that of history as theater, it is uniquely history with a difference, history as predicated on the total reality for black Americans of personal and cultural difference. For what is so truly astonishing about these plays is the degree to which, even as history presides as an enormous, epochal, inescapable presence in the world of the plays, it is simultaneously a world almost totally devoid of the conventional benchmarks of official, conventional, basically white history. To put this more directly, throughout the cycle, there are virtually no current events in the traditional meaning of that phrase. The Vietnam War sneaks in as a 1969 coda to the 1957 setting of *Fences*. *Jitney* makes some reference to brands and model years of cars. *Ma Rainey's Black Bottom* is set in a pioneering age of studio recording. There are also very few white people physically embodied. In *Joe Turner's Come and Gone*, a Jewish peddler trades in piecework manufacture from black homes. In *Ma Rainey* we meet a music promoter. More often, white America is the landlord we never see.

A rich white man, since most of the plays are set in Pittsburgh, is usually just called a Mellon. Or he is the bogey-man in a title song: the nigger-catcher Joe Turner.

Nor, it is supremely important to note from the outset, does cultural whiteness appear as in any explicit way genetic. Most specifically, racial mixing, so pronounced a theme in African American literature, goes virtually unmentioned here. Markedly absent, especially given Wilson's own racial and cultural patrimony, is Frederick Douglass's rage, for instance, at white fathers, or Harriet Jacobs's at the exercise of sexual power over the enslaved black woman and mother. Just as distinctly unpronounced is the sense of double racial otherness that so permeates the sensibilities of James Baldwin or Ralph Ellison. Throughout the plays, racial mixing is simply and plainly not an issue. Blackness is the issue. Mixing or degrees of mixing do not obtain. Or rather, mixing is assumed, but so assumed that it's not worth going into. Wilson is having no nonsense with the racial pieties of culture, academic or otherwise: "crossing," "transgression," "hybridity," and the like. One drop of blood is all it takes. Black is black. White is white. This is the message of history and the experience of culture. Blood will tell. If you have black blood in you, you are black, you know it, the world knows it, and there's hell to pay.

To be sure, the historical fact of slavery, with all its attendant horrors of blackness and whiteness, presides always in the background, along with Reconstruction, Jim Crow, and the great migrations to the cities of the North and upper Midwest: New York, Philadelphia, Baltimore, Washington D.C., Chicago, St. Louis, Detroit. Pittsburgh—up the middle, in the boundary regions of Ohio, Pennsylvania, Maryland, and West Virginia, a place of transit since the underground railway—becomes all of them, the chokepoint of the universe, diaspora town and promised land. It is the capital of the world. Simultaneously, it is the world of the plays, within which life itself—what happens in a family, a household, a neighborhood—frequently outstrips time or place, becoming in and of itself enormous, epochal, earth-shaking, cataclysmic.

How this works in the great cycle of the plays themselves may be at least suggested, initially, by two parallel listings, one ordered by year of appearance and the other re-ordered by year of represented chronology:

Jitney (1982)	*The Gem of the Ocean* (1904)
Ma Rainey's Black Bottom (1984)	*Joe Turner's Come and Gone* (1911)
Fences (1987)	*Ma Rainey's Black Bottom* (1927)
Joe Turner's Come and Gone (1988)	*The Piano Lesson* (1937)
The Piano Lesson (1990)	*Seven Guitars* (1949)
Two Trains Running (1992)	*Fences* (1957)

Seven Guitars (1996)	*Two Trains Running* (1969)
King Hedley II (2001)	*Jitney* (1977)
The Gem of the Ocean (2004)	*King Hedley II* (1985)
Radio Golf (2005)	*Radio Golf* (1997)

One begins by noticing certain simple, obvious things. It seems striking that the first play in represented historical chronology, *The Gem of the Ocean*, set in 1904, was written next to last—precisely a century later, it turns out, in 2004. The last play written in represented historical chronology, *Radio Golf*, set in 1997, on the other hand, turns out to have been the last in composition, written in 2005 and thereby bringing the twinned sagas of history and writing directly into the present. (Characteristically, when confronted with this idea of structural purpose, Wilson denied such a big idea by leaning back like the creator and looking at what he had created. "I went at this haphazardly," he claimed; ". . . then I looked up one day and saw I had only the first and last plays to do. I thought it would be perfect to relate them. The two form a kind of umbrella for the rest to sit up under.")

Certain plays oddly intersect. The titular protagonist of *King Hedley II* believes—incorrectly, it turns out—that he is the son of the strange, mad, oracular character named King Hedley in *Seven Guitars*; Harmond Wilks, the would-be communications tycoon in *Radio Golf*, is the grandson of Caesar Wilks in *Gem of the Ocean*; *Fences*, set in 1957, includes a 1969 coda relating to events contemporary with *Two Trains Running*—the very next play in represented chronology, but not in order of composition. In overall terms, as to authorial style and vision, the plays are sometimes noted as growing more mythic and less mimetic as the years of writing go on, becoming ghost dramas, the search for lost myths of history and genealogy. This may be true. On the other hand, *Joe Turner's Come and Gone* (1988) partakes most eerily of all the early works of the sad, ghostly spirituality of *Gem of the Ocean*. In turn, as remarked unhappily by a number of reviewers who lamented the lack of a signature history-haunted eloquence, *Radio Golf*, the very last of the plays to be written (2005) and the one set closest to the present, is as unhappily barren of past reference as any day-trader hedge-fund saga.

As usefully, one notices the odd, idiosyncratic fact. As is well known, *Jitney*, now considered the first work in the ten-play cycle of composition, is the single one that did not make it in initial production to Broadway, presented in 1982 at the Allegheny Repertory Theater in Pittsburgh and reaching New York production at the Second Stage Theater only in 2000. It is the shadow play, albeit now appearing to us as being as concentrated, demanding, and powerful as any of the others. Was it rejected by the big time because it was too contemporary for August Wilson in the late 1970s as he was writing it and too contemporary for early 1980s audiences who would see it as distinctly contemporary? This is to ask, was it too black? To read the play now is to believe that. The world of gypsy cabs, the people who hustle to drive them, the people who call to ride in them, a representation of the world of the times, is a world on the illegal, unregulated, shadow line of free enterprise. It uses a secret, underground economy, networking through the white man's telephones, his streets, his cars, without his approval, his franchise, his certification. It unwrites all the Public Utility Regulations of cultural visibility. (Finally reaching print in 2001, it was dedicated by Wilson to Azula, his late-life daughter.)

In a corresponding way, the literature on Wilson, scholarly and popular, abounds with anecdotes concerning his passion for the blues: how he said he had found his art while listening to an old record by Bessie Smith; how he would come sidling into a rehearsal or an interview with his latest blues discovery—softly singing and humming; how he would have to be talked out of writing it into whatever play he was trying to put into production at the time. And the music is all over the cycle: a pronounced and major element in texts as diverse as *Joe Turner's Come and Gone*, *The Piano Lesson*, and *Seven Guitars*. Perhaps the play most central to the theme, however, is *Ma Rainey's Black Bottom*, the one play to speak directly about the experience of people who all try to make their living playing the music called the blues. Written more or less simultaneously with *Jitney*, it was the first of Wilson's plays that did make it to Broadway, opening the possibility of his writing the rest of the cycle as a dramatist of major national reputation. As is well known now, it is the one play not set in the Hill District of Pittsburgh. At the same time, it anticipates the later world of the ghost plays, where a corresponding figure of woman, the legendary, oracular, Hill District matriarch Queen Ester, will frequently stand at the absolute center of everything.

From beginning to end, or from end to beginning, for that matter, it is not all that much harder to observe, in a simple way, what most of the plays are "about" in terms of basic conflict. *Gem of the Ocean*, for instance, brings together a group of freeborn blacks and former slaves at the house of Aunt Ester, somehow at once a living presence and 356 years old; *The Piano Lesson* centers on the conflict of a brother and sister over an inherited piano symbolizing their legacy of family suffering; *Two Trains Running* depicts the anguished attempts of a freed convict to re-enter the world through interactions with the regulars at a neighborhood café.

Wilson's characters operate in the same dimension of direct, concrete, elemental being. They are people: as in real people, but also as in a people and/ or *the* people. To cite Margaret Walker's tribute to an analogous resolutely independent and uncompromising predecessor, Zora Neale Hurston, we find in Wilson the sign and index of what Walker called the possibility of "racial health—a sense of black people as complete, complex, *undiminished* human beings." In Wilson, commentators have identified recurrent, signature figures. They are often middle-aged black men, angry, thwarted, hurtful, hurt-filled. They act at once cornered and disdainful, fearful of the young, the hip, the outlaw. Of the young males, as well as many of those slightly older, nearly everybody's been in jail. Then, as has been frequently remarked, there is also Wilson's fondness for old crazy bastards, prophets, and oracles, what Ben Brantley called "wild-eyed soothsayer types." Concerning women, the plays likewise attest to the powerful centrality, social and sexual, of black women in the lives of black men. As characters, the women also run the gamut of age. Frequently important as figures of power, mixed with an infinite sadness of thwarted hope, are women no longer young but not yet old, a wife, a mother, or just somebody's woman, all standing on the boundary of what the larger culture might call middle age. Here the right word would be *used*. Some are young icons of sexuality. Others are old, charmed, spiritually powerful—a Ma Rainey or a Queen Ester. There are not many very young children; those we see are hurt, bewildered, floating as if in a terrible dream. At the center of the cycle seems to come, perhaps, one strange, magical moment of coupling and conception—the old, mad, lonesome Hedley and the voluptuous, hypnotic Ruby in *Seven Guitars*. Later we find out, in *King Hedley II*, it has been a sexual and cosmological false alarm.

Character is thought and action in the plays—striving, impassioned, deep-hearted and deep-souled, but also frequently confused, gratuitous, and often startlingly violent. As Ben Brantley has written, "poltergeists, mad prophets, fatal curses, visions of unavenged dead men and roads to heaven" mix with "genealogies that twist into constellations of legend, and bloody crimes of passion that seem as inevitable as they are unnecessary." But first and last, the drama of life throughout the cycle always comes down to the words. One may attempt to describe it by using the big language abstractions. Race, History, Culture, Memory: in other plays, these might be the stuff of the great speeches; in Wilson one always begins in the great word concretions, frequently as immediate and compacted as the titles of the plays themselves. *Two Trains Running* is about exactly what it says. One runs up north. The other runs right back south, through Memphis, back to Jackson. Once an underground railroad ran north; now one can get railroaded back south. The play is set in 1969, an age in which trains have become in great measure archaic as passenger conveyances. One takes the bus or the plane— except for a people of an invisible history of the middle of America that is itself the endless story of the old migrations, up north, and then back south, then north again, then south.

One may say the same of *Fences*—so simple yet explosive a titular concretion that Wilson himself came to dislike the frequency with which it was invoked in connection with his "signature" play. (Characteristically, he seems to have felt it made the play too popular. One wonders whether he also disliked the way the theme of father–son athletic genealogy and rivalry summoned a particular kind of "white," *Death of a Salesman* accessibility— here, a father's dream, for his son, of a success foreclosed to him by older racial codes.) And here, of course, the figure does begin in the commonest of common experiences. When someone builds a fence, the builder is at once fencing in and fencing out. But here the questions become immediately more concrete: whether the fence will get built or not; what happens if it does, what happens if it doesn't. What in fact has happened to the fence project at the end? What will it have to do with being a signifier of relationships: of Troy Maxson with his younger son Cory, or of their relationships with Rose, Troy's wife and Cory's mother? Where will we find Lyons, Troy's son by an earlier marriage? Gabriel, Troy's brother? Raynell, Troy's daughter? In 1957, the year in which the main play is set, the fence is a work in progress. In the 1969 coda, it is a falling-down ruin, a piece of instant archaeology. A fence is a thing: a fence around a house or a yard or a family, but also a city job, a prison, the loony bin at a VA hospital. Troy embodies the battle of the wall, the classic order, Priam, Hector, Paris and all the rest. Troy's metaphors are always baseball, the dream of swinging for the fences. Lyons's are always jazz, the old way up and out. Cory is football, the new way up and out. In the end, *Fences* tells the old story: no way up, no way out. At the end, we see Cory, in a marine uniform, a sergeant. He has been to Vietnam and is staying in where he has gotten ahead. He is a lifer.

 Ma Rainey's Black Bottom is a play title by being a song title. It is thrown out, along with all the others, right up front: "Prove It on Me" . . . "Hear Me Talking to You" . . . "Ma Rainey's Black Bottom" . . . "Moonshine Blues." But it also embodies everything about Ma Rainey: her music; her soul; her ass. It is a song about a black bottom the way something is called a black bottom pie. But it is also a song about a black bottom the way something is called a black ass. It is about getting a piece of her sweet black ass; or maybe, for the musicians, the session players, the way the system always gets a piece of everybody's sweet black ass.

 At the end, Wilson himself admitted, as he reached the final plays in the cycle, he sometimes did start getting more mystical. *King Hedley II* queerly fulfills certain claims of prophecy ventured in *Seven Guitars*. *Radio Golf* marks a reappearance of the richly eloquent ex-convict Sterling Johnson from *Two Trains Running*. Queen Ester in *Gem of the Ocean* is also invoked in *King Hedley II*, and before that in *Two Trains Running*. Wilson called her a "conjure woman" he always knew, as with every other character in his plays, that she stood for something more. Depending on the play, she carries the history and memory of slavery at age 287, 349, 356. In *Radio Golf*, Elder Joseph Barlow, a single holdout against the building schemes of the play's slick young black entrepreneurs, now inhabits her house. Toward the end, the odd moments of the visionary in Wilson, even while remaining firmly contextual, truly did begin getting bigger and bigger, epiphanic, sometimes even cosmic.

But even as the moments got bigger, they were still made out of language in its simplest, and most direct, particular, concrete sense of human expression, of what it means to be a human person in history trying to find a sense of human community. In Wilson's cycle, there are indeed many great speeches distributed among a vast array of characters. Language is truly eloquent, moving, furious, in precisely the sense we use when we expect drama spectacularly to comprehend a whole tradition of art, comedy, tragedy, and everything between and beyond, the whole enactment of myth and ritual into great human performance. But even here, as from the very first plays produced to the end of the magnificent cycle, it was a language of performance with a big difference—indeed the difference between Wilson's characters and those even of Shakespeare, with whom he has been so frequently compared. Wilson's characters in *their* great speeches—frequently at the seemingly strangest, most unlikely, distinctly un-epiphanic times—are just overcome by the things that come out of their mouths. To put this more simply, in Wilson's plays, characters do not possess their speech. Their speech possesses them. They may get noble oratory, fine lines, quotable phrasings, but such speech quickly passes and blends in with all the other lines. There is no character who owns Hamlet's soliloquy, or Charley's rhapsody about Willy Loman riding on a smile and a shoeshine.

Language in Wilson is always made of the speaking self—experience, joy and hurt, puzzled human suffering, passion, thoughts and dreams, nightmares and imaginings, but at crucial moments it also remains beyond the speaking self in such a way as never to be contained by the speaking self. It is not too much to say that Wilson's best speeches indeed are unspeakable, unrecordable. His actors themselves, dazzled and undone by the parts he writes for them, describe an experience of being taken out of speaking as they know it. So Charles Dutton, among the many distinguished black figures who found their legitimate theater voices in Wilson's plays, said of his speeches: "It is a lingo that has an inherent rhythm of its own. Most of us have been black all our lives. But we kid each other about August's writing. We'll say, 'I've never heard anything in my life like that, have you?' " Language in Wilson is an original tongue. But it is also community—"the most valuable thing you have," Wilson was on record as saying, "in African American culture." Sometimes it can be as simple as food: "The white man knows you just a leftover," says Toledo in *Ma Rainey*. "Cause he the one that done the eating and he know what he done ate. But we don't know that we been took and made history out of. Done went and filled the white man's belly and now he's full and tired and wants you to get out of the way and let him be by himself." At other moments, as with Boy Willie in *The Piano Lesson*, it measures its risings and fallings by the pulse of everyday anger and confusion. "I got a heart that beats here and it beats just as loud as the next fellow's," he says. "Don't care if he black or white. Sometime it beats louder. When it beats louder, then everybody can hear it. Some people get scared of that." He goes on: "Some people get scared to hear a nigger's heart beating. They think you ought to lay low with that heart. Make it beat quiet and go along with everything the way it is. But my mama ain't birthed me for nothing. So what I got to do? I got to mark my passing on the road. Just like you write on a tree, 'Boy Willie was here.' "

At still other times, as with crazy old Hedley in *Seven Guitars*, amidst his mutterings and rooster killings, it can even speak a vision as exalted and loony as that of the coming of the glory of the Lord. "Ain't no grave can hold my body down," he proclaims to no one in particular. "The black man is not a dog. You think I come when you call. I wag my tail. Look, I stirreth the nest. I am a hurricane to you, when you look at me you will see the house falling on your head. Its roof and its shutters and all the windows broken." In all such moments, language is always somewhere within and beyond the speaker. One may talk of voicing, signification, empowerment, and still never catch the words. In the plays, the words circulate, inhabit, possess. Words get teased out of some characters; they pour out of others; sometimes they get squeezed or teased out and suddenly wind up pouring out of the same person. They are halting, searching, inarticulate; then, suddenly mad, wildly eloquent improvised, they pile out into each other, teeming and jostling; and then they rush into image and action, calling out to music, philosophy, religion, art. Wilson made a kind of mantra out of the set of influences he called the Four Bs—Blues, Baraka, Borges, Bearden. And he was right. His plays are black music; they are an embodied radical black aesthetic; they are postmodernist metafiction; they are painting and mixed-media collage. The representation of experience and thought, history and memory, in the plays is a totality of performance, endlessly seeking out the verbal and visual equivalents of nonverbal and nonvisual forms.

In this regard, as a matter of linguistic and theatrical representation, of pure performance, it is sometimes suggested of Wilson's plays that some characters get so loaded up, they can't carry the hoardings of vision, experience, history, and prophecy they are given. In Wilson, such work has frequently been invested in the figure of the strange, old, dirty, lonesome, crazy-talking and crazy-acting black guy. Academically, these characters have been objects of complex post-structuralist critical and theoretical understandings, frequently engrafted upon invocations of non-western myth: the shaman or trickster figure; or, specifically in the African and

African American traditions, the griot or the signifying monkey. With the famous four B's, Wilson himself supplied yet another set of figures. But then sometimes he would add Ed Bullins. As close to home were the quotations on the workroom wall: one from the white architect Frank Gehry (TAKE IT TO THE MOON); the other from the black saxophonist Charlie Parker (DON'T BE AFRAID. JUST PLAY THE MUSIC). All of this is there. But none of it really seems to be Wilson's point about origins. That point seems to be that any person can be an oracle. Among Wilson's characters, this is nearly always someone speaking out of some prison house: slavery, jail, sex, poverty, loneliness, abuse. Nearly everybody has been to jail, has left somebody in jail, has gotten somebody out of jail, or paid outrageous fines, bails, court costs. Life is endlessly extortionate. Men are beaten down and turned crazy by the everyday world. Women are beaten down and turned crazy by having to figure out what to do with all this, what is happening to their men, what it does to them, the future it spells for their sons and daughters. Holding households together, they sit mostly alone waiting, hoping, looking for a little love along the way; worn out, bred out, sung out, loved out. The young ones wind up having children, waiting for the fathers to shape up; watching the sons get in trouble; watching the daughters take up with and have more sons and daughters by boys and men who get in trouble. The annunciation of King Hedley by the voluptuous, fecund Ruby proclaims the conceiving of the new Messiah. Like everything else conceived of as a promise of history, it doesn't come true here either, although we don't find out until four plays and two decades later.

So often everything in the plays comes down not to an event or speech or even words themselves but to some collocation of language and experience barely remembered—often a song—waiting to be remembered by somebody so it can get spoken or written. And maybe paid for. In *Ma Rainey's Black Bottom*, there is the session-man Levee, with his frustration, his rage, and the band he dreams of for the songs he keeps getting swindled out of. In *Seven Guitars*, Floyd Barton is the bluesman with the dream of just one big hit. "Floyd Barton is gonna make his record," he tells us. "Floyd Barton is going to Chicago."

Or it is a song that has been endlessly paid for: the great white title anthem of the blackest and oldest of all the plays, *Gem of the Ocean*; or, more pertinently here, the title song of the play Wilson designated his personal favorite, *Joe Turner's Come and Gone*—the black song that is the title and the black title that is the song. "Joe Turner's Come and Gone" is the song that everybody tries to remember, even as it is the song that nobody ought to want to remember. It is the song of fear, of flight, of broken loves and households, of the constant nigger-catching that becomes the endless catch in the system for black Americans in the twentieth century. This one winds up being sung by a vintage Wilson crazy nigger—Landrum—to another vintage Wilson crazy nigger—Herald Loomis—now come north with his daughter Zonia, looking for the lost wife Martha, taken from him while he was imprisoned by the nigger-catcher Joe Turner. Set in 1911, nearly half a century after slavery, the drama remains the old one, of broken apart lives and families still looking for each other amidst the general dispersement. Joe Turner is the Man. Joe Turner, "brother of the governor of the great sovereign state of Tennessee," is the man who "catch niggers." He is the new slaver who has replaced the old enslaver, the Jim Crow, sharecropping, work-camp, lynch-law nigger-catcher. The song is the new song of the old pain. It is a song that Landrum has from memory. Now he helps Herald Loomis learn how to remember again. "Now I can look at you, Mr. Loomis," he says, "and see you a man who done forgot his song. Forgot how to sing it. A fellow forget that and he forget who he is. Forget how he's supposed to mark down life." It is a song, he continues, passed down from father to son, yet also made up from the hardest sort of reaching down for "pieces and snatches" of one's own life and memory and self. "It got so I used all of myself up in the making of that song," he says. But that is the work required. "See, Mr. Loomis, when a man forgets his song he goes off in search of it . . . till he find out he's got it with him all the time. That's why I can tell you one of Joe Turner's niggers. Cause you forgot how to sing your song." Joe Turner's come and gone, he says, and now come again. And he still hasn't gotten what he wanted. "What he wanted was your song. He wanted to have that song to be his. He thought by catching you he could learn that song. Every nigger he catch he's looking for the one he can learn that song from. Now he's got you bound up to where you can't sing your own song. Couldn't sing it them seven years because you was afraid he would snatch it from under you. But you still got it. You just forgot how to sing it."

Loomis replies: "I know who you are. You one of those bones people." Loomis is right. Landrum sings the song to hold onto it and not give it away. For it is the song celebrating the pain and suffering of a people, their courage, their dignity, their vitality; it is a song of the undefeatability, as individual persons—a trash collector, a jazz singer, an entrepreneur, a nutcake—they wear in their bones. It is what Houston Baker, after Langston Hughes, has called the Long Black Song.

Obituary notices and memorial essays made claims for the greatness of August Wilson and his plays that hardly need my endorsement here. In academic criticism, he requires no push either, given his status as the subject of more than two hundred articles in scholarly publications and around twenty books. In his bemused way, he seemed to tolerate, even enjoy the attempts of criticism to try to appropriate him to its sundry agendas, political and aesthetic. Nor did he savor less the intermingling of artistic renown with a biographical legend predicated on his uncompromising personality in art and life alike, with the two histories of independence and resistance irreducibly interrelated—a kind of portrait of the artist finally arriving at fame and fortune by making all the wrong moves. In the age when—for all the racial curses and slights—education promised a way out of the ghetto of segregation, Wilson simply quit school when accused of plagiarizing a term paper and went out and started reading, educating himself in the tradition of the great American literary autodidacts—Benjamin Franklin, Frederick Douglass, Herman Melville, Walt Whitman, Emily Dickinson, Samuel Clemens—into brilliant fragmentariness, sometimes complete with the divine monomania.

On the other hand, how else, one asks, could he have discovered and committed himself to a field of production totally beset, of all late twentieth-century American art forms, with notorious impossibilities: what is now called, with a completeness of admonitory implication, "legitimate" theater—a wending way through local, regional, and national arts companies, almost never reaching the celestial city, New York, let alone Broadway, and thereafter both literary and popular print? How else in turn, save through a faith in his autodidact genius, could he have compounded all those difficulties with insistence on a legendarily complex, difficult, exacting process of getting any single play, not to mention a whole ten-decade cycle, from early draft through major theater performance trial into final production? How could he have embraced the whole enterprise, as he was only too proud to announce, with a creative intelligence unsullied by any major experience or understanding of what we could call twentieth-century dramatic tradition—American, British, or Continental drama; experimental drama; the drama of the absurd; the theater of alienation; political theater; radical theater; guerrilla theater? August Wilson said once he had probably seen a total of ten plays in his life. He never went to movies.

He told the high-school teacher who accused him of plagiarism to go to hell. He told the American educational system to go to hell. He eventually told the whole American arts-funding apparatus to go to hell. He told the white American theater establishment to go to hell—and then most white American audiences along with it. He declared the independence and the freedom of his genius in the essay "The Ground on which I Stand," the famous 1997 Town Hall debate with Robert Brustein, and in every single talk he gave to an interviewer, a critic, or a popular audience.

For all these reasons, August Wilson as an American artist of our age and of ages to come will always be too important to be left to the critics, myself included. Oriented as we are toward texts and context, we ourselves will never find the language, the terms for the magnitude of his achievement:

an absolutely concentrated bravery of genius linked to an unbounded moral passion. He wrote for the stage an entire epic history of race in America in the twentieth century. And if it is largely absent of white history, it is also as frequently absent of black history in any conventional sense. Here one finds no Brown versus Kansas, Freedom Summer, "I Have a Dream" speech, or Black Power. One mainly finds individual, living, human persons, and what is left, therefore, is only everything. Everything about August Wilson's plays bespeaks the immense vitality that went into his creations and the corresponding vitality of their effect on anyone who experiences them on stage or responds imaginatively to them in print.

No matter who you are, if you see the plays of August Wilson or read them, you will hear the song. If you hear it, you will never forget it. And you will never see history again the same way. You will simply understand, as you never understood before, that race is everything in America. You will now be unable not to remember how it presides over the slavery-haunted Declaration of Independence; how no one can or should edit out of our memory of the original Constitution the insane fiction that once certain human beings constituted three-fifths of a person. You will know that all those terrible compromises, however named—the Missouri Compromise, the Compromise of 1850, the Kansas-Nebraska Act, the Dred Scott Decision—were about one thing and one thing only: the shadow of race presiding over the promised land. And that every piece of American history, literature, and culture ever since—the rise of Jacksonian Democracy, the saga of the opening of the West, the Civil War, the Gilded Age, World War I, the Great Depression, World War II, the Civil Rights Era, Vietnam, the Post-9/11 Age of Terror—lives in the land of the shadow. Life in twentieth-century America has been lived, the plays of August Wilson tell us, where it has always been lived.

I think of this now any time I make up a syllabus. I think of it as I reflect on experiences and events I have personally lived through, written about, tried to discuss as an interpreter of American life and culture: the Eisenhower 50s; the Kennedy early 60s; the Vietnam War; the era of the youth counterculture. Having lived through the 70s, 80s, 90s, and into the first decade of a new century, I think of it when I make any kind of personal or cultural generalization. For me, as for so many other Americans since August Wilson came among us, what we talk about when we purport to discuss history or culture really continues to be what we don't talk about.

August Wilson gets one entry in *Bartlett's*. "As long as the colored man look to white folks to put the crown on what he say . . . as long as he looks to white folks for approval . . . then he ain't never gonna find out who he is and what he's about." *Ma Rainey's Black Bottom* (Act I). It's the only one he needs.

Let me explain myself. When I started to write "Me and My Shadow, August Wilson," I now confess, I already knew that I was not writing about an Al Jolson shadow but a Ralph Ellison shadow. I was not writing about *a* shadow but *the* shadow that presides over white America, the shadow that Ellison called the spook. In August Wilson, I had found a contemporary who knew what Ellison knew about white people.

I had found a shadow, as in an opening epigraph to *Invisible Man*, who knew what Melville knew. "You are saved," the well-meaning American Captain Amasa Delano, with every word "more and more astonished and pained," calls out to the titular character of Melville's tale *Benito Cereno*, after he has been rescued from near-murder by mutinous slaves under the mastermind Babo; "you are saved: what has cast such a shadow upon you?" What is not written is Benito Cereno's reply; for, as Ellison knew that Melville knew, it was the answer contained in two words: "the negro."

Or, I had found a shadow, with his favorite white cocktail party anecdote, who knew somehow what even T. S. Eliot knew. This seemed to be the point now of the second epigraph to *Invisible Man*, taken not only from the most strangely white of all white writers, but from one of his strangest works—of all things, a poetic drama in blank verse actually entitled *The Cocktail Party*. Harry, a central speaker in the play, protests: "I tell you, it is not me you are looking at, / Not me you are grinning at, not me your confidential looks / Incriminate, but that other person, / You thought I was: let your necrophily / Feed upon that carcase. . . ."

In a personal and cultural encounter with August Wilson, I had been brought eyeball to eyeball with the shadow of my life as a post World War II–era white American. Beyond any cultural conceit, like the Nordic specimen violently described in Ellison's first chapter, I had been bumped into by the necrophily of my unspoken history. I had been mugged by a spook singing a song that kept asking, "What did I do to get so black and blue?"

What August Wilson said he knew about white people was recorded by John Lahr in a *New Yorker* profile. "Blacks know the spiritual truth of white America," Wilson said. "We are living examples of America's hypocrisy. We know white America better than white America knows us." He also knew the consequences for American history and memory. As phrased by his predecessor James Baldwin, "If I am not what I've been told I am, then it means that *you're* not what I thought *you* were *either*."

Wilson's age in the recent announcement of his death was sixty. It was my age exactly, our age, as was fifty-six our age that day I remembered so indelibly four years earlier when he had flown in to Birmingham—Birmingham, Alabama—from Seattle, Washington. He flew first class—a stipulation made by his assistant. He was impossible to miss. He was finely dressed and immaculately mannered. A small hint of truculence—which he knew well he had in him—came with his leaning slightly forward, walking on the balls of his feet, like a boxer. I only learned some of *those* stories later: about the punching bag by the writing table in the basement; about the old fighter, Charley Burley, who gave Wilson his first real male image; about the nickname he got from his director, Marion McClinton: the Heavyweight Champion. I saw the temper, just once, when I said something conversational—in reference to my experience teaching judicial writing seminars—that was generally flattering to the intelligence of judges; Wilson flared, citing a newspaper article I too had read recently about a notorious Texas appellate case where a judge had declared that an indigent black defendant—given a court-appointed attorney who had spent much of the trial asleep—had been provided adequate representation. Everywhere I look now, I still feel the unrelenting insistence—in Wilson's plays, his performance contracts, his travel requirements, and his conversation: what Richard Zoglin called in a *Time* article of 9 April 2005, his "principled pigheadedness."

To the end, I now find it almost impossible not to think of Wilson, in the chair in my office where he sat in that moment as I sit here, still here, with my family, my daughter, my blessed life, my conceits about clever entitling. One more time, I think, it's all about race. One more time, August Wilson gets the shitty deal, when he's the genius of the age, the one who will live on as long as plays are written and performed. But I know what he would say this time, with characteristic grace, wisdom, and forbearance. Race didn't get him. Or history. Or cultural memory. Cancer got him. Death got him. This time it was not my shadow or a shadow, as big as the shadow of race is in America. It was *the* shadow. But there, too, he doesn't need a personal or literary tribute from anybody, least of all me. I am convinced he knew who he was, what he had written, and how long it was going to last. "You are our king," Susan Lori-Parks told him in a 2005 interview. He voiced a graceful little demur, but he didn't really object. He just said thank you. He knew that he had become King August. The one and only.

MARGARET BOOKER

Radio Golf: *The Courage of His Convictions—Survival, Success and Spirituality*

Hey, you have to go forward into the 21st century. I figure we could go forward united ... I'm talking about the black Americans who share that 400-year history of being here in America. One of the things with *Radio Golf* is that I realized I had to in some way deal with the black middle class, which for the most part is not in the other nine plays. My idea was that the black middle class seems to be divorcing themselves from that community, making their fortune on their own without recognizing or acknowledging their connection to the larger community. And I thought: We have gained a lot of sophistication and expertise and resources, and we should be helping that community, which is completely devastated by drugs and crime and the social practices of the past hundred years of the country ...

If you don't recognize that you have a duty and a responsibility, then obviously you won't do that. Some people don't feel that responsibility, but I do, so I thought I would express that in the work. In the 21st century we can go forward together. That was my idea behind the play.[1]

Radio Golf (2005) is both August Wilson's Old Testament to the past and his New Testament to the future. Never one to mince words, even in the last few months of his life, he sounds his challenge to the black middle class to engage in the battle for the black man's soul.

From *The Cambridge Companion to August Wilson*, edited by Christopher Bigsby, pp. 183–192. © 2007 by Cambridge University Press.

Wilson selects a specific era out of the homogeneous course of history to illustrate a 'state of emergency' which Walter Benjamin in *Illuminations* (1969) calls the rule rather than the exception for those who subscribe to the tradition of the oppressed.[2] *Radio Golf* depicts Pittsburgh's Hill District in 1997, a year which marks the critical moment of its possible extinction in the name of progress. As the city proceeds to rid itself of blight, it also creates a 'moment of danger' which affects both the historical content of the African American tradition and its receivers. The Hill's current desolation and impending demolition could lead to a redevelopment of black culture and community or to the erasure of African American memory and history when faced with the appeal of material success, wealth and status promised by the American Dream. Wilson presents the dilemma but leaves us to contemplate the solutions.

In his entire ten-play chronicle, Wilson teaches his own community and the diverse American audience to recognize and respect the role African Americans have played in both an ethnic and a national historical context. Simultaneously proud of his cultural roots and his American citizenship, he wants to support and celebrate both. To do so, he has wisely chosen his old neighbourhood, the Hill District of Pittsburgh, as the location for all but one of his plays. Containing many landmarks, with Aunt Ester's house as its red-doored heart, it was once a lively hub made up of houses with yards, numerous businesses (Miss Harriet's fried chicken place, Hop's Construction, Sam Green's grocery, Mr Redwood's Orphanage, Wilks Realty), schools (St Richard's, Connolly Trade), hospitals, churches, entertainment and sports centres (the Crawford Grill or Kennard Field). Poverty, crime and unemployment now walk its once busy streets. Poor blacks and street gangs, pawnshops, the mission, Hill House, and busy undertakers populate the district. Even TV trucks, as Mame Wilks points out, will not drive up to the Hill unless there is a shooting. Socially mobile blacks have moved out of the inner city to Shadyside and other suburban neighbourhoods. The Hill District is the cycle's overriding "*lieu de mémoire*" to use Pierre Nora's term, the setting

> where memory crystallizes and secretes itself at a particular historical moment, a turning point where consciousness of a break with the past is bound up with the sense that memory has been torn—but torn in such a way as to pose the problem of the embodiment of memory in certain sites where a sense of historical continuity persists.[3]

What happens when the local handyman paints the front door of an old house slated for demolition and decides to invite the neighbourhood to a party? All hell breaks loose. 1839 Wylie Avenue is sacred ground, the home of the now-deceased Mother of the Race, the 'most significant persona'[4] of Wilson's ten-play chronicle of the African American experience. She is none other than the ultimate ancestor, Aunt Ester. Aptly named after the woman who saved her people in the Old Testament and as old as slavery itself, she signifies the presence of the black man in America and bears witness to his history and worth. The impending destruction of her home serves as the catalyst for the play's dramatic action.

Significantly, the stage setting for *Radio Golf* is the Bedford Hills Redevelopment Company construction office and not Aunt Ester's home. One is visible and the other invisible; one concrete, the other spiritual. One points to the future, the other connects to the past. Decorated with posters of contemporary international golf champion Tiger Woods and the 1960s icon of the civil rights movement Martin Luther King, Jr., it is a site of memory that exists within the larger one of the Hill District. The old building, a former Centre Avenue storefront, complete with antique embossed tin ceiling, belongs to Wilks Realty, the black business with a history which reaches back to Caesar Wilks, the first black constable on the Hill and the man who invaded Aunt Ester's sanctuary in 1918 (*Gem of the Ocean* (2003)). This location becomes the arena in which the drama's spiritual conflict takes place.

The play's protagonist, Harmond Wilks, is representative of the black middle class, which moved out of the Hill District years earlier to a more affluent part of the city (Shadyside) and lost touch with those left behind. He is a real estate developer, wealthy owner of Wilks Realty, local leader and potential mayoral candidate. His Cornell roommate, and the drama's antagonist, Roosevelt Hicks, is an avid golfer, soon-to-be Mellon Bank Vice-President and part owner of and golf talkshow host on WBTZ radio. The two friends have long played golf together and have just become partners in a new, black enterprise—the Bedford Hills Redevelopment, Inc. Funded by a combination of their own and government (Model Cities) money, the pair plan to revive the Hill District and make a tidy profit on their $200,000 investment in the process. The author uses their shared interest in the game of golf to contrast their personal histories, ethics and relationship to African American history and values.

Titles are always keys to an understanding of Wilson's dramas, and *Radio Golf* is no exception. The title metaphorically alludes to the aspirations of the black middle class towards the accumulation of wealth and social status, including celebrity, within the larger American context. Golf is, after all, an upper-class individual sport played on manicured greens as opposed to team baseball played on backlots in urban neighbourhoods (*Fences*) (1985). Wilson chooses golf—a professional sport once inaccessible to blacks—to

examine the erosion of African American cultural values in the pursuit of
success as defined by the dominant white society. Ever since '22 noblemen
and gentlemen' at St Andrews, Fife, Scotland set up the Society of St Andrews
Golfers in 1754 and adopted its present name of the Royal and Ancient
Golf Club of St Andrews by permission of William IV in 1834, the game
of golf has been associated with upper-class society both in Great Britain
and later in America. Historically, African Americans were the caddies,
not the players, on American courses. The Professional Golf Association
did not admit blacks until Charlie Sifford, first black in the World Golf
Hall of Fame and author of *Just Let Me Play* (1992), pioneered the way in
1961. Wilson issues a warning: 'We're all trying to imitate the British to
become lords and aristocrats, have a bunch of servants and a gardener . . .
We were founded as a British colony.'[5] Wilson is a typical Pittsburgh sports
fan who admires the athletic excellence of Tiger Woods, Muhammad Ali,
Joe Louis and others who pioneered the way for blacks in professional sports.
Simultaneously, he criticizes the conversion of their talent and heritage into
mass-marketable products, such as the Nike endorsement or, much earlier,
Ma Rainey's recorded songs. This commodification[6] is tantamount to stealing
their heritage, like Aunt Ester's house, in the name of progress.

The play's language and music capture this commodification and
shattering of history. Harmond and Mame speak with near-perfect grammar
about marketing and business deals and their relationship. Harmond, like a
true politician, can adjust his speech pattern to his constituency. Roosevelt
retains the poor grammar and colourful swearing of his youth in addition to
the vocabularies he learnt in college. Ben Brantley, in his *New York Times*
review of *Radio Golf*, describes what Wilson is doing as an artist:

> The inspiring antiseptic slang of much of the dialogue in 'Radio
> Golf' is deliberate . . . Mr Wilson intends that at least three of
> his characters sound as out of place as they do. They may be
> transacting business in that section of Pittsburgh known as the
> Hill, . . . but they have forgotten its language, an organic poetry
> shaped by decades of hard living. They are people who've lost
> their natural voices. In Mr Wilson's world, that's the same thing
> as losing their souls.[7]

Old Joe and Sterling possess the 'Shakespearean richness that Mr Wilson
has devised for residents of the hill . . . the wayward anecdotal vigor that is
Mr Wilson's blissful specialty'.[8]

Wilson signifies a break in the African American tradition with the
noticeable absence of the blues, a 'way of remembering, a congenital instinctive
force that reaches back through the centuries to the first slave ships'.[9] Old

Joe Barlow pawned his guitar in 1970. The two developers sing white man's music: 'Hail, Hail the Gang's All Here' and 'Blue Skies'. Harmond, who has lost the way to 'leave his mark on life'[10] in a unique song of his own, will eventually transform the notion of 'gang' into a new alliance with Sterling, the war-painted Cochise of the play's close, in a last-ditch effort to celebrate the history contained in Aunt Ester's house.

Wilson utilizes contrasting attitudes towards the game of golf in the drama's five characters to explore the dilemma of entrepreneurial self-interest versus community welfare. The five characters are living embodiments of chronological history ranging from 1918 through 1997, and reference back to the founding of America as a nation. Wilson includes allusions to the Indian Wars, African ancestry in Ethiopia, the Middle Passage, slavery, the underground railroad, abolition and reconstruction, black northward migrations, the industrial revolution, the Depression, World War II, middle-class black flight from the inner cities and the residue of poverty and crime left behind, the demise of the steel mills and small businesses, the civil rights and Black Power movements, and the consequent advancement of blacks into positions of prominence in entertainment, sports, business and politics.

Both Harmond Wilks and Roosevelt Hicks are beneficiaries of the expanding opportunities for blacks made available through the civil rights movement and affirmative action policies of the 1960s, 1970s, 1980s and 1990s. Both are graduates of one of the nation's finest private universities, Cornell. While Harmond inherited wealth, Roosevelt is still scrambling to amass it. Harmond's monogrammed golf set, bought 'before taxes' twelve years earlier, is now a part of him. He is comfortable with government officials (both city and federal) and experienced in urban politics. His hero and champion of the community is Martin Luther King, Jr. At the play's beginning, Roosevelt is hungry for financial success and recognition and is comparatively naïve, as is evident by his elation over an invitation to play golf with a set of white Pittsburgh businessmen for the first time. His hero is Tiger Woods. Aided by the notion that golf has taught them how to succeed in life, both men believe that a world of opportunity lies before them. They are excited by the possibility of erecting a driving range at Kennard Field and a golf camp for kids which could give young, poor blacks a head start.

Wilson delineates three other nongolfing *dramatis personae* to fill out the spectrum of characters inside his geographical Hill District/*lieux de mémoire*. He brings us Harmond's wife Mame, a public relations professional and future spokesperson for the governor's office as well as loyal, loving spouse. She prefers the posh neighbourhood of Shadyside to the downtrodden Hill and views Harmond's golf clubs as 'stuff', easily replaceable if you have insurance and file a police report. The two Hill denizens—Elder 'Old Joe' Barlow (World War II veteran, divorced father of eight children, vagrant with a criminal record, the son of Caesar Wilks's sister Black Mary and Citizen Barlow of *Gem of the Ocean* and the current owner of Aunt Ester's house) and Sterling Johnson (local handyman, Aunt Ester protégé, ex-con and warrior spirit who first appeared in *Two Trains Running* (1990))—can view golf clubs only as useless weapons or stolen goods for sale, especially in a neighbourhood which cannot boast the necessary grass to play on. They carry the history of the neighbourhood through personal memories in vigorous anecdotal voices, speaking a language lost to the three strangers—Harmond, Mame and Roosevelt. History, however, conflicts with the process of gentrification.

Wilson focuses on the two black business partners to build the conflict which powers the drama. The real estate developers are, by definition, erasers of history and memory. And there is not much of the old Hill District left to preserve, as Sterling points out: 'How you gonna bring it back? It's dead. It take Jesus Christ to bring it back. What you mean is you gonna put something else in its place. Say that. But don't talk about bringing the Hill back. The Hill District's dead.'[11] Harmond tells him about the plan to rebuild the whole neighbourhood with shops, houses and stores (later revealed to be a 180-unit apartment building and chain businesses like Starbuck's, Barnes and Noble, and Whole Foods (one exists in Shadyside today)). He tempts Sterling with potential construction work. Wilson, however, has other plans for his central character. As he begins a journey to acknowledge the importance of African American history, Harmond will discover the real meaning of that 1960s anthem 'We shall overcome', and what inclusive civic leadership really demands.

As the grandson of Caesar Wilks, the Hill's first black policeman, Harmond inherits his ancestor's belief in the structure provided by the rule of law. He sees golf as a game of honour, concentrated individual effort and skill governed by an international, uniform set of rules. He declares, 'You teach the kids how to play golf and they have all the rules they need to win at life' (93). A man of integrity, Harmond has played by the rules. He follows his father into the business, remains loyal to his wife, and believes some things are not replaceable or for sale, like the embossed tin roof, the decorations in Aunt Ester's house, or a family bloodline. Citizens' rights and responsibilities are very important to this man. He views the law as a means to set standards for everyone (black and white), curb violence, protect individual rights and ensure social order and well-being. He protests about police brutality in his candidacy speech in the face of his wife's resistance and promises to attract future employers, such as Wilson Sporting Goods, to provide jobs and a means to combat poverty. He wants to be the mayor for all Americans. He holds to the notion that 'The law protects you when you own your house and pay the taxes. But the law also protects the city when a property's left abandoned' (96).

The currently controversial concept of 'eminent domain', which permits the state to seize private property for the 'public good' or a city to remove someone's home and turn it over to a private developer, goes one step further. Ironically, Harmond's one illegal act, buying derelict houses from the city before public auction, hoists him on his own petard in a way he could not have predicted at the outset. He discovers his own complicity in buying stolen property, whether it be the club set from Sterling or the house belonging to his cousin, Old Joe Barlow. Wilson puts Harmond to the test; he must make a choice between hiding his fraudulent activity, thereby ensuring huge financial success and social prominence if the development moves forward, or eliminating the corruption by rescuing Aunt Ester's house from demolition and risking the ruin of his career. Ultimately, he confronts Mame and Roosevelt with his moral dilemma:

> HARMOND: Bedford Hills acquired 1839 illegally. It bought it from me but I didn't own it. I bought the house before it went to auction. That's against the law. That's corruption. I'm going down to the courthouse and file an injunction to stop the demolition.
>
> MAME: Harmond, if you do that you're throwing everything away. All your hard work. Your career. Your reputation.
>
> HARMOND: All I'm trying to do is save Bedford Hills Redevelopment. You got to have rule of law. Otherwise it would be chaos. Nobody wants to live in chaos. (105)

While Harmond believes 'I've got the law on my side', it is Sterling who knows from experience that rules change, especially if you are not the one making them. Even Old Joe recognizes the uselessness of protest if you are 'invisible'. Sterling, who went to Black Power leader Malcolm X's rally in *Two Trains Running*, spells out the nature of the game:

> You got too big too fast. They don't like that. If you hadn't did it to yourself they was laying for you. They don't mind you playing their game but you can't outplay them. If you score too many points they change the rules. That's what the problem was … you scored too many points. If things had kept on going like that you was gonna have to buy you a gun. Time this is over you ain't gonna be able to walk down the street without somebody pointing at you. If they point and whisper you in trouble. You'd have to move out the state. Start over again somewhere fresh. That is if you still wanna play the game. If you still wanna play the game you gonna have to relearn the rules. See … they done

changed. If you relearn the rules they'll let you back on the
playing field. But now you crippled. You ain't got but one leg. You
be driving around looking for handicapped parking. Get back on
the field and every time you walk by somebody they check their
pockets. That enough to kill anybody right there. If you had to
take a little hit like that all day every day how long you think you
can last? I give you six months. (107)

Roosevelt, on the other hand, has to be 'in the game', no matter what
the cost. He tells his partner:

I hit my first golf ball, I asked myself where have I been? How'd
I miss this? I couldn't believe it. I felt free. Truly free. For the
first time. I watched the ball soar down the driving range. I
didn't think it could go so high. It just kept going higher and
higher. I felt something lift off of me. Some weight I was
carrying around and didn't know it. I felt like the world was
open to me. Everything and everybody . . . I must have hit a
hundred golf balls trying to get that feeling. But that first time
was worth everything. I felt like I had my dick in my hand and
was waving it around like a club: 'I'm a man! Anybody want
some of this come and get it!' That was the best feeling of my
life . . . That's why I keep my golf clubs in the trunk of my car
just in case I drive by a golf course. I keep looking for that
feeling. That's what I want these kids to have. That'll give them
a chance at life. I wish somebody had come along and taught
me how to play golf when I was ten. That'll set you on a path
to life where everything is open to you. You don't have to hide
and crawl under a rock just 'cause you black. Feel like you don't
belong in the world. (90–1)

Sounding like Boy Willie in *The Piano Lesson* (1987), Roosevelt associates
golf with freedom and self-respect, making money (Tiger Woods's Nike
endorsement), achieving celebrity status, and playing the game with white
heavy hitters. Because his need to belong is so strong, he believes that
success in America comes through playing by the white man's rules, just
as in golf. To transact business on the green, he prints his new business
cards as Vice-President of Mellon Bank and partner in the Bedford Hills
Redevelopment Company because 'Without them cards they'll think I'm
the caddie' (92).

Roosevelt naïvely believes that the white businessmen included him at
their table because of his great golf game:

> I was the center of the table and the conversation was going as
> good as my game. There I was holding my own, breaking out
> ahead of the pack at a table of millionaires. Then I look up and
> it was just me and Bernie sitting there. Man to man. I thought
> to myself, This is where I've been trying to get to my whole life.
> And then it happened. Bernie Smith wants to partner with me
> to buy WBTZ radio ... I'd be in charge. Bernie wants to be a
> silent partner ... (97)

The more practised Harmond recognizes their manipulation of his partner's
love for golf and need to belong. Bernie's payment of green fees, drinks, etc.
is not much of an outlay when compared with the profit margin possible via
media or urban redevelopment.

Roosevelt, however, is more than happy to trade on his 'black face' to
garner government subsidy to buy the local radio station at a reduced price.
Particularly when he can both make money and be the host of a programme
about his favourite sport. As he says:

> This is how you do it! This is how everybody does it. You don't
> think Mellon has ever been used? We're talking about an eight
> million dollar radio station! This is the game! I'm at the table!
> There was a time they didn't let any blacks at the table. You
> opened the door. You shined the shoes. You served the drinks.
> And they went in the room and made the deal. I'm in the room!
> Them motherfuckers who bought and traded them railroads ...
> how do you think they did it? This is business. This is the way it's
> done in America ... I get to walk away with a piece of an asset
> worth eight million dollars. I don't care if somebody else makes
> some money 'cause of a tax break. I get mine and they get theirs
> ... Harmond, I have to take this. This is not going to come along
> again. The window of opportunity is already starting to close. If I
> don't do this Bernie will get somebody else. (97–8)

As an old friend, Harmond supports him with advice about lawyers, deal
percentages and a promise to watch his back. Roosevelt wants to celebrate
with another round of golf, but, in a funny, ironic and prophetic twist,
Harmond cannot play. His golf clubs have been stolen by members of his own
African American community. At the play's close, Roosevelt will sacrifice his
best friend to the lure of wealth and status promised by a new partnership
with the same Bernie Smith in the Bedford Hills Redevelopment project.
Roosevelt follows his own radio broadcast advice. He knows he is 'one hole
from disaster' (101) if he sticks with Harmond and decides to eliminate the

handicap (1839 Wylie) which threatens the entire redevelopment scheme. Ultimately, he does not care whose rules he plays by, if he wins the game and gets his cut. He is, as Sterling declares, a 'Negro':

> Sterling: [*to Roosevelt*] ... You a Negro. White people will get confused and call you a nigger but they don't know like I know. I know the truth of it. I'm a nigger. Negroes are the worst thing in God's creation. Niggers got style. Negroes got blind-eyetist. A dog knows it's a dog. A cat knows it's a cat. But a Negro don't know he's a Negro. He thinks he's a white man. It's Negroes like you who hold us back. (107)

Unlike Roosevelt, Harmond discovers the value of history and memory contained within the community whereas Roosevelt threatens its very existence.

Harmond takes action testifying to his newly evolved community loyalty. He attempts to pay Old Joe for his house, recognizes the Wilks family role in supporting Aunt Ester, and tries to include 1839 Wylie in the new redevelopment plan. He learns that rules change when the court denies his temporary injunction against the demolition of Aunt Ester's house. When all else fails, he significantly gives Roosevelt his Tiger Woods poster in a painful goodbye and destroys his participation in a partnership that would later include Bernie Smith. At the end of the play, Harmond, paintbrush in hand, joins Sterling, war-painted like Cochise, the Apache chief who resisted white colonization of the tribe's homeland in the Southwest. Theirs is a grassroots uprising in the style of Malcolm X. Harmond's actions cost him his political career and Roosevelt's friendship, but redeem his soul. He is one of the gang, one of Aunt Ester's children, and the proud possessor of '[t]he wisdom and tradition she embodies which are valuable tools for the reconstruction of their personality and for dealing with a society in which the contradictions, over the decades, have grown more fierce, and for exposing all the places it is lacking in virtue'.[12]

Wilson's characters

> still place their faith in America's willingness to live up to the meaning of her creed so as not to make a mockery of her ideals. It is this belief in America's honor that allows them to pursue the American Dream even as it remains elusive. The conflicts with the larger society are cultural conflicts ... in what has been a difficult and sometimes bitter relationship with a system of laws and practices that deny us access to the tools necessary for productive and industrious life.[13]

In the final analysis, the Harmond/Roosevelt conflict embodies and crystallizes in time (the turn of the century) the moment of danger in which the unique African American history and cultural values could disappear, if those in leadership positions do not assume responsibility for their continuance. It is time for the next generation of Aunt Ester's children to step up.

NOTES

1. Suzan-Lori Parks, 'The Light in August', *American Theatre* (November 2005), pp. 22, 24.

2. Walter Benjamin, *Illuminations*, ed. Hannah Arendt, trans. Harry Zohn (New York: Schocken Books, 1969), p. 263.

3. Pierre Nora, *Les Lieux de Mémoire* (*Realms of Memory: Rethinking the French Past*), ed. Lawrence D. Kritzman, trans. Arthur Goldhammer (New York: Columbia University Press, 1996), vol. 1, p. 284.

4. August Wilson, 'Aunt Ester's Children: A Century On Stage', *American Theatre* 22:9. (November 2005), p. 26.

5. Parks, 'The Light in August', p. 24.

6. Paul Gilroy, *The Black Atlantic: Modernity and Double Consciousness* (Cambridge, MA: Harvard University Press, 1993).

7. Ben Brantley, 'Voices Warped by the Business Blues', *New York Times*, 30 April 2005, p. B11.

8. *Ibid.*, p. B15.

9. *Ibid.*, p. B11.

10. August Wilson, *Joe Turner's Come and Gone* (New York: Penguin, 1988), p. 10.

11. August Wilson, *Radio Golf*, in *American Theatre* (November 2005), p. 91. Further quotations will be cited parenthetically in the text.

12. Wilson, 'Aunt Ester's Children', p. 30.

13. *Ibid.*, p. 28.

HARRY J. ELAM, JR.

Gem of the Ocean *and the* Redemptive Power *of History*

G*em of the Ocean* (2003) ends with the benediction and instruction offered
by Mr Eli, Aunt Ester's gatekeeper, over the newly deceased body of his
friend Solly. As he pours a drink and raises it in a toast, he says, 'So live.'[1]
It is a noble petition of hope for the future of the gathered community and
a purposeful plea for African Americans to live a life founded on personal
integrity and committed to the collective struggle for truth. 'So live.' And so
ends the beginning of August Wilson's history plays, the first play in his ten-
play cycle, set in 1904 at the dawn of the first migration of blacks from the
South to the North. Wilson has situated this play at this precise moment just
as he has positioned every work within the cycle at critical historical junctures,
key transitional moments in the story of Africans in America. Within such
moments Wilson reviews the choices that blacks have made in the past.
Yet in *Gem*, as well as his other works, Wilson is not simply reviewing this
past and reevaluating history. His project is so much more proactive as he
considers how this past now impacts on the African American present.

In *Gem of the Ocean*, Citizen Barlow is haunted by his past. He comes
to the home of Aunt Ester, at 1839 Wylie Avenue in Pittsburgh, seeking her
assistance. There he finds her tended by Mr Eli, who maintains and watches
over her and Black Mary, who cooks and cleans for her. The desperate
Citizen has heard that Aunt Ester has the ability to wash people's souls

From *The Cambridge Companion to August Wilson*, edited by Christopher Bigsby, pp. 75–88.
© 2007 by Cambridge University Press.

and, racked with guilt, he badly needs some form of spiritual sustenance and moral forgiveness. In order to help Citizen save himself, Aunt Ester, with assistance from Mr Eli, Black Mary and her friend and suitor Solly, a former conductor on the Underground Railroad, takes him on an eerie, symbolic and spiritual journey, back through time and space, to the City of Bones, a place deep down in the middle of the ocean, where, we are told, African slaves who never made it across have built a kingdom of bones. Through the psychic process of travelling to this city, by confronting his past in this site and making his peace, Citizen Barlow is able to move forward.

In Wilson's dramas characters repeatedly return to their history in order to move on with their lives and into their future. Wilson delves into and rewrites the African American past, addressing and righting the wrongs of historical amnesia and social oppression, ritualistically reconnecting African Americans to the blood memories and cultural rites of the African past. For him, black people are not tangential to the central motion of history. He places them at the centre of his attention. His history is not simply a linear line of progression but one that stops and starts. In his plays, and in the construction of his twentieth-century cycle, history is reworked for contemporary purposes. Most significantly, in Wilson's project history becomes redemptive. This concern with the redemptive power of history is critical to *Gem of the Ocean* and to the entirety of the cycle. The idea of going back and confronting the past, as Citizen Barlow must do in *Gem*, initiates redemptive processes. Working through his relationship with history transforms him. Accordingly, history is not simply a lesson. In *Gem* the relationship to history is vertical. Citizen Barlow and the others do not learn from the past in a simple way. Redemption suggests a level of deeper understanding.

The critical figure mediating the redemptive power of history in *Gem of the Ocean* and the cycle as a whole is Aunt Ester, a woman as old as the African American presence in America. Before her appearance onstage in *Gem*, Wilson first mentions her in *Two Trains Running* (1990) and then again in *King Hedley II* (1999). In the final play of the series, *Radio Golf* (2005), set in 1997, Aunt Ester's home is scheduled for demolition as part of a redevelopment project. Born with the arrival of Africans in America, Aunt Ester is the actual site of the African American legacy; history and memory co-mix in her body. In fact, her name, in a riff of aural signifyin', sounds similar to 'ancestor'.[2] 'Aunt Ester' is in fact the 'Ancestor', the connection to the African American past which is both personal and collective, material and metaphysical. Rather than abstract signifier, she is blood, she is family, the aunt of her people. By communing with Aunt Ester, others have the potential to rework their relationship to the past and find redemption.

According to Wilson, 'Aunt Ester has emerged for me as the most significant person of the cycle. The characters after all, are her children.'[3] Yet, in the list of characters for *Gem of the Ocean* Wilson describes Aunt Ester only as 'A very old, yet vital spiritual advisor for the community' (*Gem*, List of Characters) and thus does not simply downplay her advanced age, 285 years, but minimizes the full register of her powers. The idea of the characters all being children of Aunt Ester speaks to the inherent interconnectedness of black people and black lives but also recalls the legacy of slavery and the condition of the mother. According to the slave law, children inherit the mother's condition regardless of the baby's father. As a result, black mothers became the repositories of blackness. Aunt Ester represents such a traditional picture of black womanhood, but she might also be Wilson's most feminist construction, for through her behind-the-scenes presence, through her invisibility before her appearance in *Gem*, Aunt Ester finds and expresses voice and power. She empowers the other characters, including Citizen Barlow in *Gem*, to find the force of god within themselves.

Africanist allusions abound with Aunt Ester, and Wilson is always conscious of an African presence in African Americans. Entrance to Aunt Ester's home is through a red door, and the colour red represents 'the supreme presence of color' for many of Nigeria's Yoruba people.[4] Her 'faith-based practice', her laying on of hands, has a direct relationship to the Yoruba goddess Oshun or Osun, one of the wives of the powerful thunder god Shango, who, when she died, fell to the bottom of the river and became the divinity of the rivers. At the festival for the river goddess Oshun, at Oshogbo in Nigeria, the celebrants praise her by throwing 'flowers into her stream'.[5] In keeping with the river goddess's realm of authority, Aunt Ester asks all those who come to her for counsel to throw their offering into the river. Her city, Pittsburgh, is known for its three rivers, the Allegheny, the Monangahela and the Ohio. Oshun is a spirit of wisdom and generosity. Also known occasionally as the Yoruban 'love goddess', she controls all that makes life worth living, such as marriage, children, money and pleasure.[6] Correspondingly, Wilson's characters come to Aunt Ester when they have trouble over such issues. Going to *see* Aunt Ester requires faith and the engagement of their inner eye. They then come to reconstruct their physical reality and to see the world anew.

In the earlier plays, where she is not physically present, Aunt Ester does not dictate a course of action; she asks that her parishioners be proactive in their lives. As Holloway scolds West in *Two Trains Running*, 'That's what your problem is. You don't want to do nothing for yourself. You want someone else to do it for you. Aunt Ester don't work that way. She say you got to pull your part of the load'.[7] Aunt Ester does not act for the souls who seek her counsel but rather enables them to determine their own way. She explains to Citizen Barlow in *Gem of the Ocean*, before she guides him on his journey to the City of Bones, that she could 'take him to that city, but you got to want to go' (2.1.54). Aunt Ester dispenses advice in parables that compel her supplicants to interpret them, to think and then act. The spiritual and practical healing she initiates is internal, and psychological. She does not provide salve for the external wounds of oppression and racism. 'She make you right with yourself'.[8] This inwardly focused theology is reevolutionary and distinctly Creolized. Only by being touched by the past, by re-membering the lessons of the ancestor, can the characters move forward. The African spiritualism conjoins with the practical American reality.

Aunt Ester's death in *King Hedley II* reverberates loudly. It creates fissures within the community and constitutes a loss of history that requires its own healing. She dies of grief due to the desperate conditions of African American life in the 1980s. More than a testimony to the benign neglect of the Reagan-Bush administration, or the power of external forces corrupting African American existence, her death marks the continued movement of blacks away from their 'songs'. What happens when the spirit of a people passes away, when Aunt Ester, the living symbol of the past, the 'ancestor', or Aunt Ester of all African America, dies? Wilson foregrounds Aunt Ester's death visually and aurally. It causes all the lights to go out in Pittsburgh's Hill District. A voiceover newsflash tells of her passing. Stool Pigeon reports that crowds are lined up inside Aunt Ester's house and outside on the streets below. Following the African tradition, they will remain with the body until she is buried and crosses over to the world of the ancestors. Solly is scheduled to be one of her pallbearers.

Stool Pigeon senses the magnitude of the loss, celebrates her passing and enacts rituals that reaffirm her significance and facilitate her eventual resurrection. The death of Aunt Ester means the evacuation of spirit and Stool Pigeon's rituals over her cat's grave are intended to revive and renew this spirit. As Wilson suggests, through the ceremonies performed by Stool Pigeon at her cat's gravesite, Aunt Ester's is a soul we cannot afford to let die. Her death signals the urgent need for an immediate infusion of social change; it is a call for African American rebirth and reconnection. Her voice—eventually heard in her cat's meow at the play's conclusion—cries out loudly from the grave. The spirit cannot die but must find resurrection through rites of faith and through a ritual return to the past.

In the next play that Wilson wrote after *King Hedley II*, *Gem of the Ocean*, Aunt Ester is quite literally reborn. History is undone and created as Wilson brings a 285-year-old woman on to the stage. How should we read the material presence of the previously invisible Aunt Ester? How should spectators react, for certainly there must be some disjuncture when they see her and hear of her age? In fact, in the earlier draft, and in the first production of *Gem* in Chicago 2004, her age was stated by Aunt Ester and other characters several more times than it is now in the published script, and with each mention the audience laughed, perhaps out of incredulity, perhaps out of nervousness. Does her embodied presence on stage merely require that audience to realize the power of theatre to make possible the impossible and suspend their disbelief? Should they, upon seeing her enacted on Broadway by the beautiful and immensely talented Felicia Rashad, recognize the ageless quality of black skin and the fact that black folk just do not wrinkle like white folk? Does the Chicago audience's unease and laughter reveal that they just did not know what to make of this old, old woman? If Aunt Ester exists symbolically between the world of the spirit and the world of the flesh, can placing her on stage potentially dissolve this imaginative, metaphysical power?

For Wilson, Aunt Ester's power does not simply emanate from the fact that she was previously disembodied. She is far from a static site of remembrance. She is a living force, actively urging spiritual and cultural change. She is a conjure woman with spiritual power and otherworldly authority. She is a woman who has loved and lost, who has been married and given birth. She embodies not only a collective history but also a personal history. Hers is an embodied knowledge, then, that she shares with others. She tells Citizen Barlow, upon his arrival at her home through the upstairs window after she has caught him in the act of pilfering bread, 'You remind me of my Junebug he was the only one of my boys that cause me trouble' (1.1.20). She understands and imagines her new child Citizen Barlow through the eyes of one past, lost and gone. Her point of reference is the past. History and remembrance become a force of authority to enable change in the present and to precipitate an understanding of current circumstances. Her embodiment makes the metaphysical an element of the everyday, and this is critical to Wilson and his drama. Aunt Ester is not merely a spirit unseen but a material force. Her actions have weight.

The City of Bones, the site of Citizen Barlow's redemption, is also a material presence in *Gem of the Ocean*. An actual city below the surface of the water where black souls have come to rest, it is built from the bones of those who perished on the perilous journey across the ocean that was the Middle Passage. Aunt Ester explains to Citizen:

> It's only a half mile by a half mile but that's a city. It's made of bones. Pearly white bones. All the buildings and everything is made of bones. I seen it, I been there, Mr. Citizen. My mother live there. I got an aunt and three uncles live there down there in that city made of bones ... That's the center of the world. In time it will all come to light. The people made a kingdom out

of nothing. They were the people that didn't make it across the
water. (2.1.52)

The City of Bones actively remembers the loss of those that did not make it
across the water. In a proactive act of reconstructing history at the bottom of
the sea, those seemingly forgotten black travellers—those who were too infirm
for the journey, those who mounted unsuccessful insurgencies, those who
jumped into the cold, uncertain water rather than face the cold uncertainties
ahead—have built a city. In a poem in the Africa section of *Wise, Why's, Y's*
(1995) Amiri Baraka, one of the most important dramaturgical influences
on Wilson, writes:

> It's my brother, my sister.
> At the bottom of the Atlantic Ocean there's a
> Railroad made of human bones.
> Black ivory
> Black ivory[9]

Baraka's poem notes the loss of black bodies below the sea but, more
importantly, suggests that through the image of an underground railroad
one can connect to those lost black family members. The tracks of history
are made out of black ivory. Its construction is an act that reunites or
remembers the collective black body, those old bones making them into a
unified structure, a communal site, a city that joins past to present and that
overcomes loss by recuperating and actively maintaining a living African
American history. Aunt Ester reports that she has relatives who live there,
not who rest there but who live. Thus the City of Bones functions not simply
as memorial to the Middle Passage but as embodiment, a vibrant place, a
destination that Citizen Barlow, the other characters and we, as spectators,
can visit. The Middle Passage has traditionally been conceived as a fixed
moment in time, as a significant event in the collective memory of African
Americans that marks the difficult transition from free peoples to captive
Africans in America, but not as a place. In *Gem of the Ocean*, however, the
City of Bones is a locality.

Significantly, Citizen Barlow's journey to the City of Bones occurs
at the beginning of the second act of *Gem of the Ocean*, literally the
middle passage of the play. His journey, then, embodies the idea that it
symbolizes, repeating and revising Wilson's earlier plays, even as it speaks
to the specifics of this play. In addition, the title, *Gem of the Ocean*, is a
signifying revision. Aunt Ester tells us that the 'Gem of the Ocean' was
the name of a slave ship but is also the title of a song, 'Columbia, the
Gem of the Ocean', written in 1843 by David T. Shaw. This song was

extremely popular during Abraham Lincoln's Civil War administration and later became a staple of the United States Marine Corps marching band. Even earlier, back in 1775, the slave Phillis Wheatley wrote poems about 'Columbia', celebrating the new nation. Almost 200 years later, in 1973, Baraka wrote a play called *Columbia, the Gem of the Ocean* about efforts to free blacks from the psychological tyranny of white hegemony and to build black solidarity. With its discussions of slavery, of nation and of spiritual healing, Wilson's *Gem of the Ocean* revisits and revises the work of Wheatley, Baraka and even Wilson himself. Fittingly, as they travel to the City of Bones, Citizen Barlow and the others hear the people singing 'Remember me' (2.2.66). Wilson asks that the trauma of these Bones People be re-membered, in order to address the unfinished business of the past within the circumstances of the now.

As Aunt Ester declares that this City of Bones is 'the center of the world' and that 'In time it will all come to light', she enters substantively into contemporary intellectual discourse on the black diaspora and the symbolic capital of black cultural traffic. Paul Gilroy's seminal work of the early 1990s, *The Black Atlantic*, powerfully theorizes how the historical circuit of the Black Atlantic transit makes manifest intersections between the black experience in America and Europe. Most significantly, Gilroy, through his examination of the Black Atlantic, inserts black people as central participants in the creation of the modern world.[10]

More recently, Joseph Roach and others have built on Gilroy in their discussion of a 'Circum-Atlantic', insisting on the centrality of 'the diasporic and genocidal histories of Africa and the Americas North and South' to the creation of a New World.[11] Aunt Ester's proclamation about the City of Bones takes this argument even further. For these scholars who have recognized the significance of the movement between Africa, America and Europe in terms of cultural progress, the Atlantic Ocean functions not as a material site but merely as a transitional passageway connecting these bodies of land. Wilson, on the other hand, through Aunt Ester, plunges down into the water, recovering, reclaiming and reconnecting the bodies discarded there, constructing this liminal site as the 'center of the world'. In this way he refigures not just the black Atlantic but the world by proposing the City of Bones as its centre. This enables him to uncover or, as David Palumbo-Liu phrases it, to 'un-forget' that which had been previously covered up in historical accounts.[12] Not merely the centre of the black world, or seminal just to the collective memory of African Americans, the City of Bones is the place from which the power of the world, its intellectual and cultural thinking, its humanity emanates. Hence black history can no longer be seen only as a footnote or a chapter at the end of the history book. Rather, it must be read as constitutive to all history.

Significantly, the conduit for Citizen Barlow's journey to the City of Bones is a paper boat, modelled after the *Gem of the Ocean*, which Aunt Ester moulds out of her documents of indenture that identify her as a slave. She hands it to Citizen Barlow, who balks at it, complaining, 'This is a piece of paper'. Aunt Ester replies, 'Look at that boat, Mr. Citizen. That's a magic boat. There's a lot of power in that boat. Power is something. It's hard to control but it's hard to stand in the way of it' (2.1.54). Indeed, papers of indenture were very powerful instruments as they declared that Aunt Ester and other black people constituted property that could be bought and sold. The power these papers once had over her life Aunt Ester now employs to her own ends. Her documents of indenture are at once material, symbolic and functional. Part of the historical record of black enslavement and of her personal memory of slavery, the medium of enslavement becomes now the method of transcendence.

Repeatedly in *Gem of the Ocean*, and elsewhere in the cycle, Wilson reminds us that the battle to remove the shackles of slavery is not simply an external struggle but an internal one. Later in the play, when the black constable Caesar brings another piece of paper, a warrant for Aunt Ester's arrest, charging her with aiding and abetting the fugitive, Solly, Aunt Ester asks him to read the same papers that earlier served as Barlow's magical boat:

> I see you got a piece of paper. I got a piece of paper too ... Sit down there Mr. Caesar I want to show you something ... Tell me how much that piece of paper's worth, Mr. Caesar ... That piece of paper say I was property. Say any body could buy or sell me. The law say I need a piece of paper to say I was a free woman. But I didn't need a piece of paper to tell me that. (2.4.78)

Aunt Ester differentiates between the legal authority of these papers to dictate black freedom and the spiritual and psychological power she already possesses to determine her own identity and self-worth.

In *Gem of the Ocean*, the symbol of the white legal system is the black constable, Caesar, who lords his authority over the black mill workers and chastises them for their ignorance: 'People don't understand the law is everything. What is it not? People think the law is supposed to serve them. But anybody can see you serve it. There ain't nothing above the law. You got to respect the law.' (1.3.36). Caesar's claim that nothing functions above the law stands in stark contrast to the figure of Aunt Ester and the portrait of black struggle throughout the cycle. Somehow, Wilson insists, justice can prevail for black America. Caesar's name echoes not only Julius Caesar but the blaxploitation film of 1973, *Black Caesar*, written and directed by the white filmmaker Larry Cohen and featuring Fred 'the Hammer' Williamson, in which the figure of Black Caesar, with the help of a corrupt white police officer, became the power broker, ruling over Harlem. Caesar similarly wields his own form of power but his name also signals his demise and his failure to understand the will of the people. His name recalls as well the legacy of slave naming. Southern masters often gave their slaves ancient Greek and Roman names, such as Pompey and Caesar, as a means of ridiculing slave pretensions and belittling them, preemptively satirizing black attempts at dignity or pride. In the aftermath of slavery, these names were generally rejected by the newly freed blacks as slave designations.[13] Citizen was named after Emancipation. Solly rejected his slave name of Uncle Alfred once free:

> I used to be called Uncle Alfred back in slavery. I ran into one fellow called me Uncle Alfred. I told him say 'Uncle Alfred dead.' He say, 'I'm looking at you.' I told him, 'You looking at Two Kings. That's David and Solomon'... But my name is Two Kings. Some people call me Solomon and some people call me David. I answer to either one. I don't know which one God gonna call me. If he call me Uncle Alfred then we got a fight. (1.3.27)

Solly thus subverts the former process, finding his identity in this biblical history of greatness, his naming himself King recalling those earlier Wilson kings, King Hedley I and II, who, like Solly, exemplified an oppositional spirit, a warrior energy out of step with the constraints of white hegemony but also out of step with the social status quo. Wilson, who himself grew up as Frederick August Kittel only to become August Wilson after taking his mother's maiden name, as a statement of his affinity to her and his black roots, is profoundly interested in names and the power of naming. His Citizens, Heralds, Kings, Roses all speak to how a name can convey not only a sense of individual identity, but a history, and a culture. In like manner, Negroes became coloureds then blacks then Afro Americans then African Americans, with and without the hyphen.

Caesar exemplifies internalized racism. Unwilling to see the humanity within his black brethren, and settling for the rule of law, he calls Solly by his legal name, his slave name, Alfred Jackson, as he comes to arrest him, rather than Solomon or David. As is evidenced by his relationship with his sister, Caesar has separated himself from his collective history. He tells a story of his personal past but not his ties to family or to a communal spirit. Like West in *Two Trains Running*, he has accepted the rewards of money over the possibilities of collective action and consciousness. He exploits his own people, once selling them magic bread that would supposedly make them twice as full. While West refuses to follow through on Aunt Ester's directives to throw twenty dollars into the river, Caesar takes his alienation from Aunt Ester, the ancestor, a step further. He comes to arrest her and removes her from the house calling the law and the penal code his bible. As a consequence he is bereft of the sort of spirit and spiritual justice that Wilson ultimately promotes. He has no sense of the black spirit necessary to find redemption.

One of the more complex and even contradictory believers in Aunt Ester is the white peddler Rutherford B. Selig, a character we have earlier encountered in Wilson's play set in 1911, *Joe Turner's Come and Gone* (1986). Selig frequents Seth's boarding house and ingratiates himself within black lives even as he capitalizes on them. We learn in *Joe Turner* that Selig, whose surname is German for 'holy',[14] has been nicknamed 'the People Finder' for his skill in retrieving souls presumably lost. Yet, unlike the spiritual meaning of his name, Selig's people-finding skills are based on practical material methods rather than metaphysics. Bertha, Seth's wife and co-proprietor of the boarding house, intimates that Selig's skills at people-finding are built on his manipulation of black lives and their dependence on his white privilege. In *Joe Turner*, and in a room full of black people, Selig proudly and shamelessly announces his family business: 'we been finders in my family for a long time. Bringers and finders. My great-granddaddy used to bring Nigras across the ocean on ships'.[15] In *Gem of the Ocean*, Selig is willing to carry the fugitive Solly back down south hidden in his wagon on the request of Aunt Ester and in the face of the law, as represented by Caesar. 'I ain't never know you to be on the wrong side of anything,' Selig tells her. 'I ain't scared of Caesar' (2.4.75). As a white man of this time, certainly Selig need have no fear of Caesar and his black codes. In his construction of Selig, Wilson underlines his previous history even as he creates a new one. Selig functions as a participant on a redirected Underground Railroad. Rather than heading north, he plans to take Solly south, despite the fact that the roads are blocked and passage will be difficult. The plan is to go back and save Solly's sister. Solly and Selig must go back to move forward, repeating Wilson's central trope. And Wilson himself returns to Selig to chart a new course for the complicated relationships between black and white people within the economics of slavery.

For Citizen Barlow, going to the City of Bones is a ritual act of cleansing in which the spiritual, the political and the historical all combine. He undertakes this journey to cleanse his soul after another man, Garrett Brown, had died for Citizen's crime of stealing a bucket of nails. Accused of the theft and unwilling to go to jail for a crime he did not commit, Brown ran into the river and remained in the cold, potent current until he drowned. In a repetition, with revision, of Christian doxology, he died for the Citizen's sins. Citizen is free because of Brown's fateful action. With the water as his grave, Brown now resides in the City of Bones, a spiritual place of sacrifice, where all the residents have died sacrificial deaths so that others, the Bones People that Herald Loomis describes in *Joe Turner* as rising up out of the water and walking on the land, can survive. While Christianity, in its ritual of communion, remembers the body and blood of Christ, Wilson, in his ritual of remembrance, calls for the souls of Brown and those lost in the perils of the Middle Passage to find eternal life as they are re-membered by the living.

Barlow must confront Brown at the City of Bones, for he is the gatekeeper. 'The gatekeeper . . . the gatekeeper . . . it's Garrett Brown the man who jumped in the river' (2.2.69). And, as Aunt Ester explains, only by confessing his story to Brown can he cleanse his guilt-ridden soul and enter the City of Bones. 'You got to tell him, Mr. Citizen. The truth has to stand in the light' (2.2.69). Barlow must confess. This ritual act of confession is good for his soul. Yet, unlike Catholicism where confession is followed by admonition and acts of contrition, Citizen's confession is linked to the mandate uttered by Solly, to 'live in truth'. The notion of living in truth requires an acknowledgement of the past. This opens up a history to Barlow, the redemptive power of collective history present in the City of Bones. The gates of the city now stand open and, overwhelmed by its glory, he sits down and cries. Citizen Barlow experiences the presence of the past as he goes back to move forward.

Significantly, Wilson brings the African past and African American present into relation with each other in the figure of Citizen Barlow. Overcome by the atavistic power, the emotional weight of his spiritual odyssey, as Wilson's stage direction for an earlier version of the play indicates, he '*begins to sing to himself an African lullaby*'.[16] Wilson provides no information on where this son of a slave would have learnt this lullaby. It is simply part of his blood memory. Similarly, Wilson provides no detail for the actor or director staging the play as to exactly which lullaby from which African country should be sung. In Wilson's work Africa functions as Gunilla Theander Kester suggests, 'as a native soil and empirical abstraction and a metaphorical space'.[17] The idea of Africa as metaphor enables Wilson's 'Africa' to be constructed within the context of the moment or within each different production of a play such as *Gem of the Ocean*.

Africa is also made symbolically present for Citizen when Solly gives him a link of chain to carry with him on his journey. Aunt Ester tells him that he needs to carry a piece of iron for protection, as iron will keep strong. Iron, historically, has been the metal associated with the Yoruba god Ogun. Robert Farris Thompson notes that, Ogun 'lives in the piercing or slashing action of all iron. Lord of the cutting edge, he is present even in the speeding bullet or the railway locomotive'.[18] Fittingly, Pittsburgh, the steel city, the

site of all Wilson's plays save *Ma Rainey's Black Bottom* (1984), seems the
logical pace for Ogun, the god of metallurgy, to resurface on the shores of
America. In fact, the spirit of Ogun, the god of iron, suffuses and infuses
the world of Wilson's dramatic cycle. The link of iron that Barlow receives
from Solly was one of the pieces of the chain that enclosed his ankles and
imprisoned Solly as a slave. He keeps this remnant of the past as 'a good luck
piece'. Thus, as he bestows it on Barlow, it functions not simply as a link
to Ogun, but as a material connection to the collective memory of African
Americans and a synthesis of their history within a single symbol. The ritual
journey to the City of Bones at the centre of *Gem of the Ocean* resonates
with both African and Euro-Christian rites of communion. In its unique
syncretism and in its social and symbolic meanings, it represents an act that
is decidedly African American.

Wilson's characters embody spirit and spirituality, as evidenced in
Barlow's confession and redemption. This proves crucial to his dramaturgy
and its processes of cultural healing and regeneration. Citizen's journey is
itself an embodied ritual. He sees himself as reacting to the forces around
him but also as shaping these circumstances. His embodied rite produces a
complex interaction with systems of power, history and knowledge. He is
linked to powerful external spiritual forces but also locates the force of god, of
spirit, within. For Wilson, such spiritual salvation as that of Citizen Barlow
is not antithetical to but a necessary component of a progressive historicism
and a revolutionary politics. Invoking rites which connect the spiritual, the
cultural, the social and the political does not simply serve to correct the past
but also serves to interpret it in ways that impact powerfully on the present.

For Citizen Barlow, redemption through history and spiritual
cleansing is a step to self-empowerment. In its aftermath he determines to
take revolutionary action. He will travel down south with Solly and Selig in
the reverse Underground Railroad pilgrimage, to reach Solly's sister and aid
Solly in escaping Caesar. With a new recognition and appreciation of the
need to be right with oneself, Citizen tells Black Mary, 'Black Mary, is you
right with yourself? Cause if you is I believe when I come back from down
Alabama, I'd come by and see you. If I was still right with myself. Then maybe
we could be right with each other' (2.4.76). Their budding relationship is,
then, to be built not simply on the mutual desire expressed earlier in the play,
but on an awareness of the power of self-realization. Black Mary has taken
steps in this direction when she stands up to Aunt Ester for the first time,
asserting that after trying to please her and follow her will for three years she
will now do things her own way. Aunt Ester responds, 'What took you so
long' (2.3.74)? Through a form of tough love, Aunt Ester has moved Black
Mary, too, towards self-empowerment.

Perhaps the leading advocate of black self-determination in the play is Solly, the former conductor on the Underground Railroad, who lives out the principle of Frederick Douglass that without struggle there is no progress. For Solly, his life is a constant battle not only to live in truth but to realize the hard-earned freedom that he and other slaves have achieved. 'You got to fight to make it mean something' (1.3.28). Thus Solly is willing to burn down the mill in the name of justice and as a strike against oppression. Ultimately, he is willing to die for his beliefs. For Solly, a willingness to risk death rather than continue to endure oppression is built on his experience in slavery and the understanding by the enslaved that nothing, not even death, is worse than slavery. 'Ain't nothing worse than slavery! I know. I was there' (2.2.56). The choice of death does not represent an act of Western rationality, or acceptance of the present social reality, but rather a revolutionary action aimed at a utopian vision of a liberated future. For Wilson, the key to defining a new liberatory vision lies in the steps his black figures take towards self-determination.

Freedom by itself is not enough. Early in the play, Solly asks, 'What good is freedom if you can't do nothing with it?' (1.3.28). This question informs Solly's own determination to resist as he recognizes that for African Americans the new condition of freedom poses new challenges. The play makes clear that the act of Emancipation by itself did not make black people free. The task for Solly and the other characters is to find a way to make the word freedom have concrete meaning. Unfortunately, Solly is killed for his efforts. Gunned down by Caesar, he attempts to commit one final act of civil disobedience.

Solly's death near the end of the play, and the trajectory of *Gem of the Ocean* as a whole, suggests that this question, 'what good is freedom?', is not simply one left in the past. For Wilson, in this play and throughout his canon, asks that this question continually be reconsidered. Throughout Wilson's interrogation of the conditions of African American freedom there is a recognition of the racism that persists and keeps blacks at the bottom of the economic system in America. He asks, however, how responsible blacks are for their own condition, how complicit they are in their own oppression. He wonders what actions African Americans can take in the present that will change their future. How are black people to redefine themselves and determine their own history? In many ways *Gem of the Ocean* can stand as a paradigm for Wilson's entire ten-play cycle in which he explores the psychological, emotional, political and spiritual dimensions of this struggle for freedom. And so the cry goes out from *Gem* and from Wilson's canon to black America past, present and future: 'So live'.

NOTES

1. August Wilson, *Gem of the Ocean* (New York: Theatre Communications Group, 2006), p. 85. Further quotations will be cited parenthetically in the text.

2. I thank Margaret Booker for bringing this to the class's attention during our seminar at Stanford University on August Wilson in spring 1997.

3. August Wilson, 'Sailing the Stream of Black Culture', *New York Times*, 3 April 2000, Section 2, p. 1.

4. Robert Farris Thompson, *Flash of the Spirit: African and Afro-American Art and Philosophy* (New York: Vintage Books, 1983), p. 6.

5. *Ibid.*, p. 79.

6.. Sharon Holland, *Raising the Dead* (Durham: Duke University Press, 2000), p. 55.

7. August Wilson, *Two Trains Running* (New York: Plume, 1993), p. 76.

8. *Ibid.*, p. 22.

9. Amiri Baraka, *Wise, Why's, Y's* (Chicago: Third World Press, 1995).

10. Paul Gilroy, *The Black Atlantic: Modernity and Double Consciousness* (Cambridge, MA: Harvard University Press, 1993).

11. Joseph Roach, *Cities of the Dead* (New York: Columbia University Press, 1996), p. 4.

12. David Palumbo-Liu, 'The Politics of Memory: Remembering History in Alice Walker and Joy Kugawa', Amritjit Singh, Joseph T. Skerrett, Robert Egan and Appaduria Arjun, eds., in *Memory and Cultural Politics* (Boston: Northeastern University Press, 1996), p. 215.

13. See Herbert G. Gutman, *The Black Family in Slavery and Freedom 1750–1925* (New York: Pantheon Books, 1976), pp. 185, 186.

14. Observation from Margaret Booker in May 2000.

15. August Wilson, *Joe Turner's Come and Gone* (New York: New American Library, 1988), p. 41.

16. August Wilson, *Gem of the Ocean*, unpublished playscript, 6 December, 2004. Act 2, scene 2, p. 69.

17. Gunilla Theander Kester, 'Approaches to Africa: The Poetics of Memory and the Body in Two August Wilson Plays', in Marilyn Elkins, ed., *August Wilson: A Casebook* (New York: Garland Press, 1994) p. 108.

18. Thompson, *Flash of the Spirit*, p. 53.

Chronology

1945	Born as Frederick Kittel on April 27 in Pittsburgh, the fourth of six children of Frederick Kittel, a German immigrant baker, and Daisy Wilson Kittel, an African-American cleaning woman.
Late 1950s	Mother, now divorced, moves family to Hazelwood, a white suburb. At approximately this time, mother marries David Bedford, a black man.
1960–61	After being accused of turning in a term paper that wasn't his, drops out of Gladstone High School as a tenth-grader.
1962–63	Enlists in the U.S. Army for three years but leaves after one.
1965	Discovers the blues. Father dies. Adopts the name August Wilson. Buys a typewriter, determined to become a writer. Begins to write poetry. Moves to a rooming house, living among writers and painters and supporting himself for the next twelve or thirteen years on odd jobs.
1968	With Rob Penny, founds a theater in Pittsburgh, Black Horizons on the Hill, where Wilson acts and sometimes directs plays by an assortment of writers.
1969	Stepfather dies. Marries Brenda Burton.
1970	Daughter, Sakina Ansari, born.
1972	Marriage ends.

1978	Moves to St. Paul, Minnesota. Works at Science Museum of Minnesota writing children's plays.
1981	*Black Bart and the Sacred Hills* is produced at the Penumbra Theatre in St. Paul. Marries Judy Oliver, a social worker.
1982	*Jitney* is produced at Pittsburgh's Allegheny Repertory Theatre. Lloyd Richards, then dean of the Yale School of Drama and artistic director of Eugene O'Neill Theater Center's National Playwrights Conference, reads *Ma Rainey's Black Bottom*, which is given a staged reading at the conference.
1983	Mother dies.
1984	*Ma Rainey* opens at Yale Repertory Theatre in April and at Cort Theatre on Broadway in October.
1985	*Ma Rainey* wins New York Drama Critics' Circle Award. *Fences* opens at the Yale Repertory Theatre.
1986	*Joe Turner's Come and Gone* opens at Yale Repertory Theatre.
1987	*Fences* opens at 46th Street Theatre in New York and wins Pulitzer Prize, Tony Award, and New York Drama Critics' Circle Award. *The Piano Lesson* opens at Yale.
1988	*Joe Turner's Come and Gone* opens at Ethel Barrymore Theatre on Broadway and wins New York Drama Critics' Circle Award.
1990	*The Piano Lesson* opens at Walter Kerr Theatre on Broadway and wins Pulitzer and New York Drama Critics' Circle Award. *Two Trains Running* opens at Yale. Second marriage ends. Moves to Seattle.
1992	*Two Trains Running* opens at Walter Kerr Theatre on Broadway.
1994	Marries costume designer Constanza Romero.
1995	Television adaptation of *The Piano Lesson* airs.
1996	*Seven Guitars* opens at Walter Kerr Theatre in New York. Receives New York Drama Critics' Circle Award. Gives controversial speech at the Theatre Communications Group's conference at Princeton University, which leads to 1997 debate at New York's Town Hall with Robert Brustein, former dean of the Yale School of Drama and a theater critic.
1997	Daughter, Azula Carmen, is born.

2000	*King Hedley II* premieres at Pittsburgh Public Theater. *Jitney* opens off-Broadway at New York's Second Stage Theatre and wins New York Drama Critics Circle Award.
2003	*Gem of the Ocean* opens at Chicago's Goodman Theatre.
2004	*Gem of the Ocean* opens at New York's Walter Kerr Theatre.
2005	*Radio Golf* opens at the Yale Repertory Theatre. Dies on October 2 of liver cancer. Later that month, Broadway's Virginia Theater is renamed in his honor.

Contributors

HAROLD BLOOM is Sterling Professor of the Humanities at Yale University. He is the author of 30 books, including *Shelley's Mythmaking*, *The Visionary Company*, *Blake's Apocalypse*, *Yeats*, *A Map of Misreading*, *Kabbalah and Criticism*, *Agon: Toward a Theory of Revisionism*, *The American Religion*, *The Western Canon*, and *Omens of Millennium: The Gnosis of Angels, Dreams, and Resurrection*. *The Anxiety of Influence* sets forth Professor Bloom's provocative theory of the literary relationships between the great writers and their predecessors. His most recent books include *Shakespeare: The Invention of the Human*, a 1998 National Book Award finalist, *How to Read and Why*, *Genius: A Mosaic of One Hundred Exemplary Creative Minds*, *Hamlet: Poem Unlimited*, *Where Shall Wisdom Be Found?*, and *Jesus and Yahweh: The Names Divine*. In 1999, Professor Bloom received the prestigious American Academy of Arts and Letters Gold Medal for Criticism. He has also received the International Prize of Catalonia, the Alfonso Reyes Prize of Mexico, and the Hans Christian Andersen Bicentennial Prize of Denmark.

PATRICIA GANTT is a professor at Utah State University and chairperson of the department of English education. She is the coeditor of *Body My House: May Swenson's Work and Life* and *Teaching Ideas for University English*.

SANDRA G. SHANNON is a professor of drama in the English department at Howard University. She has written extensively on August Wilson. Her books include *The Dramatic Vision of August Wilson* and *August Wilson and Black Aesthetic*, of which she is a coauthor.

179

KEITH CLARK is associate professor of English at George Mason University. He is the editor of *Contemporary Black Men's Fiction and Drama*.

WILLIAM W. COOK is a professor of English and African American studies at Dartmouth. In addition to writing about Wilson, he has written chapters about poetry that appeared in various texts.

ÇIĞDEM ÜSEKES is associate professor and chairperson of the English department at Western Connecticut State University.

AMANDA M. RUDOLPH is an assistant professor at Austin State University. She is the author of *Techniques in Classroom Management*.

LADRICA MENSON-FURR teaches in the English department at the University of Memphis. Aside from the work of August Wilson, her research interest includes the dramas and short fiction of Zora Neale Hurston and the dramas of Ed Bullins.

PHILIP D. BEIDLER is a professor in the English department at the University of Alabama. Among his many published works are *American Wars, American Peace* and *American Literature and the Experience of Vietnam*.

MARGARET BOOKER is the author of *Lillian Hellman and August Wilson: Dramatizing a New American Identity*.

HARRY J. ELAM, JR. is a professor in the drama department at Stanford University and director of the Institute for Diversity in the Arts. He is the author of *The Past as Present in the Drama of August Wilson* and coeditor of four titles, including *Black Cultural Traffic* and *Fire This Time: African-American Plays for the 21st Century*. Additionally, he has directed professionally for more than eighteen years.

Bibliography

Anderson, Douglas. "Saying Goodbye to the Past: Self-Empowerment and History." *CLA Journal* 40, no. 4 (June 1997): pp. 432–57.

Berkowitz, Gerald M. *American Drama of the Twentieth Century*. London: Longman 1992.

Bigsby, Christopher. *Modern American Drama, 1945–1990*. Cambridge: Cambridge University Press, 2000.

———. *Writers in Conversation*. Norwich: Arthur Miller Centre for American Studies, 2000– .

Birdwell, Christine. "Death as a Fastball on the Outside Corner: Fences' Troy Maxson and the American Dream." *Aethlon: The Journal of Sport Literature* 8, no. 1 (Fall 1990): pp. 87–96.

Blumenthal, Anna S. "'More Stories Than the Devil Got Sinners': Troy's Stories in August Wilson's *Fences*." *American Drama* 9, no. 2 (Spring 2000): pp. 74–96.

Boan, Devon. "Call-and-Response: Parallel 'Slave Narrative' in August Wilson's 'The Piano Lesson.'" *African American Review* 32, no. 2 (Summer 1998): pp. 263–272.

Bogumil, Mary L. *Understanding August Wilson*. Columbia: University of South Carolina Press, 1999.

Booker, Margaret. *Lillian Hellman and August Wilson: Dramatizing a New American Identity*. New York; Frankfurt: Lang, 2003.

Brustein, Robert. *Reimagining American Theater*. New York: Wang, 1991.

Clark, Keith. *Black Manhood in James Baldwin, Ernest J. Gaines, and August Wilson*. Urbana: Illinois University Press, 2002.

Elam, Harry J., Jr. "August Wilson, Doubling, Madness, and Modern African-American Drama." In *Modern Drama: Defining the Field*, edited by Ric Knowles, Joanne Tompkins, and W.B. Worthen. Toronto; Buffalo: University of Toronto Press, 2003.

———. *"Ma Rainey's Black Bottom*: Singing Wilson's Blues." *American Drama* 5, no. 2 (Spring): pp. 76–99.

———. *The Past as Present in the Drama of August Wilson*. Ann Arbor: Michigan University Press, 2004.

Elam, Harry J., and David Krasner, ed. *African American Performance and Theater History: A Critical Reader*. New York: Oxford University Press, 2001.

Elkins, Marilyn, ed. *August Wilson: A Casebook*. New York and London: Garland, 1994.

Goddu, Teresa A. "Blood Daggers and Lonesome Graveyards: The Gothic and Country Music." *South Atlantic Quarterly* 94, no. 1 (1995): pp. 57–80.

Hampton, Gregory. "Black Men Fenced in and a Plausible Black Masculinity." *CLA Journal* 46, no. 2 (2002): pp. 194–206.

Hanlon, John J. "'Niggers Got a Right to be Dissatisfied': Postmodernism, Race, and Class in *Ma Rainey's Black Bottom*. *Modern Drama* 45, no. 1 (2002): pp. 95–124.

Hannah, John M. "Signifying *Raisin*: Hansberry's *A Raisin in the Sun* and Wilson's *Fences*." In *Reading Contemporary African American Drama: Fragments of History, Fragments of Self,* Trudier Harris, ed.; Jennifer Larson, assistant ed. New York: Peter Lang, 2007.

Harrison, Paul Carter, Victor Leo Walker II, and Gus Edwards. *Black Theatre: Ritual Performance in the African Diaspora*. Philadelphia: Temple University Press, 2002.

Herrington, Joan. *I Ain't Sorry for Nothin' I Done: August Wilson's Process of Playwriting*. New York: Limelight Editions, 1998.

Maufort, Marc, ed. *Staging Difference: Cultural Pluralism in American Theatre and Drama*. New York: Peter Lang, 1995.

McDonough, Carla J., *Staging Masculinity: Male Identity in Contemporary American Drama*. Jefferson, N.C.; London: McFarland & Co., 1997.

McKelly, James C. "Hymns of Sedition: Portraits of the Artist in Contemporary African-American Drama." *Arizona Quarterly* 48, no. 1 (Spring 1992): pp. 87–107.

Menson-Furr, Ladrica. "What He Learned from Zora: August Wilson as Ethnographer." *Zora Neale Hurston Forum* 19 (2005): 15–27.

Morley, Sheridan. "High Society and Slumming It: Sheridan Morley on Conflicts of Colour in Noel Coward and August Wilson." *New Statesman* (January 6, 2003).

Nadel, Alan, ed. *May All Your Fences Have Gates.* Iowa City: University of Iowa Press, 1994.

Pereira, Kim. *August Wilson and the African-American Odyssey.* Urbana and Chicago: University of Illinois Press, 1995.

Plum, Jay. "Blues, History, and the Dramaturgy of August Wilson." *African American Review* 27, no. 4 (Winter 1993): pp. 561–567.

Shafer, Yvonne. *August Wilson: A Research and Production Sourcebook.* Westport, Conn.; London: Greenwood Press, 1998.

Shannon, Sandra G. "Blues, History, and Dramaturgy." *African American Review* 27, no. 4 (Winter 1993): pp. 539–559.

———. *The Dramatic Vision of August Wilson.* Washington, D.C.: Howard University Press, 1995.

———. *August Wilson's Fences: A Reference Guide.* Westport, Conn.; London: Greenwood Press, 2003.

Tibbetts, John C. "August Wilson Interview." *Literature/Film Quarterly* 30, no. 4 (January 2002): pp. 238–42.

Vorlicky, Robert. *Act Like a Man: Challenging Masculinities in American Drama.* Ann Arbor: University of Michigan Press, 1995.

Wang, Qun. *An In-Depth Study of the Major Plays of African American Playwright August Wilson: Vernacularizing the Blues on Stage,* vol. 6 of *Black Studies* series. Lewiston, New York; and Queenstown, Ontario: The Edwin Mellen Press, 1999.

Wessling, Joseph H. "Wilson's Fences." *Explicator* 57, no. 2 (Winter 1999): pp. 123–27.

Wilde, Lisa. "Reclaiming the Past: Narrative and Memory in August Wilson's *Two Trains Running.*" *Theater* 22, no. 1 (Fall/Winter 1990–91).

Williams, Dana A., and Sandra G. Shannon, ed. *August Wilson and Black Aesthetics.* Basingstoke; New York: Palgrave Macmillan, 2004.

Wolfe, Peter. *August Wilson.* New York: Twayne Publishers, 1999.

Acknowledgments

Patricia Gantt, "Ghosts from 'Down There:' The Southernness of August Wilson." From *August Wilson: A Casebook.* Copyright 2000 by Taylor & Francis Group LLC—Books. Reproduced with permission of Taylor & Francis Group LLC—Books in the format other book via Copyright Clearance Center.

Sandra G. Shannon, "Audience and Africanisms in August Wilson's Dramaturgy: A Case Study." From *African American Performance and Theater History: A Critical Reader*, edited by Harry J. Elam Jr. and David Krasner, 149–167. © 2001 by Oxford University Press. Reprinted by permission.

Keith Clark, "Race, Ritual, Reconnection, Reclamation: August Wilson and the Refiguration of the Male Dramatic Subject." From *Black Manhood in James Baldwin, Ernest Gaines, and August Wilson.* Copyright 2002 by the Board of Trustees of the University of Illinois. Used with permission of the University of Illinois Press.

William W. Cook, "Members and Lames: Language in the Plays of August Wilson." From *Black Theatre: Ritual Performance in the African Diaspora*, edited by Paul Carter Harrison, Victor Leo Walker II, and Gus Edwards, pp. 388–396. © 2002 by Paul Carter Harrison, Victor Leo Walker II, and Gus Edwards. Reprinted by permission.

Çiğdem Üsekes, "'We's the Leftovers': Whiteness as Economic Power and Exploitation in August Wilson's Twentieth-Century Cycle of Plays." From

African American Review 37, no. 1 (Spring 2003): 115–125. © 2003 by Çiğdem Üsekes. Reprinted by permission.

Amanda M. Rudolph, "Images of African Traditional Religions and Christianity in *Joe Turner's Come and Gone* and *The Piano Lesson*." From *Journal of Black Studies*, 33, no. 5 (May 2003): 562–575. Copyright 2003 by Sage Publications Inc. Journals. Reproduced with permission of Sage Publications Inc. Journals in the format other book via Copyright Clearance Center.

Ladrica Menson-Furr, "Booker T. Washington, August Wilson, and the Shadows in the Garden." This article originally appeared in *Mosaic*, a journal for the interdisciplinary study of literature, vol. 38, issue 4, (December 2005), pp. 175–192. Reprinted with permission.

Philip D. Beidler, "'King August': August Wilson in His Time." From *Michigan Quarterly Review* 45, no. 4 (Fall 2006): 575–597. © 1996–2008 by ProQuest LLC. Reprinted by permission.

Margaret Booker, "*Radio Golf:* The Courage of His Convictions—Survival, Success and Spirituality." From *The Cambridge Companion to August Wilson*, edited by Christopher Bigsby, 183–192. © 2007 by Cambridge University Press. Reprinted with the permission of Cambridge University Press.

Harry J. Elam, Jr., "*Gem of the Ocean* and the Redemptive Power of History." From *The Cambridge Companion to August Wilson*, edited by Christopher Bigsby, 75–88. © 2007 by Cambridge University Press. Reprinted with the permission of Cambridge University Press.

Every effort has been made to contact the owners of copyrighted material and secure copyright permission. Articles appearing in this volume generally appear much as they did in their original publication with few or no editorial changes. In some cases, foreign language text has been removed from the original essay. Those interested in locating the original source will find the information cited above.

Index

187